STRAIGHTFORWARD STATISTICS

Patrick White

D1477388

P

First published in Great Britain in 2023 by

Policy Press, an imprint of
Bristol University Press
University of Bristol
1–9 Old Park Hill
Bristol
BS2 8BB
UK
+44 (0)117 374 6645
bup-info@bristol.ac.uk

Details of international sales and distribution partners are available at
policy.bristoluniversitypress.co.uk

British Library Cataloguing in Publication Data
A catalogue record for this book is available from the British Library

ISBN 978-1-4473-6368-2 hardcover
ISBN 978-1-4473-6325-5 paperback
ISBN 978-1-4473-6326-2 ePub
ISBN 978-1-4473-6327-9 ePDF

Cover design: Matthew Perks and Clara Tsang
Cover image: Patrick White

Bristol University Press and Policy Press use environmentally responsible
print partners

Printed and bound in Great Britain by CPI Group (UK) Ltd,
Croydon, CR0 4YY

This book is dedicated to the memory of Jim Grant, an inspiring teacher and dear friend, who introduced me to sociology and a lot of good music.

Contents

List of figures and tables

Figures

Tables

Acknowledgements

Most of my academic career has been spent teaching statistical analysis to students who wouldn't have signed up for a statistics class if they'd had a choice. On reflection, this has been the best way for me to learn how to teach statistics. It's forced me to think about how to explain concepts and techniques to students who aren't confident about their numeracy and also how to show them that these concepts and techniques are important and useful. This book is the culmination of many thousands of interactions I've had with my students over the years. All these students have played a part in shaping this book, regardless of how they felt about having to take my class. For that, I'd like to thank them.

As someone who came to statistical analysis quite late, it's important for me to thank Stephen Gorard, the teacher who sparked my interest in statistics and showed me that statistical analysis wasn't as difficult as it often appeared. His early mentoring greatly influenced my own teaching and practice.

Many people have read parts, or all, of this text at various points in its development. I would like to thank the anonymous reviewers for all their feedback. The text is definitely better for their input. Several friends and colleagues generously agreed to read chapters of the final draft, and some of them even read the whole manuscript. Thank you to David Bartram, Jilly Kay, Rebecca Morris and John Williams for taking time out of your busy schedules to help me. Thank you to Matthew Perks and Clara Tsang for their hard work and patience with my many requests when they designed the cover. Thanks also to the authors and designers who either made their work available through a Creative Commons license or gave me permission to use their illustrations in this book.

Finally, thank you to Emma Smith, who not only read the whole manuscript, but who also put up with me during the more frustrating and stressful periods of pitching, writing and editing this book.

Introduction:
Why this book *actually is* different

Who is this book for?

This book is for anyone learning statistical analysis for the first time. You might be learning statistics as part of your studies or because you need to do some analysis and don't know where to start. Whatever your reason for learning statistics, this book provides a gentle introduction to the basic concepts and techniques you need to know as a beginner.

If you are being taught statistics, you might have been recommended this book by one of your teachers. But even if it hasn't been recommended to you, it might still be useful to fill in any 'gaps' in the texts on your reading list. I have written it to work well as a stand-alone resource, but it can also be helpful as a supplement to other learning materials.

If you need to conduct some statistical analysis for the first time – for whatever reason – this book will get you off to a good start. You'll need to use some software to do the actual calculations, but there are many resources available to help you with this, including videos on my own YouTube channel (see www.youtube.com/@patrickkwhite/videos). The most important concepts and techniques needed to start doing basic statistical analysis are covered here.

Why do we need another statistics textbook?
And how is this one different?

Many people find learning statistics both difficult and unenjoyable. If you're one of these, don't worry, you're certainly not alone. As someone who has taught statistical analysis to students for over 20 years, I have met thousands of students studying many different subjects, and lots of them were nervous about taking my class. In fact, most of them wouldn't have been taking my class at all if it wasn't a compulsory part of their studies. So I'm very familiar with the kind of anxieties students have, and I've learned from experience about the things that they find difficult.

Some of the students I teach have taken statistics classes before. Most had managed to pass their assessments, but often felt that they hadn't understood enough about the subject to do their own analysis, and certainly didn't feel excited about doing statistics. What these students are often surprised to learn is that I had the same experience. I also had to take statistics classes, passed the exams, but didn't feel confident to *do* statistical analysis, and I didn't really understand what statistics could *do* for me.

It was only later that I started to learn more about statistics. This was thanks to a chance meeting with a teacher who made all the concepts I found so difficult much easier to understand. This started a journey that led to me teaching introductory statistics to students of all kinds. Because I had initially struggled to understand what I was taught in statistics classes, I could empathise with students when they didn't understand things, and this allowed me to relate closely to their experience.

I only started to *really* learn statistics quite late on, after I already had some academic experience under my belt. By that time, I had the confidence to question how things worked and why we did them in a particular way. This mindset has informed my approach to teaching, where I focus on what I believe to be the most important concepts and skills for getting students ready to do their own analysis, rather than simply covering what has traditionally been taught.

Although I've very much enjoyed teaching statistical analysis, one of my frustrations has been that I've never found a textbook that fits well with this goal. My reading lists for students were largely made up of short sections from a range of texts, but there weren't any texts that matched up well with what I wanted to teach. Eventually I gave up waiting for someone to write a book that would fill this gap, and decided that the best thing was to write one myself.

What I found lacking in many introductory texts was a straightforward explanation of basic statistical concepts. While I believe that the fundamentals of statistics can be explained in a way that almost everyone can understand, certain ideas and concepts can be tricky for some people to understand at first. But it's vital that students fully understand these ideas before moving on to more advanced techniques. My experience is that many students move on to much more complicated statistical analyses before they have a complete understanding of some of the basics. In this book I concentrate on the fundamental concepts and techniques that will allow you to look for interesting patterns in your data, and try to ensure that you develop a good understanding of what you're doing and why you're doing it.

(Almost) no equations and no screenshots

Something else that frustrated me as a teacher was the number of unnecessary equations, even in 'introductory' textbooks. Because computers have been used to 'do the math' for us for over half a century, you don't need to know any of these equations to do statistical analysis. Including lots of equations in a textbook can put some students off the whole area of statistics and, importantly, it can distract from the conceptual understanding that is much more important. There *are* a few equations in this book – but *only* a few – and they're very simple ones. I've only included them when there's no alternative and when they are needed to understand something I'm trying to explain. And even if you skip over these equations, you'll still be able to do almost all of the analyses I cover, and also interpret the results.

Lots of books are tied to particular software packages, which means that they're of limited use if you don't have access to that program (some of which can be expensive). Including software screenshots means that these books tend to be longer, cost more to buy and go out of date when the software is updated. It seems a bit odd to still be publishing books with software tutorials in them when there are thousands of videos available on YouTube and elsewhere on the internet (including some made by me!). Learning to use software from a video tutorial is, anyway, much easier than learning it from a book.

You'll be able to conduct the techniques covered in this book using any statistical software package, or programming language, that's available to you. My YouTube videos cover IBM's Statistical Package for the Social Sciences (SPSS®), but there are good video tutorials covering all the software packages out there, and they're mostly available for free.

What can statistics do for me?

Many students I teach are only learning about statistics because they have to: they probably wouldn't have chosen to take my class if it wasn't compulsory. I imagine that lots of people reading this book are in a similar situation. But understanding statistics can be both useful and empowering. Even if you never do any statistics again, knowing about how statistics work means that you'll be better informed when you read anything that has statistical information in it. And using statistics gives you the power to find things out about the world that are useful and important. There are, of course, many other valuable ways of doing research, but there are some things that we can only discover by using statistical analysis.

Learning statistics doesn't have to be difficult and unenjoyable. Some of my students who take my classes reluctantly admit that, although they were dreading it, they actually find it to be fun. I hope that you not only find this book useful in terms of developing your skills and knowledge, but also that it increases your confidence and sparks your enthusiasm to use and understand basic statistical analysis. And while this book may not turn every reader into a fan of statistics, I hope that you will at least be left with a feeling that statistics can be useful, and that many of the fundamental concepts and techniques are actually quite *straightforward*.

How to use this book

This book is intended to be used in two different ways. If statistics is completely new to you, it's probably best to start at the beginning and read each chapter sequentially. Some of the later chapters build on what's covered in earlier chapters and, after the first two chapters that introduce the basic concepts, Chapters 3 to 8 move from simple to more complicated analyses.

However, if you've done some statistics before, and want to brush up on or revisit certain topics, I've written all the chapters so they work as a 'stand-alone' resource that can be read separately.

Glossary, exercises and boxes

I've provided a glossary (and index) at the end of the book, and some exercises throughout the book, to support your learning. It's not necessary to use either of these features, but some of you may find them helpful.

Glossary

You'll notice that some of the words in the main text are in **bold type**. Each of these terms has a corresponding entry in the glossary at the end of the book. The glossary gives a brief definition of each term, and also lists the page numbers where this term is mentioned throughout the book. The glossary may be particularly useful if you are 'dipping into' particular chapters or sections, rather than reading the whole book from start to finish.

Exercises

Some of the chapters include exercises. The answers to these can be found at the end of each chapter. These exercises are intended to consolidate your learning and also to link the concepts and techniques covered in each chapter to your own interests and the topics that you study.

Boxes

In each chapter there are a number of boxes. These boxes were designed to answer questions that my students sometimes ask. You don't need to read the contents of the boxes to understand the topics covered in each chapter, but they contain additional information that you might find interesting and/or useful.

Accompanying resources

Although this book is written to work as a stand-alone text, I have provided links to other resources that compliment what it provides, including datasets and software tutorial videos.

Datasets

Most of the analyses in this book were conducted using data from open access datasets that are available to the public. You can download these and replicate my analyses or try out some of your own. I have included full details of these at the end of each chapter, but most can be found at: https://ukdataservice.ac.uk/learning-hub/teach-with-real-data

Software tutorial videos

Although none of the content of this book is tied to any particular software package or programming language, the videos on my YouTube channel (www.youtube.com/@patrickkwhite/videos) show you how to do most of the analyses covered in this book using software published by IBM called SPSS® (Statistical Package for the Social Sciences). I originally recorded these videos for my own teaching, and at the time I write this (April 2023) they have had over 912,000 views. I used SPSS® because it is the most user-friendly software package available at the university where I teach, and it is one of the most widely available packages for statistical analysis, and not because I necessarily believe it to be better or worse than any other software on the market. All the analyses covered in this book can be conducted using any software that you have available, including Microsoft Excel and free-to-use software such as JASP and Jamovi (although doing statistics in Excel is a bit awkward at times).

1

Everybody's talking about it: important terms explained in everyday language

WHAT IS THIS CHAPTER FOR?

In this chapter I introduce you to some language that researchers use when they discuss methods, research design and data analysis. Understanding this language is important because, although I try to avoid 'jargon' wherever possible in this book, there are some technical terms that you need to be familiar with if you're going to conduct your own research or read other people's. And you'll also find these terms used in other research methods and statistics textbooks, so it's useful to know what they mean. I try to explain these terms in everyday language and to keep the discussion as simple and as straightforward as possible.

WHAT DOES IT COVER?

Most of the terms covered in this chapter relate to research methods in general, rather than being specific to statistical analysis. However, these ideas aren't always explained fully or clearly, either in general methods or statistics textbooks. I have covered what I think are the most important concepts to understand when you're conducting or reading reports of statistical analysis. Many other terms are included in the glossary at the end of the book.

WHAT WILL YOU LEARN?

You'll learn about what the following terms mean and why they are important:

case	population	sample
variable	relationship	dependent and independent variables
cause and effect		

Before we start thinking about statistical analysis, it's important to make sure we're speaking the same language about research in general. In this chapter I introduce some important terms that you'll come across when reading about data collection and analysis. These terms are explained in detail here and other common terms (highlighted in bold in the text) are explained more briefly in the glossary at the end of the book. If you're already familiar with all the terms listed above, you might want to go straight to Chapter 2. Or if you are familiar with most, but not all, of them, you can skip to the relevant sections before moving on.

Key terms

Social researchers use particular words when they write about their methods, research design and analysis. Although some – or all – of these may be familiar to many of you, in my experience students often find them confusing. To make sure you can follow the discussions in the rest of the book, I want to make sure that you understand the most important terms before we go any further. The first three terms – case, population and sample – all relate to who (or what) is being studied in our research. The next group of terms are about how things are different and similar (variables and relationships). The last terms – cause and effect – are important for all kinds of research, and we'll get a bit philosophical when we discuss these, because they're still argued about fiercely by philosophers, statisticians and social researchers alike.

Case

In social research we usually look at more than one example of the thing we're interested in. This is because we're often interested in how things differ or vary – what's called 'variation'. Lots of research focuses on people as individuals, and so in these studies it's people who are our 'cases'. Each person is a case, and we collect information from, or about, every one of them. But cases don't have to be individual people. They can also be groups of people, such as families or work teams. Or they can be institutions, such as schools, prisons, hospitals or businesses. They can be streets, cities, regions or countries. They can even be events, such as crimes, medical operations, school lessons or car journeys. The most appropriate case for your research will depend on exactly what you're trying to find out.

You might have more than one type of case in your research. National censuses, for example, often collect data on more than one type of case. While some questions are asked about each individual in a household, other questions are asked about the household as a whole.

It's important to be clear about what your cases are before you do any analysis. This is because your cases are the units that will be used in your analyses, what's called your **unit of analysis**. For example, if you wanted to compare the differences in people's educational qualifications, then individual people would be your cases because each person has a particular set of qualifications, and your analyses would be based on the differences between these people. But if you were interested in researching household income, both your case and unit of analysis would be households rather than individual people. Although every person in that household might have a different income (and some may have no income at all), the unit of analysis would be the household, so the income of all those living in each household would have to be combined before comparing the income of different households.

Educational attainment could also be researched using different units of analysis, depending on the question you wanted to answer. I have already used the example of comparing the attainment of individuals, but we might want to compare attainment between schools, regions or even countries. Even though the results for a school would be made up of the combined attainment of the students in that school, if we want to compare schools, then each school would be a single case that could be compared with other institutions. The 'units' we analysed would therefore be schools.

Population

When you hear the term 'population' in everyday life, it usually refers to the people who are living in a country, region or city. It's common to hear news stories about the size of the world's population, or reports about how fast the population of Kuwait, for example, is growing. And we might talk about the population of London, New York or Beijing to refer to the residents of those cities.

In social research, the term 'population' *can* refer to the people who live in a particular geographical area, but it has both a wider and more specific meaning than this. Although we often just say 'population', the term 'population of interest' is a better description of what the concept actually refers to.

I explained in the last section that there are different types of 'case', and what your cases are in a particular study will depend on exactly what you're trying to find out. Broadly speaking, your population – or population of interest – contains all the cases you're interested in. So, if you were interested in looking at the attainment of young people currently in compulsory schooling in the UK, your population wouldn't be the entire population of the UK, because most of these people aren't still in school. Ideally, it would be every student who is still in compulsory schooling, and your cases would be individual students.

If, on the other hand, you were interested in the economic performance of businesses in the US state of Wisconsin, your population would be every business in that state, and your cases wouldn't be people but businesses. Each business would be a single case. Or you might be interested in the number of car accidents in the city of Tokyo in the past year. Your cases would be accidents rather than the people or cars involved in the accidents, and your population would be made up of all the accidents occurring in that year.

While the idea of a population – or population of interest – might sound reasonably straightforward, it's important to make a distinction between what our *ideal* population might be and what our *actual* population is for a particular study. When the term 'population' is used in its strict, technical sense, it either refers to all the cases for which you have data, or all the cases that had a chance of being included in your research.

Although it's becoming more common, it's still quite unusual for researchers to use every case in a population in their research. This is either because data on every case are not available, or because it would be too expensive and time-consuming to collect these data. As I explain in the next section, it's more likely that researchers will select a number of cases from that population to make up what is called a sample. But if you don't have – or don't collect – data on the whole population of interest, ideally all the cases in this population should have had *some* chance of being included in your study.

So although you may ideally be interested in finding out about every school student in the UK, if every student doesn't have a chance of ending up in your study, strictly speaking your population isn't 'school students in the UK'. Depending on who could have been included in your research, it may be 'school students in the London borough of Hackney', or 'students in six secondary [high] schools in Oxford', but it wouldn't be all school students in the UK.

But why is this important? Isn't this just splitting hairs? Does it really matter how we use the word 'population'? Isn't the main thing to let people know who or what we're interested in studying?

It's actually very important to use – and think about – the term 'population' in the correct way. This is because the concept of a population is connected to two closely related topics in research: sampling and generalisation. In the next section we'll look at these terms in more detail, and I'll explain how they're linked to the idea of a population.

Sample

Research can be very expensive and time-consuming, especially if the data you need don't already exist and you have to collect them as part of your project. Because of practical considerations – usually involving the time and money available to us – we often have to make compromises. One of the most common compromises is not collecting data from everyone in our population of interest, but only from a selection of cases.

Selecting cases from a population is called 'sampling'. The cases that have been selected are called a 'sample'. There are several different ways of selecting a sample, each with its own advantages and disadvantages. There isn't the space in this book to discuss them in any detail, but I have recommended some resources on sampling at the end of the chapter.

Whatever method of sampling you have used, it's important to be clear about exactly what population you have selected your sample from. Having a sample is never as good as having data on your whole population, because with population data you don't have to worry about how well your sample 'represents' your population. If you have data on every case you are interested in, you can say something definitive about your population as a whole. But if you only have a sample, you have to think about **representativeness**: whether the results of your research would be the same as the results you would have got if you'd collected data from every case in your population.

Most research is carried out using samples, rather than population data. Even very large and well-funded studies, such as the Crime Survey for England and Wales (CSEW) or the US National Longitudinal Study of Adolescent to Adult

Health (Add Health), rely on samples. There are some exceptions, such as censuses and some administrative datasets, but sample-based studies still dominate most areas of social research.

Because population data is relatively uncommon, and social researchers are so reliant on sample data, it's important to understand the concepts of populations and samples. These terms are used in relation to statistical analysis, and you'll come across them in research methods and statistics texts, as well as in reports of research findings.

Variable

A variable is just something that varies: something that is different for different cases. Ethnicity is a variable because not everybody belongs to the same ethnic group. Time spent in full-time education is also a variable because some people continue in education for longer than others. Income is another example, as different people have different amounts of money coming in each week, month or year. Statistics is all about variation, and that's why the idea of a variable is central to statistical analysis.

Understanding the idea of a variable can be easier if you think about what the opposite would be. In many countries, government agencies and other organisations have encouraged cyclists to wear helmets to reduce the risk of serious head injuries in the event of an accident. Publicity campaigns have often included statistics showing that when cyclists are involved in an accident, those wearing helmets are less likely to be killed or suffer serious head injuries compared to those who weren't wearing helmets.

In most countries wearing a helmet is a choice left up to the individual. A study looking at whether wearing a helmet is beneficial might involve, among other things, comparing the injuries of cyclists wearing helmets with those not wearing them. In such research, helmet wearing is a variable: some people will wear helmets and others will not. However, in some countries – such as Australia – it's against the law not to wear a helmet. In these countries it wouldn't really be possible to conduct the kind of research I just described because everyone (apart from, presumably, a few law-breakers) has to wear a helmet. So, while wearing a helmet in the USA or the UK is a variable – some people do and some don't – in Australia it's a **constant**: everybody has to do it. We couldn't compare the injury rates between cyclists who do and don't wear helmets in Australia because everyone wears one.

The idea of a constant is used in some of statistical analysis – as I explain in Chapter 8 – but it's not something you need to worry about too much at this stage. The important thing for the moment is that you understand what a variable is.

Some of my students confuse cases with variables, so it's useful to clarify the difference between the two. Your cases are the individual units of analysis – such as people, groups, places, events or institutions – that you're interested in studying. Variables are the characteristics or qualities of those cases. If your case is an individual person, a variable relating to them might be their age or their ethnicity. If your case is a prison, a variable might be the number of inmates in that prison or its geographic location. Whatever kind of research you do, it's likely that you will have a number of different cases. There will also be some variables that you're interested in. Ideally, for each of your cases there will be information about all of these variables. One of the things you'll learn to do later in this book is to examine the relationships between those variables. You might find Exercise 1.0 helpful to practise making the distinction between these ideas.

EXERCISE 1.0

Think back to some research that you've read about, and consider the following questions. Being able to answer them will depend on the authors having provided all the necessary information, but being able to notice if important information is missing from research reports is a valuable skill to develop:

a) What were the cases (or units of analysis) in the study?

b) What was the population of interest?

c) Did the authors have data on all cases in the population of interest, or did they select a sample?

d) What were the variables that the researchers analysed in the study?

Relationship

A relationship is simply a link between two (or more) variables. This is probably the most common way social researchers describe a link between two things, but other words such as **association** are also used. When we look at one variable at a time, we're examining variation, but we're not finding out anything about a relationship, because a relationship can only exist between at least two things. But if we analyse two or more variables together, we're able to examine the relationship between them.

Looking at one variable at a time is called univariate analysis, and in Chapters 3 and 4 we'll see why this can be useful, and look at common ways of doing this type of analysis. Many of the other chapters cover techniques to look for relationships between two variables – what's called bivariate analysis. Although I don't cover **multi-variable analysis** in any detail in this book, I do recommend some resources for this group of techniques, which are used to look at the relationship between more than two variables.

'Relationship' is a word that can describe quite different sorts of connections between variables. As I explain in later chapters, the type of statistical analysis you need to do will vary depending on the type of data you have, but regardless of which technique you use, you can still describe any link between two or more variables as a relationship. 'Relationship' is a fairly general term, so as long you're describing some sort of connection between variables, it's unlikely that you'll be using it incorrectly.

There are, however, words that are specific to certain types of relationship, and you need to be much more careful when using these. Probably the most misused term is **correlation**. This should only be used to describe the results of a particular method of statistical analysis that we cover in Chapter 7. This analysis can only be used on data of a certain type, and produces a particular kind of description of a relationship between variables. In media reports, journalists often use the term 'correlation' to describe any relationship between variables, but I would encourage you to avoid doing this. People will probably understand what you mean if you use the term like this, but I hope that what you learn in this book will help you to use technical language correctly.

Dependent and independent variables

When you conduct analysis into the relationship between variables, you usually need to be clear about which of your variables are dependent variables and which are independent variables. Students often find these two terms confusing, but the difference is important for several reasons. First, it helps you think about your analysis and what is called the 'direction' of any relationship you are examining. (We'll look at this later.) Second, these terms are used in textbooks, research reports and software packages, and you'll need to understand them to use these resources effectively. And lastly, you'll need to use these terms to explain your analysis in your research report.

Unless you have had some research methods training, the terms 'dependent variable' and 'independent variable' probably don't mean much to you. They're not particularly intuitive and new researchers can find them difficult. Luckily, there are some alternatives: outcome variable and explanatory variable. Because 'outcome' and 'explanation' are words that we use in our everyday lives, it might be easier for you to think in these terms.

In our research, we're often interested in a particular *outcome* – such as how much people get paid in their jobs – and so could look for *explanations* as to why some people get paid more or less than others. Possible explanations might be: the type of work someone does; their educational qualifications; how much experience they have; the hours they work; and so on. So the outcome variable would be their pay and the explanatory variables would be their job type, education, experience and any other factors that we think might affect how much someone gets paid.

So how are outcome and explanatory variables related to dependent and independent variables? 'Outcome variable' and 'dependent variable' are different names for the same thing, as are 'explanatory variable' and 'independent variable'. If you find the terms 'dependent' and 'independent' difficult, it may be easier for you to first think in terms of outcomes and explanations and then translate these to dependent and independent variables as and when you need to. Another way of thinking about these terms is that the dependent variable *depends* on the independent ones. Using our example from above, how much you are paid *depends* on your qualifications, experience and working hours.

Cause and effect

As we have been thinking about relationships, it's a good idea to have a brief discussion of cause and effect, or what is also known as causality. Textbooks often warn about the dangers of assuming that one thing is directly *caused* by something else. It's always important to remember that just because we might observe a difference between groups or an association between variables, this doesn't necessarily mean that differences in one thing are being *caused* by a difference in the other.

To use a common textbook example, fire engines are more likely to be seen outside burning houses than outside houses that aren't on fire. But even young children don't think that this means that fire engines cause fires. As we all know, fire engines arrive at a burning building because people call the fire service to extinguish a fire. But it also makes no sense to say that fires 'cause' fire engines. In reality, there is a chain of events in which the sight (or smell) of a fire 'causes' people to phone the fire service, which, in turn, 'causes' fire engines to be despatched to the site of the fire. Even this description is a bit of a simplification, and you could probably break these events down into many more stages.

Causality is a tricky area and in social research we're sometimes dealing with variables whose relationship is much less clear than the appearance of fire engines at fires. Having said that, it's important to remember that if we label variables as 'dependent' and 'independent', or 'outcome' and 'explanatory', we're *implying* that there is some kind of causal relationship between them. And when we say that one variable *depends on* another, or that differences in one variable can be *explained* by variation in another, we're using causal language to describe these relationships.

There's a big difference between looking for causal relationships and providing evidence demonstrating a causal link between two (or more) things. But it's important to remember that the terms we use in our research, and the analyses we conduct, are often linked very closely to the idea of causality. And although we must be careful about making causal *claims*, it's important to remember that we're often looking for causal links between variables.

Descriptions can be very valuable, and we need to make sure we've described something accurately before we try to explain why it has occurred. However, descriptions only get us so far. For example, we might discover that people with higher levels of qualifications tend to earn more money than those with lower levels of qualifications. But this would only be interesting if we thought that people earned more *because* they had higher levels of qualifications (or, alternatively, because their higher earnings had allowed them to study for higher qualifications). If we're only prepared to describe this situation, and not even speculate about a causal connection, then we are just pointing out what might be a coincidence.

Most importantly for readers of this book, however, is the fact that when you are conducting particular statistical analyses, you have to specify which of your variables is the dependent variable and which are independent variables. To work this out you need to think about the possible causal relationships between the two. Exercise 1.1 will help you think through causality in your own research.

EXERCISE 1.1

If you are carrying out your own research, or have been asked to produce a research proposal or some research questions, you might find this exercise helpful:

a) Look at your research questions and examine all the words you have used very carefully. Identify any words that suggest causal links between two variables.

b) Think about which of the variables would be the dependent and independent variables. What has led you to think that the dependent variable is an effect (or outcome) and why do you believe that the independent variable, or variables, could be causes (or explanations)? Why wouldn't it be the other way around?

Thinking about your research in terms of dependent and independent variables

One of the benefits of thinking about your data in terms of dependent and independent variables is that it forces you to reflect on how you think the world works and the implications of this for both the analyses you conduct and the conclusions you draw. To follow up on the earlier example about earnings, if you looked at the working-age adult population of most countries, you would find that there is a relationship between earnings and age. There is what is called a **positive relationship** between these two variables, which means that as one goes up, so does the other, and vice versa. If I asked you which of these two variables was the dependent variable and which was the independent variable – or the outcome variable and the explanatory variable – hopefully you would conclude that earnings had to be the outcome, and age might explain that outcome. So earnings would be the dependent variable and age would be the independent variable.

But why do you come to this conclusion?

What you already know about the world would lead you to think that there was something about getting older that allowed you to earn more. (But you probably wouldn't conclude that moving to a lower paid job could slow down, or reverse, the ageing process!) In fact, you might have gone a bit further than this and started thinking about what exactly it is about getting older that allows most people to earn more. You know that you don't earn more simply by ageing, but you may know that workers are sometimes rewarded for long service, for increased experience, because of promotions or career changes, and so on. So the relationship between age and earnings isn't a direct one, but gaining experience and moving up the career ladder takes time, and workers will get older while doing this.

Sometimes it's not quite as clear which is the independent and which is the dependent variable. Several years ago, there was a great deal of media coverage of a research finding that eating fast food was linked to depression. There's a link to information about the study at the end of this chapter, but before you look at this, it's useful to think about the ways that these two things could be linked.

One possible relationship between fast food and depression is that eating fast food makes suffering from depression more likely. It could be one of many different things that increases the risk of depression. Here, depression would be the outcome and fast food would be an explanatory factor: the dependent variable would be depression and the independent variable would be eating fast food.

However, there are other ways in which these two variables could be related. It could be that if you are suffering from depression, you are more likely to eat fast food. In this case, eating fast food would be the outcome and depression would be the explanation. The relationship would be in the opposite direction to the first possibility, and so eating fast food would be the dependent variable and depression would be the independent variable.

The key question for researchers in this area is 'which came first?' Sometimes this is easy to answer. For example, educational qualifications gained at school usually come before income from a full-time job, so if we were looking at the relationship between these two things, it would be clear that income would have to be the outcome, as it came later. However, as with the example of fast food and depression, it's not always as easy to work out. In fact, the study collected data over time, and was designed to see if eating fast food preceded developing depression. But, as a commentary on the findings warns:

> The tendency to consume fast food and develop depression may both have stemmed from some common factor, rather than fast food directly causing depression. For example, participants with the highest fast food consumption were generally all single, younger and less active, which may have influenced both their diet and their risk of depression. (NICS Well, 2023)

As this example shows, there can be pairs (or groups) of variables where it's not clear which are the dependent (outcome) or independent (explanatory) variables. Exercise 1.2 gives you a chance to think about two more pairs of variables.

EXERCISE 1.2

Think about the relationship between each of the two pairs of variables listed below. Can you come up with explanations as to why each variable in a pair could be either the dependent or independent variable?

a)   The political party that people vote for and where they read about news and current affairs.

b)   The strength of people's religious belief and their attendance at organised religious events.

From the examples I have discussed in this section, you can see that when we conduct an analysis, we not only have to think about the techniques that we are going to use; we also have to think about how the relationships we are investigating fit into what we already know about how the world works. This is true for all analysis of any type but, as we will see in later chapters, it is something you must decide *before* conducting certain types of statistical analysis.

Summary

This chapter has introduced you to some of the key terms you'll come across when reading about research. It's important that you understand them all properly before reading the chapters that follow, as I'll go on to use many of these terms. In the next chapter we'll look closely at numbers, think about what they represent, and consider how they can be used as 'tools' that can help us find things out.

References
NICS Well (2023) 'Fast food "linked" to depression', www.nicswell.co.uk/health-news/fast-food-linked-to-depression

Useful resources
Robert de Vries provides a very good discussion of why sampling is important in research and how it can affect the conclusions that you can draw:

de Vries, R. (2019) *Critical Statistics: Seeing Beyond the Headlines*, London: Red Globe Press [Chapter 3: 'Samples, Samples Everywhere…'].

A useful short discussion of different methods of sampling by Stephen Gorard can be found here:

Gorard, S. (2013) *Research Design: Creating Robust Approaches for the Social Sciences*, London: SAGE [Chapter 6: 'Identifying the Sample or Cases']. The same book has an in-depth discussion of causality.

Answers to exercises

Exercise 1.0
Your answers to these questions will depend on the particular study that you are thinking about. However, this is a useful set of questions to think about when you are reading any research report, and also when you are planning your own research.

Exercise 1.1
Your answers to these questions will depend on your own research questions. However, hopefully you'll have found this exercise useful. You can use this set of questions any time you are carrying out your own research.

As I won't know your research questions, I can't anticipate your answers to question (b). However, for question (a), there are a number of commonly used words and phrases (apart from 'cause') that suggest some kind of causal link:

effect of	affect	shape
led to	bring about	give rise to
engender	induce	result in
result in/of	produce	trigger
generate	make	create

This list is far from exhaustive, but I hope it gives you an idea of how many of the words and phrases we use in research suggest some kind of causal relationship.

Exercise 1.2
a) As with the example of fast food and depression, in this example there is no obvious order to these behaviours. Although in most countries you can't vote until you're 18, but you can access news outlets at almost any age, it might seem that reading news comes before voting and so would be an explanatory (independent) variable. But being able to do something and actually doing it are two different things. Not many school children will be regular readers of the news. To make things more complicated, people don't always vote at their first opportunity, and so the age at which someone votes for the first time may vary.

Because different news outlets have particular political leanings, it's plausible that they influence people to vote for particular parties or candidates. But it's also reasonable to believe that people might read certain news sources because they reflect their political views. It's likely that, to a certain extent, both things happen. Because of this, it's hard to say which is the most obvious dependent or independent variable.

b) People with strong religious beliefs may be more likely to attend organised religious events, such as services and other rituals. People with less strong beliefs, and those who have no beliefs at all, might be less likely to attend these. If, for the sake of argument, we accept that this is the case, does this help us with working out the causal order of these two variables? It could be the case that going to organised religious events strengthens people's religious beliefs. If you go to these events, you may learn more about your religion and mix with other members of your faith, and this could lead to stronger religious beliefs.

But it's very difficult work out which comes first. Although you could argue that people are unlikely to attend a religious event if they had *no* religious beliefs to start with, they may just be curious, accompanying friends or family members, or attending a wedding or other social event. For example, very young children are often taken to religious events by their parents well before they can understand what these events are about. As with the previous example, it's not easy to work out which would be the dependent and independent variable. It is plausible to say that religious beliefs (as an independent variable) explain attendance at religious events (the dependent variable). But it also makes sense to say that attendance at religious events (as an independent variable) leads to stronger religious beliefs (the dependent variable). The important thing is that we think these things through before we do any analysis, and discuss any difficult issues when we write up our results.

2

What are numbers *really* about?

WHAT IS THIS CHAPTER FOR?
In this chapter I introduce the idea of numbers as tools that you can use whenever they are helpful. I look at the different ways in which numbers are used in both research and everyday life. I also examine the limitations of numbers, and show how they can be used inappropriately or in misleading ways.

WHAT DOES IT COVER?
I start the chapter by explaining the different ways we use numbers as 'tools' to help us record and understand the things around us. Next, I explain how these differences in how we use numbers affect how we can analyse our data, and I introduce the idea of 'level of measurement', which is central to statistical analysis.

WHAT WILL YOU LEARN?
- When using numbers is useful and when it's not
- How to recognise when numbers are being used in different ways
- How to distinguish between numbers that have real numeric value and those that are being used as labels
- What 'levels of measurement' are, and how this can affect the analyses you conduct

It might seem strange to dedicate a whole chapter of a book about statistical analysis to looking at numbers. After all, you're probably reading this book for one of the following reasons:

1. You have to learn about statistics for a course you are studying.
2. You're conducting some research and need to know how to analyse the data.
3. You might even just be interested in learning about statistics!

Regardless of which category you fit into, you either want to or have to conduct some statistical analysis. So why don't I just get on with it and show you how to do statistics?

There are two good reasons. First, I want to spend a bit of time pointing out what I think are some important misconceptions about using (or not using) numbers in research. And second, you need to be clear about the different ways we use numbers before you can do any statistical analysis at all. But if you're short on time, or just really want to do some statistics as soon as possible, you can skip to the section called 'Three ways we use numbers' later in the chapter.

Two types of research? Two types of researcher?

If an alien visitor arrived on Earth and was quarantined in the research methods section of a university library, they might end up thinking that there are two types of human: those who are just interested in numbers and those who are only interested in other types of information, such as words and pictures. Depending on what they read, they might also discover a third group: people who tried to convince the two other groups that you could use numbers alongside other types of information and that doing so wouldn't cause the sky to fall in.

This isn't a world you would recognise as a native inhabitant of Earth, but it might be familiar from the research methods classes you have taken, or from the many textbooks in which research designs, methods of data collection and analysis, and even researchers themselves are divided into 'quantitative' or 'qualitative' types.

This division is very common and I'm sure many of you will be familiar with these terms. However, I don't believe that this is a very useful division, and it often results in many students and researchers completely avoiding the use of statistics or even very simple numeric data. The message often seems to be that if you aren't a 'quantitative' researcher, there is no reason to use numbers (and lots of reasons not to use them!).

A divide between 'quantitative' and 'qualitative' research seems to be 'baked in' to a lot of thinking about research, but it's also an idea that's been widely criticised, and many commentators have argued that it prevents us from doing the best possible research. I feel that the disadvantages of this division outweigh its advantages and that it acts as a barrier to using statistics for many students and researchers. (The qualitative–quantitative divide has been fiercely debated for a very long time. I've included some references to further reading on this topic at the end of the chapter, in case you are interested in finding out more about this debate.)

Exercise 2.0 is designed to help you see the problems with dividing up research in this way, and to show those of you who are nervous about statistics that you probably use numbers in your daily life more than you think.

My guess is that, whenever you are trying to find something out, and whatever you are trying to find out, you use the information that you think is the most relevant. I would be surprised if you rejected information just because it either did or didn't contain numbers. Doing so would be rather odd, wouldn't it?

EXERCISE 2.0

a) Think about the last time you did some research in your daily life to find something out. This might have been choosing a course at university, finding the best way to visit a friend who lives far away, or anything else.

    i.   What different types of information did you use?

    ii. Why did you choose each piece of information?

    iii. Did you ignore any information because it contained numbers?

    iv. Did you reject any information because it didn't contain numbers?

b) Now answer the same questions ((i) to (iv)) for something you wanted to find out as a social researcher.

So, if you are trying to find the best way to visit a friend, you might compare different types of public transport. Some of the data you'd come across would be numeric, such as the time of the journey, the cost of the fare, how frequently the service runs, and how far away the stations or stops are from your home and your destination. But you'd also have to combine this information with some non-numeric data, such as whether you prefer travelling by bus or train, whether you'd have to change trains, or if you get travel sickness sitting in the back of the bus. You might also consider whether your friend could meet you at the time that you are scheduled to arrive.

You would combine these pieces of information and use your judgement to come to a decision. The important point is that, in most areas of research – whatever you are researching – there are usually useful data that are numeric as well as useful data that aren't. Being able to use that numeric data can help you find out more about what you're interested in, and knowing more about numbers and statistics can help you with this.

One way to think about numbers – and statistics – is as tools that we can use when they are helpful to us and that we can ignore when they're not the right tools for the job.

Three ways we use numbers

Although it's something you probably take for granted and haven't given much thought to, we generally use numbers in three different ways. It's important to be clear about the differences between these three uses because they have implications for how we do statistical analysis. The ways that we use numbers can be summarised as: counting, measuring and labelling.

Counting

One way we use numbers is to count things. Counting is probably one of the first things you learned to do as a small child, and it's incredibly useful. It forms the basis of some important types of statistical analysis and, especially in the social sciences, is often the only way we can quantify particular things. For example, criminologists might want to know how many burglaries were recorded in a particular city over the course of the last year. To find out whether burglaries are 'common' or 'rare' they may go on to compare the number of burglaries with the number of other types of crime. These numbers can then be used to calculate other measures such as percentages, proportions, ratios and crime rates, all of which we discuss in more detail in Chapter 3. There are also statistical techniques for looking at the relationships between the different things that have been counted, and we'll look at those in Chapter 5.

Measuring

A second way we use numbers is to measure things. Measuring is different to counting, because it's only possible if we have a scale we can use to measure the thing we're interested in. Throughout history, people have developed many scales that have become almost universally accepted, such as those used to measure distance, money and time. We could use metres, miles or feet to measure distance, height or length: it wouldn't matter which measure we used, as each one of these can be converted into any of the others. It also wouldn't matter if we used US dollars, Japanese yen or Indian rupees to measure monetary value; while their value in relation to each other is affected by exchange rates, at any one time we could convert one currency to the other. We could also measure time in seconds, minutes, hours, days or years.

Natural scientists use lots of different scales to measure things. Some of these are controversial, but many have become universal. In the social sciences, things are a little different. Apart from those relating to time, distance and money, there are relatively few widely accepted scales available to social researchers, possibly because of the nature of the things we study. Researchers in the field of health use measures such as weight, blood pressure, calories consumed, and so on, but most of these have been developed in the natural sciences. Social psychologists have developed scales to measure attitudes or aspects of personality, but it's often the case that different scales are used by different researchers, and there can several competing measures in a particular area of study. Unlike in the natural sciences, there are few measures that have been adopted universally within psychology itself, let alone outside of it.

We'll look at some of the problems that can be encountered when creating scales and measures later in this chapter. The important point to make here is that many of the things we study in the social sciences can't easily be measured with scales and, as we'll see in later chapters of this book, this affects the kinds of analysis that we can do.

Labelling

The last way we use numbers is to label things. These numbers are not 'real numbers' but are used to identify things and distinguish them from each other. One example is phone numbers. If your friend has a higher phone number than you, this doesn't mean they have a better phone line than you – these numbers just distinguish your phone line from theirs. Your 'phone number' could just as well be made up of letters as numbers. It could even be a sequence of colours or pictures. As long as there were enough combinations to differentiate between everyone's phone lines, we could use any system we wanted.

Another example is the number printed on the back of a sportsperson's jersey or vest. In some sports, particular numbers indicate the position the player has taken on the field or court, but this isn't universal, and certain numbers have become identified with particular players (such as the number 23 for the basketball player Michael Jordan). You can't do meaningful calculations with these numbers. It's not the case that the player with number 20 on their jersey is twice as a good as the player with number 10 on their back; they're just playing in different positions or have chosen (or been given) different numbers. In either case the 'number' has no numeric value – it's just a label to help spectators and commentators identify players.

It's important not to confuse 'numbers' that are used to label things (phone lines, players, etc) with 'real numbers' that represent a measurement. This might sound like a mistake that you'd never actually make, but, because of the nature of the software that we use to help us conduct statistical analysis, it's often the case that we have to label our data with numbers in exactly this way. In a spreadsheet containing all our data, we're likely to have some numbers that represent measurements and some that are just used as labels. This can sometimes be confusing, so you need to be aware of it and recognise when numbers actually represent numerical values and when they are just being used as labels.

In the next section we'll look closely at how these different ways of using numbers affect what kind of analyses we can conduct. I show you how, by asking some simple questions, you can identify exactly which way numbers are being used. You'll then be in a good position to choose the most appropriate analyses to conduct.

Types of number and types of variable

So how do these different ways in which we use numbers affect the analysis we do? The answer to this question relates to something called **levels of measurement**. I've already touched on this topic when we looked at the difference between 'measuring' and 'counting' in the last section. As long as we recognise when numbers are being used as labels – and don't treat these as 'real numbers' – the most important distinction is between counting and measuring.

Continuous and discrete data

If you're measuring a variable using a true scale, then your data is likely to be continuous. What this means is that a value for that variable could be anywhere along a continuum. To use a simple example – if you're measuring someone's height with a tape measure, in theory their height could fall anywhere along the tape. If you could measure with enough accuracy, there are an infinite number of possible values between the tallest person alive and the shortest. Another example would be the time it takes to run 100 metres. World records are usually only specified to the nearest hundredth of a second, but it's possible to measure time more accurately than this in practice, and theoretically time could be measured with infinite precision. Money is another example. When you buy something in a shop or online, you usually only pay in whole units – such as pennies or cents. But in banking and trading currencies are sometimes calculated to a fraction of the smallest unit available as cash. These are all examples of continuous data and so, measured in these terms, height, time and money can be considered to be continuous variables.

Another kind of data, called discrete data, is very similar to continuous data. The difference between continuous data and discrete data is that discrete data can only take on certain values (often, but not always, whole numbers). So, to use the example above, if we are paying for something in cash, usually we can only pay to the value of a whole penny or cent.

Another example might be marks awarded to a student in an assessment. It's common for tests to be marked out of 100, with the result given as a percentage. When I mark essays, I give marks as a whole number (for example, 67%). These marks aren't really continuous, as I don't award marks that include a fraction of a per cent or that are expressed to a number of decimal places. So, my marking produces discrete data because there are only 101 possible different marks (from 0% to 100%), rather than the (theoretically) infinite number with a continuous scale.

Some statistical techniques have been designed to be used with variables that are continuous. However, in most cases you can also use these techniques with discrete data. This is because, although cash might only be available in whole units of currency, and marks may only be awarded as whole percentages, fractions of a cent or percentage make sense to us. Although there aren't any coins that are smaller than a penny or cent, the idea of 'a quarter of a cent' or '0.73 cents' isn't something that is confusing to us. If we have a savings account, we'd want our bank to give us all the interest we'd earned, even if the calculation hadn't ended up on a whole number. The same applies for when we combine the results of more than one assessment to calculate a student's overall mark. Even though I only award marks in whole percentages, we understand what it means when a student gets an average mark of 66.5% once the results of more than one assessment have been combined, and we would consider them to have a higher mark than someone who only got 66%.

If you have continuous or discrete data, every case should have a number of its own, and that number should be a 'real number' that we could use to do meaningful calculations (more on this later). So, for example, each of my students would have a particular mark in their test. Or each runner in a race would have their own finishing time. This is important, as it's not the same as when we have a different type of data – called 'categorical data'.

Categorical data

Categorical data are different to continuous and discrete data because for any individual case, there *isn't* a 'real number' associated with the thing that you're interested in. Rather than assigning each case a number (like we might for someone's age in years, or their annual salary), each case can only be given a label or put into a category.

A simple example of categorical data is the type of fuel that a car runs on. Every car runs on a particular fuel or a combination of different fuels. The categories might be, for example: petrol, diesel, electricity and hybrid. If I asked you what type of fuel your car ran on, you would use one of these words (or say something similar) to describe the fuel. You would be unlikely to give me a number for the type of fuel, as this wouldn't make any sense (although some fuels do have numbers attached to them). Because you (and everyone else in my study) are providing me with data in the form of a label or category, the data I am collecting would be categorical data. You have told me what category of fuel your car runs on.

If, on the other hand, I asked you how economical your car was, you could give me an answer in miles-per-gallon or litres-per-100 km. As you are giving me a number – one that I could sensibly do arithmetic with – these data would be continuous, because we could assign a meaningful number to each respondent's car, and that number could be anywhere along a continuum. It would make sense, for example, to say that your car gets 45 miles to the gallon.

Lots of the variables that social researchers are interested in are categorical. Many of these relate to people's backgrounds and social characteristics, such as social or occupational class, gender, sexual orientation, religious affiliation, employment status, and so on. For example, it's common for social researchers to be interested in how people's race or ethnicity affects their lives. Participants in surveys are often asked to assign themselves to a category that is closest to their racial or ethnic identity or background. As I explain in Box 2.0, researchers don't always agree about what these categories are, how many there should be, and what they are called – and there are often differences between countries and over time. But, however race and ethnicity are conceptualised and defined, the important thing for our discussion is that people would identify with a label or description rather than a number. A participant in the 2011 UK Census might choose to identify as British Indian, but they couldn't put a number on their ethnicity: that just wouldn't make any sense.

Box 2.0: How categories of race and ethnicity vary between countries and over time

As the ideas of race and ethnicity aren't straightforward, the categories available to respondents have changed over time and vary between countries. For example, the 2011 UK Census provided respondents with 13 different ethnic categories that they could choose from, as well as a chance to specify an answer that was not listed. The 2010 US Census was quite different. It included five categories for 'race', but respondents could specify more than one of these, including the option of 'writing in' a category that wasn't listed. As well as picking a category for race, they could specify 'Hispanic or Latino' or 'Not Hispanic or Latino' as an additional 'ethnicity'. Previous censuses in both countries have had different numbers of categories available for respondents and have also labelled some of these categories differently. How race and ethnicity is categorised not only varies between countries but has also changed over time. This reflects the different histories of these countries but has also been influenced by changes in the way that we think about the concepts of race and ethnicity.

Two types of categorical data: nominal and ordinal

Working out whether your data are categorical, or whether they are continuous or discrete, is the first step towards working out what kind of analysis you need to do. For most techniques that I cover in this book, this is probably the most important consideration.

However, there are two different types of categorical data – nominal data and ordinal data – and this difference sometimes matters when choosing analyses or when presenting your results. But the difference between the two types is easy to understand, and you'll be familiar with it from the way you think about categories in your daily life.

The key difference is that nominal data is divided into categories that don't have any order or hierarchy, while ordinal data is also divided into categories that do have a clear order. The examples below should help you see the difference between the two.

Ethnicity is an example of **nominal data**. If we produce a list of different ethnic groups, there wouldn't be any clear order that we would put them in. We might group some categories together, but none of them would be seen as being 'higher' or 'lower' than any other group. Data on educational attainment, however, might be different. If you asked people about their highest level of educational attainment, you might give them the following options:

• PhD or doctorate
• Master's degree

- Undergraduate degree
- High school diploma
- No qualifications

Ignoring for a moment whether this covers all the available options, there is a clear hierarchy here. In most education systems, a PhD is a higher level of education than a Master's degree, which is, in turn, higher than an undergraduate degree, and a high school diploma is lower than all of these. But having a high school diploma is a higher level of attainment than having no qualifications at all. Because there is a clear order to these categories, these data are known as **ordinal**.

So, we have two types of categorical data: nominal and ordinal. What these have in common is that data for a particular case will fit into a category (such as an ethnic group or level of education). This is different from continuous or discrete data, where each case will have a meaningful number attached to it (such as age in years, or a percentage score in a test).

Labelling categories using numbers

Earlier in this chapter I pointed out that one of the things that confuses students when they first start doing statistical analysis is that we sometimes label categories with numbers. This is sometimes just to save us writing out category names in full, but it is often because the spreadsheets in statistics software only accept numbers, or are designed to be used most effectively with numeric data.

Box 2.1: More levels of measurement?

Most statistics textbooks tell you about at least four different levels of measurement: ratio, interval, ordinal and nominal. This typology was first suggested by Stanley Stevens in 1946, and has become a standard element in most curricula and textbooks.

Ratio and interval measurements are both continuous, and so the difference between them doesn't matter when you are choosing your analysis. Distinguishing between them makes things more complicated but doesn't affect what analysis you do, so I haven't explained the difference here. If you're interested, you can have a look at the original article or read a shorter explanation on Wikipedia.

To take an example I used earlier, we might have data on the type of fuel used by different cars. This is categorical data, but these categories might be labelled with different numbers to enable the data to be easily processed by the software we are using:

1. Petrol (gasoline)
2. Diesel
3. Hybrid
4. Electricity

The numbers attached to each category of fuel don't have any numerical value at all. It's not the case that 'Hybrid' is worth 'three times' more than 'Petrol', as this wouldn't make any sense. They are simply labels, just like a phone number or a number on a sports jersey. In this example, they don't even tell us anything about order, as the data on fuel type is nominal, and we could have attached any number to each of the four categories. All the numbers do is allow the software to distinguish between the separate categories without using words.

The example of level of education is slightly different because it is ordinal data:

1. PhD or doctorate
2. Master's degree
3. Undergraduate degree
4. High school diploma

Although these numbers show the *order* of a hierarchy, they are not the same as the numbers in continuous or discrete data, and shouldn't be confused with them. Again, they don't have any real numeric value and are only used here as labels for those categories. They shouldn't be used for doing any arithmetical calculations as the data is still fundamentally categorical.

In the discussion that follows I'm going to contrast using numbers as labels with assigning what I will call 'real numbers' to each case. When I talk about a 'real number', what I mean is that this number is something we could sensibly use to do calculations. This includes things like someone's age in years, their income, the distance they travel to work, and so on. But it wouldn't include someone's phone number or their bank card number, which are just used to differentiate their phone line or bank account from someone else's.

Telling the difference between different levels of measurement

If you're trying to work out whether data are categorical, discrete or continuous, the first thing to do is ask yourself the following:

> Can I assign a 'real number' to each case?

If you can answer 'yes' to this question, then your data are continuous or discrete. If you answer 'no', then your variable is probably categorical. Let's go back to the example about which fuel powers a particular car:

Can I assign a 'real number' to the type of fuel a car runs on?

No. We can only talk about types of fuel in terms of categories: petrol, diesel, electricity and hybrid combinations. We can't assign a number to each case that we could do maths with. Any number we assigned would just be a label.

We have answered 'no' to the question. We can therefore conclude that these are categorical data.

Compare this with the next example, which was the fuel consumption of a particular car:

Can I assign a 'real number' to the fuel consumption of a car?

Yes. Each car has a particular fuel consumption that could be measured as miles per gallon or litres per 100 km. We could assign a number to each case and use these numbers for calculations.

We have answered 'yes' to the question. We can therefore conclude that these are continuous or discrete data.

These examples are quite straightforward, but it's not always so easy to work out whether some variables are categorical or whether they are continuous or discrete. Age is a good example of this, as it is often collected and presented as both discrete and categorical data.

Some variables can have different levels of measurement depending on how the data is collected

If I asked you how old you were, you would probably give me an answer in years. Age in years is a 'real number' that we could use to do calculations, as it would make sense to say that someone who is 20 years old is twice the age of someone who is only 10 years old. It's also true that the difference between age 7 and 10 is three years, and that this is the same absolute distance as the difference in years between 10 and 13. Fractions of a year also make sense – lots of children will tell you that they are four-and-a-half or five-and-three-quarters years old!

So, age in years qualifies as discrete data. (It could be continuous data, but as we tend to collect it in whole years – at least from adults – it only takes discrete values.) You have a number for each person and you can use this number to do mathematical calculations that make sense. You could also use it with statistical techniques that require continuous data, because it makes sense to think of fractions of a year or people being at various points between their birthdays.

But it's not always this simple. Data on age are often collected or presented as age groups. You've probably filled in a form or questionnaire where the answers you can select from look something like this:

What is your age?	Under 18	☐
	18 to 24	☐
	25 to 34	☐
	35 to 44	☐
	45 to 54	☐
	55 to 64	☐
	65 and over	☐

If we collect our data like this, do we still end up with continuous or discrete data? Or are these data categorical? Let's see by using our test:

Can we assign a 'real number' to the age of a person?

We've seen that we can do this if we collect the data for age in years. However, by collecting data using the question format above, we don't get an exact age for each person. In fact, we get a mixture of numbers and words. If we have continuous or discrete data, we should be able to do some calculations with it and come out with a sensible answer. But for someone placed in the '18 to 24' category, we wouldn't know which number to use. People in this category could be 18, they could be 24, or they could be any age in between. So, '18 to 24' is the *label* for a category, rather than a numeric value.

When we collect data as age groups we actually end up with categorical data. There are some good reasons why you might decide to collect data on age as categorical data rather than continuous or discrete data, but it's important to bear in mind that how you collect your data can have implications for how you can analyse them, and so you need to think about your analysis right at the beginning of your research. (If you are using data that someone else has collected, you don't get any choice in this. But it's still important to work out what the level of measurement is, because you'll need to know this to work out what analysis you can use.)

Don't be caught out when looking at data that have already been analysed

One of the things that sometimes catches my students out is when they see categorical data that have already been analysed. Occasionally, they look at these results and mistake categorical data for continuous or discrete data.

Table 2.0 shows the number and proportion of students enrolled on different degree programmes who take one of my classes:

Table 2.0: Number and proportion of students enrolled on different degree programmes

Degree programme	Sociology	Criminology	Politics	Total
Number of students	43	94	27	164
Percentage	26.2	57.3	16.5	100.0

If we wanted to decide whether data on degree programme studied was categorical, or continuous or discrete, we need to apply our test:

> Can we assign a 'real number' to the choice of degree programme?

Looking at Table 2.0 you might be tempted to say that we can. After all, we can see some numbers in the table that have already been assigned to these data. And we could use these numbers to do calculations. It would make sense to say that there are more than twice as many criminology students as there are sociology students in my class. We can see from the table that 94 (57.3%) of my students are on criminology degree programmes, but only 43 (26.2%) are studying sociology. We have some real numbers for these data, so data on degree programme must be continuous or discrete, right?

Well, no. The confusion here is between assigning a meaningful number to *each case* and using numbers to summarise what is happening with the cases as a whole (after they have been counted up). Our question should really have been:

> Can a 'real number' be assigned to *each student's* choice of degree programme?

When we answer this question, and think about the answer that a student would give when asked about what degree subject they are studying, we soon realise that they couldn't give a number, only a label such as 'politics'. A 'real number' can't be assigned to *each case*, and so the data must be categorical.

If you want to practice working out whether a variable is categorical or continuous, Exercise 2.1 might be helpful.

EXERCISE 2.1

Think about the following variables that might be used in a research project. For each one, decide whether it is categorical, discrete or continuous:

a)   The amount of time students spent studying in the library in a single semester.

b)   The number of times students visited the library in a single semester.

c)   The religion that a person currently identifies with.

d)   An employee's occupational group.

The use of rating scales: when are data really continuous?

Now that we've looked at the difference between categorical and continuous data in some detail, you'll hopefully have the skills you need to be able to work out what kind of data you have before you start doing any analysis. But before we move on to another topic, we need to look at a common way in which data are collected that makes this decision a bit more difficult.

You've probably seen a question in a questionnaire set out like this:

Question 2.0
Raising taxes for those earning salaries of over £100,000 is a fair way of generating income for essential services.

Strongly disagree	Disagree	Don't know/ Undecided	Agree	Strongly agree
☐	☐	☐	☐	☐

This type of question often asks people how much they agree or disagree with a statement, but it can also take slightly different forms. They are used for everything from asking people how happy they feel about some aspect of their life to how much they like using a particular product. In the Crime Survey for England and Wales (CSEW), for example, respondents are asked to select answers about the level of worry they have – from 'Very worried' to 'Not at all worried' – about being the victim of different types of crime.

On the face of it, the data produced by this kind of question are clearly categorical. If you asked Question 2.0 to someone verbally, they would answer with one of the five words or phrases provided. They might say 'Agree', for example. And as there's a progression in levels of agreement from 'Strongly agree' at one extreme to 'Strongly disagree' at the other, we can also say that these data are ordinal.

As we'll see in Chapter 3, one way of starting your analysis with the data produced by this item could be simply to count how many of your respondents selected each category and perhaps also calculate the percentages. You could then use these figures to work out both the strength and direction of feeling about raising taxes for high earners.

However, some researchers go further than this and attach numbers to each response. This is sometimes done alongside the answer options, as can be seen in Question 2.1, or sometimes data are collected from questions that look like Question 2.0, and the numbers are added by the researchers after the data have been collected.

Question 2.1
Raising taxes for those earning salaries of over £100,000 is a fair way of generating income for essential services.

Strongly disagree	Disagree	Don't know/ Undecided	Agree	Strongly agree
1	2	3	4	5

There are many variations on this type of question, both in terms of the number of possible responses and how many of these responses are **anchored** to labels (such as 'Agree'). In Question 2.2 there are 10 answer options, but there isn't what is called an 'anchor label' for each possible response – only one at each end to indicate the direction the numbers take. This type of scale is called **unanchored**, in contrast to Questions 2.0 and 2.1, where the responses are 'anchored' to labels describing what they represent.

Question 2.2
Raising taxes for those earning salaries of over £100,000 is a fair way of generating income for essential services.

Disagree									Agree
1	2	3	4	5	6	7	8	9	10

Unanchored scales are more difficult than anchored ones to interpret in terms of their 'real world' meaning, because it's not exactly clear what each response means and how it is different from the other options. When you choose an option that is marked 'Agree', it's fairly clear what your answer means. But, for Question 2.2, how should we interpret an answer of '3'? And how is this answer different to '2' or '4'? This is an issue I'll return to below.

Seeing these numbers is usually an indication that the researcher plans to treat the data generated from this question as continuous (or at least discrete) data. Doing this allows them to do different types of analyses. They can go further than counting up the number of respondents who selected each option and do things such as calculating mean averages and other statistical analyses that we cover later in the book. These analyses can not only be conducted for all the respondents' answers to a particular question, but can also be used to calculate the respondents' scores for all or some of the questions combined.

Box 2.2: Use and abuse of the term 'Likert scale'

The most famous versions of these items and scales are named after a psychologist called Rensis Likert (pronounced 'Lick-ert') who first proposed using them, in the early 1930s, to measure people's attitudes (Likert, 1932). Likert had some very strict rules about the use of these scales, but nowadays the term 'Likert scale' is often used more loosely to describe any type of rating scale.

If you're interested in reading the debate about what does and doesn't count as a 'Likert scale', you might want to read a short critique of these kind of 'rating' scales by Jamieson (2004), and a much longer response by Carifio and Perla (2007), who go into some detail about what counts as a true Likert scale. I've listed these articles at the end of the chapter.

But what kind of data is being produced here? Is it really continuous (or discrete), or is it actually categorical? The best way of working this out is to look at how these numbers are created and whether we think they behave as 'real numbers'. But there are also some issues about the wording of the answers provided in this kind of question that we need to think about.

Let's use Question 2.1 as an example. All the answers relate to levels of agreement and disagreement. Unlike something like time, money or distance, there's no widely accepted scale for agreement and disagreement. But if we say that we agree with something, or that we disagree with it, or that we're undecided, most people will understand what we mean by this. We aren't likely to confuse the meaning of any of these answers with each other: they are all different in ways we can easily understand. Three of the five answer options in Question 2.1 are both easily understood and clearly different from each other.

If we treat the data produced by Questions 2.0 or 2.1 as categorical in our analyses, this would be reasonably straightforward. Leaving aside for a moment the issue of how useful it is to distinguish between 'Agree' and 'Strongly agree', treating the data as ordinal is fairly uncontroversial. People answering 'Strongly disagree' obviously have different views than those answering 'Strongly agree', and the options between are placed in a sensible order between the two extremes.

However, if we treat the data as continuous or discrete, we are making some much stronger assumptions about the relationship between the different possible answers. Let's look at Question 2.1 again.

Question 2.1
Raising taxes for those earning salaries of over £100,000 is a fair way of generating income for essential services.

Strongly disagree	Disagree	Don't know/ Undecided	Agree	Strongly agree
1	2	3	4	5

If we treat the numbers attached to each answer option as 'real numbers', and analyse them in the same way as we would sums of money or periods of time, we are treating these numbers the same as, for example, US dollars or kilometres. It's fine to say that someone with US$1,000 has twice as much money as someone with US$500, or that a train journey of 60 km is half as long as one taking 120 km. But what about saying that someone who answered 'Agree' to Question 2.1 having twice the 'agreement' of someone who answered 'Disagree'? And would they agree four times as much as someone who answered 'Strongly disagree'? Can we really 'measure' degrees of agreement in this way?

Having options that aren't anchored to labels, such as in Question 2.2, makes things even more difficult. We've already considered that there may be a problem with people's understanding of what, for example, an answer of '3' really means to different people. But this becomes even more important if we're going to do some calculations with this figure. This is because now we're not just saying that an answer of '3' is different to an answer of '4', but that this difference has a precise numerical value of one unit (or, to put it differently, that the numbers are 'equal interval').

Question 2.2

Raising taxes for those earning salaries of over £100,000 is a fair way of generating income for essential services.

Disgree									Agree
1	2	3	4	5	6	7	8	9	10

If we treat data produced with this type of question as continuous or discrete, we're making two important assumptions:

1. Each option means exactly the same to each respondent.
2. There are equal intervals between the answer options that we give them.

If we then combine the answers to these questions to make a scale, we also assume that:

3. All the questions are of equal importance.

It's very common for researchers to use 'rating scale' questions like this. And many researchers treat the answers given by respondents as continuous or discrete data in their analyses. It's also common for these answers to be combined to produce a scale that is intended to measure, for example, someone's fear of crime, their trust in the government or attitude to drug use. However, it's important to understand that when we do this we are making assumptions, both about people's shared understanding of the question-and-answer options as well as the relationship between these different answer options.

There has been a great deal of debate over the years about whether data produced by these types of questions can be treated as continuous or not. If you're unsure whether data like this really is continuous, it may be safer and simpler to either treat these data as categorical, or even to use a different method to collect data on this topic.

Summary

In this chapter we looked in detail both at what numbers really are and at the different ways we use them. I hope it has given you the knowledge to make the most important distinction between the types of data – or 'levels of measurement' – we use for statistical analysis: categorical and continuous data. As we have seen, sometimes it's easy to work out what kind of data you have, but in some cases it's more difficult or ambiguous.

In the next chapter we get started with the 'nuts and bolts' of analysis by looking at why you would want to analyse a variable on its own, and how you do this with different kinds of data.

References
Likert, R. (1932) 'A technique for the measurement of attitudes', *Archives of Psychology*, 140: 1–55.
Stevens, S.S. (1946) 'On the theory of scales of measurement', *Science*, 103(2684): 677–80.

Useful resources
Susan Jamieson provides a brief summary of why she believes Likert scale data should not be treated as continuous:

Jamieson, S. (2004) 'Likert scales: How to (ab)use them', *Medical Education*, 38: 1217–18.

James Carifio and Rocco Perla respond to Susan Jamieson's article with a very detailed account of what counts as a true Likert scale and a defence of their use:

Carifio, J. and Perla, R.J. (2007) 'Ten common misunderstandings, misconceptions, persistent myths and urban legends about Likert scales and Likert response formats and their antidotes', *Journal of Social Sciences*, 3(3): 106–16.

Alan Bryman has written a great deal on the relationship between 'quantitative' and 'qualitative' methods. One of his most accessible discussions can be found here:

Bryman, A. (2010) 'Quantitative vs Qualitative Methods?', in A. Giddens and P. Sutton (eds) *Sociology: Introductory Readings* (3rd edn), Cambridge: Polity Press, Chapter 9.

Answers to exercises

Exercise 2.0
a) This exercise is intended to get you to think about how you use numbers in everyday life, and in what situations we tend to use numbers and in what situations we don't. Thinking about the differences between these situations, and the reasons why we use numbers in some of them but not in others, is good practice for when you are doing research, when you will be faced with decisions about when it's sensible to quantify something and use numbers to represent it (and when it's not).

b) This question asked you to think specifically about some of the things we might study as social researchers. Although this is a slightly different context, your thinking should be similar. Just because you're now thinking about things we're interested in as researchers, rather than your day-to-day life, there's no need to change the way you come to a decision about whether it's sensible to use numbers or not. After all, as social researchers, we study the same world we live in!

Exercise 2.1

In this exercise we asked you to decide whether each of four variables was either categorical, discrete or continuous.

a) These data (and therefore the variable) would be continuous. The amount of time a student spends in the library could be measured – at least in theory – to the smallest fraction of a second.

b) The number of times students visited the library in a single semester is a discrete variable. You might go to the library 21 times and one of your friends may only go 7 times. It makes sense to say that you've visited the library 14 more times (or three times as often). You can't have a fraction of a visit – you either went to the library or you didn't. So this variable would also be discrete, because the number of visits can only take certain values – in this case, whole numbers.

c) If I asked you what religion you identified with you would have to give me a label, rather than a number, even if this was to say that you weren't religious. Because of this, the variable 'religious identification' would be categorical: we don't 'measure' religion; we describe religious groups using their names. But is it nominal or ordinal data? Ordinal data, as the name suggests, has an order, and as it doesn't make sense to put religions in any kind of order, this would be a nominal categorical variable.

d) Occupational groups are usually labelled (for example, 'professional', 'administrative', etc), and so are categorical. These labels can be numeric ('114', '242', in the Standard Occupational Classification 2000 classification, for example), but they are not 'real' numbers. (Think of them in the same way as telephone numbers or the numbers on the back of sports jerseys.) Whether these data are ordinal or nominal will vary between different classifications. Some classifications are hierarchical and have an order – and so are ordinal – and others do not – and so are nominal.

3

Absolute beginnings: starting statistical analysis one variable at a time

WHAT IS THIS CHAPTER FOR?

Following on from the last chapter, where we looked at the different ways we use numbers, in this chapter I introduce some techniques for analysing one variable at a time. This is called univariate analysis. You usually need to start your analyses by using univariate techniques, so this chapter helps you begin the process of 'doing statistics'.

WHAT DOES IT COVER?

I explain why these kinds of analyses should be the starting point for the analysis of any dataset, and show you some of the different statistical techniques for examining categorical and continuous data. In this chapter we look at using frequencies and percentages with categorical data and using averages with continuous and discrete data.

WHAT WILL YOU LEARN?

- Why you always need to start with univariate analysis
- Which univariate statistical techniques you can use with categorical and continuous or discrete data
- What these techniques can (and can't) tell you about the distribution of a variable
- How to choose the best statistics to use in different circumstances

WHAT CONCEPTS AND TECHNIQUES ARE COVERED?

- Frequency counts
- Percentages and other proportional measures
- Averages: the mean, median and mode

This is statistical analysis!

In Chapters 1 and 2 I introduced some important terms and concepts that you need to be familiar with before you start analysing your data. In this chapter we're finally going to start learning how to conduct some statistical analyses. Even if you've never done any statistics before, you might be surprised to see how many of the techniques we cover are familiar to you already, perhaps from school or work, or just from life in general. There are a couple of trickier ideas towards the end of the chapter, but not all the concepts and techniques I discuss are likely to be completely new to you. As with quite a few of the things I cover in this book, you might have already done some statistical analysis without even realising it.

Why look at only one variable?

However good you become at doing statistical analysis, and however sophisticated the techniques you go on to use, you should always start your analysis by looking at each of your variables separately. Looking at one variable at a time is called univariate analysis. When we look at the relationship between two variables, this is called bivariate analysis, and when we look at the relationship between three or more variables at once, this is called **multi-variable analysis**. It's quite easy to remember what these terms mean because a unicycle has one wheel and a bicycle has two. And if a piece of clothing is multi-coloured, then it's usually more than two different colours.

But why do we have to start by looking at each different variable separately? Aren't we most interested in the relationships between variables? So shouldn't we start doing bivariate or multi-variable analysis as soon as possible?

It's true that most reports of research using statistical analysis focus on the relationships between variables. The 'story' of the research that is written up usually concentrates on these relationships. However, you'll see that these reports usually also include the results of some univariate analyses, even if only in a single table or hidden away at the end, in an appendix. Researchers include these results because they are a vital part of the process of analysis *and* because they know that other researchers might want to see them.

There are three main reasons why univariate analysis is important. Some univariate analyses can produce useful findings in themselves, especially in new areas of research where there isn't much existing data. But univariate analysis serves two other vital purposes: helping the researcher 'get to know' the data they are using and identifying any problems with the data early on.

Sometimes one variable is important

There are times when data on a single variable can be important and useful. The number of people currently unemployed, the average house price or the longest time someone has waited for an operation are all figures that tell us something important about the society we live in. During the coronavirus pandemic that started in late 2019, the number of new cases, the number of hospital admissions and the number of deaths each day were all statistics that were crucial for informing the government's and the public's response in each affected country. All these figures are the results of univariate analyses.

But univariate analysis is usually just the starting point for further analyses. For example, we might want to know how unemployment has varied over time, so that we can see how good or bad the current situation is in relative terms. We could be interested in how house prices vary between regions. Or we may want to know the differences in waiting times for different operations. Finding out these things would require the bivariate analyses we look at in later chapters. But for now, we're going to concentrate on why you need to look at each variable separately, and what doing this can tell you.

Getting to know your data

It's often the case that univariate analysis – on its own – won't reveal any particularly interesting stories in your data. The unemployment rate might be well known, for example, and what you are really interested in is finding out how unemployment varies between people from different social backgrounds. You'd need to use bivariate (or multi-variable) analysis to do this. But, as I'll explain, this doesn't mean that you won't need to conduct any univariate analysis.

Whatever kind of research you do, and whatever type of analysis you plan to conduct, it's always good to become familiar with your dataset. This is the case whether you are going to do some statistics or use another analytical technique. For example, if you had conducted some interviews, you would probably read through the transcripts a few times before starting doing any kind of **coding**. The same is true for conducting statistical analysis: you need to get to know your data before looking at the relationships that you're interested in. Univariate analysis can help you with this.

Getting to know your data using univariate analysis can give you an idea about what each of your variables 'looks like'. For a categorical variable, this can tell you how many cases are in each category, and whether there are any categories that have no cases in them at all. For continuous or discrete variables, it can tell you where the 'middle' of the data are, how spread out the data are, and what the largest and smallest values are.

In your dataset you will have both dependent (outcome) and independent (explanatory) variables. My examples of univariate analysis so far have focused on dependent variables – the outcomes we are interested in. Even if you think you have a good idea what the data for these variables will look like, you'll still need to do some analysis to check. But you'll also need to look at each of your independent variables in order to 'get to know' them, too.

Knowing what your data look like can also help you make assessments about how **representative** your dataset is of your population. Even if you start with population data or a random sample, you might not end up with a representative sample, for various reasons. If you've used a non-random sampling strategy, it's quite likely that your sample will be different from your population in some way. Using univariate analysis to find out about the distribution of each of your variables can help you with this. Smith (2008) shows you how you can compare the **demographic characteristics** of your sample with **aggregate data** to judge the representativeness of your data.

Are there any potential problems?

Univariate analysis can also alert you to issues that might affect the analyses you conduct later. The most obvious potential issue is **missing data**. Regardless of how you collected your data, or whether you are using data collected by someone else, it's likely that you don't have data for every variable for every case. This will affect your analysis, because if there isn't data on a particular variable for a particular case, that case cannot be included in any of the analyses using that variable. If you're planning on doing multi-variable analysis, this is even more of a problem, as you have more variables being analysed at any one time, and you can only include cases that have data on every one of these variables.

Reporting missing data is good practice when you write up your results. You need to report what proportion of your cases was included in each of your analyses, and how many could not be included because of missing data. You also need to think about how missing data may have affected your results. Gorard (2021) gives some useful advice about this.

An issue that can cause slightly different problems is an **implausible value**. An implausible value is one that is either impossible or very unlikely. For example, if you collected data on people's age in years, a value of 256 would be implausible because nobody lives that long. A value of 108 is possible, but unlikely. For the first value, you would have to try to find out what the real age of this person is, perhaps by checking if there was a mistake when the data was transcribed or entered. If this is not possible, this value would have to be removed from the dataset and you would effectively have missing data for age for this particular case. For the second value – 108 – ideally you would confirm whether this is a correct value, but again, this may not be possible. If you doubt that the value is correct, you may want to consider removing it. This is only a concern for continuous or discrete variables, but can also mean that a case may not be able to be used in certain analyses.

One issue that can affect the categorical variables in your dataset is small numbers of cases – or no cases at all – in certain categories. If there aren't any cases in a category, this won't cause problems for the mechanics of your statistical analysis, but it may mean that your dataset isn't representative of your population of interest. For example, if your population includes people from a particular ethnic group, but no one in your sample belongs to that ethnic group, then this group won't be represented in your findings. Very small groups are more likely to be missing from your sample, and unless your sampling strategy has taken this possibility into account, it's not unheard of for a whole group to be unrepresented in a sample.

It's more common to end up with a sample that has a small number of cases in some categories. It is the **absolute number** of cases in a category that is important for statistical analysis, so don't worry about there being an imbalance of cases in different categories (that's exactly what we'd expect for many variables in a completely representative sample). But small numbers of cases in categories can be a problem for some analyses. I'll discuss this problem in greater detail in later chapters, but it's worth making a note of any groups containing small numbers of cases when you're doing your univariate analysis, so that this doesn't surprise you later on.

So what do you need to do to 'get to know' your data? In the next section we'll start to look at the different techniques that are available for different types of data.

Two types of data, two approaches to analysis

In the last chapter we saw that there are two main ways in which we use numbers. We either put cases into categories, creating categorical data, or we assign numbers to each case by making some kind of 'measurement', creating continuous or discrete data. Although we discussed other ways we use numbers, these two are the most common, and working out whether a variable is categorical or continuous is the first thing you have to do when deciding what statistical techniques you can use.

I have a categorical variable: what can I do?

If you have a categorical variable, there are only a small number of tools for univariate analysis, but the good news is that you'll probably already be familiar with them. They will usually be the same whether your categorical data is **nominal** or **ordinal**, so you don't need to worry about that difference; if you've got data where you've assigned cases to categories, then these are the techniques you can use.

Imagine that I wanted to find out about people's religious affiliations in the city where I worked at the time of the 2011 Census. We can double-check that religious affiliation is a categorical variable by asking what sort of answer people would give if we asked them about their religion: they would give you a label or description (in words) rather than a real number, so this means that the variable is categorical. We can also check that I should be doing univariate analysis. I'm only interested in data for a single year (rather than, say, change over time), so only one variable is involved, and univariate analysis is what is required.

Univariate analysis of categorical variables can give us information on two things: the number of cases in each category (frequencies or counts) and the proportion of cases in each category (often shown as percentages). As I discuss below, both of these can be useful in different ways in different circumstances.

Looking at percentages

Table 3.0 shows data from the UK Census on the religious affiliation of people living in Leicester for the year 2011. These are population data, rather than data collected from a sample, so include almost everyone living in the city in that year. Looking at the percentages in the column on the right of the table is the easiest way to understand the relative size of each of the religious groups. Because the

Table 3.0: Population of Leicester, by religious affiliation, 2011

	Number	Percentage
Christian	106,872	32.4
No religion	75,280	22.8
Muslim	61,440	18.6
Hindu	50,087	15.2
Religion not stated	18,345	5.6
Sikh	14,457	4.4
Other religion	1,839	0.6
Buddhist	1,224	0.4
Jewish	295	0.1
Total	**329,839**	**100.0**

Note: Data may not add up to exactly 100% due to the rounding of decimal places in each group.

percentages add up to a total of 100, the proportions can be understood quite easily, simply because 100 is a relatively small number that we're all familiar with.

Percentages are also easy to convert into fractions. One per cent is actually one-hundredth, so percentages are already fractions, but some percentages are easier than others to translate into other fractions. You might have worked out that the 32.4% of Leicester residents who identify as Christian represent just under one-third of the population of the city. And those with no religion make up somewhere between one-fifth and one-quarter of the population, at 22.8%. Percentages and fractions are both proportional measures that make it easier for us to understand how cases are shared out – or distributed – between categories.

Box 3.0: Other measures of proportion

Although percentages and fractions are probably the most common proportional measures, and perhaps the ones you are most familiar with, there are other measures that can be more helpful in particular circumstances.

Relatively rare events, such as being a victim of a particular crime, are sometimes expressed in rates per 1,000 people. For example, in data from the 2020/21 Crime Survey for England and Wales (CSEW), 2 in 1,000 people had their vehicle stolen. If this was expressed as a percentage, it would be 0.2%. Using rates per 1,000 people allows us to visualise this in terms of 'whole' people, which is a bit more intuitive.

You aren't restricted to just using rates per 1,000 cases either. You can use any number that's useful. You might have noticed that, during the COVID-19 pandemic, infection rates were often reported as rates per 100,000 people. As with rates per

1,000, this allows us to end up with whole numbers of cases, which are easier to visualise. On the day I'm writing this (in 2022), in Portugal there were 67 new cases of coronavirus per 100,000 members of the population. If this was expressed as a percentage, it would be a much less user-friendly 0.00067%.

How useful are frequencies?

In the middle column of Table 3.0 there are data on the number of people in each religious group. Here the title of the column is 'Number', but this is often shortened to 'N'. As I explained earlier, these numbers are also referred to as frequencies or counts. As we shall see, whereas we look at the data on proportions to tell us how the cases are shared out between categories, how we use the data on frequencies can vary depending on what those cases represent.

Because the data in Table 3.0 are from the UK Census, they are not a sample but represent (very close to) every person living in Leicester in that year. So we can see that 1,224 people described themselves as Buddhist. This is the actual number of people in this religious group, and although it might be affected by non-response and missing data, it is hopefully a reasonably accurate estimate. The key point here is that, because these are population data, we can treat the numbers in each category as estimates of the absolute size of each of the religious groups.

When we are dealing with data for a sample, we have to treat these figures slightly differently. If we have a perfectly representative sample, we can treat the percentages as representative of the wider population that the sample was drawn from. However, we can't treat the frequencies in the same way, as they reflect the sample size rather than the actual number of cases in the population the sample was drawn from. Without some extra information, and some further calculations, the frequencies for categories in research using samples can't tell us about the absolute size of those groups. The example below will help show you exactly what I mean by this.

Table 3.1 shows the results of an analysis I conducted with Crime Survey for England and Wales (CSEW) data for the closest year to the UK Census data I used in Table 3.0. As with the Census data, the variable I analysed was religious affiliation. However, the CSEW uses sample data, so it doesn't include everyone in England and Wales. But it does have a very large sample – more than 46,000 cases in 2011–12 – and this sample is carefully designed to be as representative as possible.

So it's reasonably safe to assume that the CSEW data is representative of England and Wales more widely, and that the percentages in each category reflect the wider population. However, the frequencies (in the middle column) are different from those in Table 3.0 in that they don't represent the actual number of people in England and Wales with a particular religious affiliation, only the number in the sample. There are 228 Buddhists in our sample, but there will be many more than this in the population of England and Wales.

Table 3.1: Respondents' religious affiliation (frequencies and percentages)

	Number	Percentage
Christian	34,516	75.2
No religion	8,805	19.2
Muslim	1,211	2.6
Other religion	642	1.4
Hindu	518	1.1
Buddhist	228	0.5
Total	**45,920**	**100.0**

Source: Crime Survey for England and Wales 2011–2012

So how do we use this information? If these frequencies don't reflect the actual number of people in each religious group, is it okay just to ignore them? Not quite. It's still important to look at the frequencies in each category in sample data, but for a different reason: you need to look out for categories with small numbers of cases.

The problem with small numbers

As we will see in later chapters, when you go on to do bivariate or multi-variable analysis involving categorical variables, a small number of cases in a category can be an issue. It can cause problems for some analyses or mean that you can't use a particular type of analysis at all. This is because small numbers are **volatile**: a small change in absolute terms can be a very large change proportionally. For example, if I started a new religion and could only convince one of my friends to join, we would have a membership of two. But if the next year I convinced another of my friends to join, I would have increased the membership by 50%. Just one new person joining my new religion made a very large proportional difference. However, if someone living in Leicester in 2011 had changed their religious affiliation to Muslim, the number of Muslims would change from 1,211 to 1,212, an increase of less than 0.1%. Changes to, or differences in, the frequency of cases in a category have a very different effect in categories with small and large numbers of cases. In categories with very small numbers of cases, this can make a change or difference look much more dramatic than it actually is. And with sample data, it also raises questions about whether this proportional difference or change would be reflected in the population that the sample had been selected from.

It's important to point out that the *relative number* of cases in each category doesn't matter for most analyses. Many of my students assume that for any analysis to be 'fair', all the groups need to include the same number of cases. But if you think about what most societies looks like, you really wouldn't expect all the categories in many variables to have the same number of cases. In a representative sample – or in population data – the number of people in each religious group isn't likely to be the same because, in each society, some religions are more popular than others. This would also be true for ethnic groups, social classes and many other commonly used variables. As we will see in later chapters, statistical analyses using categorical data take into account that the number of cases in different categories is often not equal. The only thing you need to worry about is if there is a very small absolute number of cases in a particular category.

I have a continuous or discrete variable: what can I do?

As you have seen, looking at the distribution of categorical variables is relatively straightforward. When you have a continuous or discrete variable, however, things are a little more complicated. There are more techniques available to you, some of which are alternatives to choose between and some of which are complimentary.

If you think about the differences between categorical and continuous variables, it's easy to see why we need to use different techniques for continuous data. Categorical variables have a finite number of categories, so we can look at the number of cases in each category, count them up, and calculate proportions. In the Census data in Table 3.0 there are nine different categories for religious affiliation (including 'No religion'). It's possible to have more than nine groups – we could create categories for the individual religions in the 'Other religion' group, for example – but we would eventually get to a point where all the religions had been accounted for, and we'd end up with a set number of categories.

Continuous variables are different because there is an infinite number of possible answers that can be associated with each case (in theory, at least). For example, if we were interested in people's annual income from their jobs, it could take any value from zero upwards. It was reported that in 2021 the CEO of the travel company Expedia was the world's highest paid employee, with a salary of US$94.6 million. Although it is clearly unusual to earn anywhere near that amount (this is an example of an **outlier** – an idea we'll be discussing later in this chapter), the amount people earn could – even in practice – be anywhere between zero and this incredibly large figure.

Because there are so many different possibilities for people's income, counting the number of people who earn the same amount isn't likely to be helpful. In fact, there is so much variation in what people earn that it's unlikely that very many people would earn *exactly* the same as someone else (apart from, perhaps, those working full-time minimum-wage jobs). If we used each different income as a category, we could end up with thousands of categories. Many of these might only have one case in them, so clearly this wouldn't be very useful.

As we use frequencies to calculate percentages, if we're not going to count how many people earn the same amount, then we won't be using any percentages either. And if we're not using either of the two techniques we used with categorical variables, what can we do?

There are two groups of statistical analyses that we can use with continuous (and discrete) variables. They help us understand two different things about how a variable is distributed:

- What the average value is
- How spread out the data are

In this chapter we're going to concentrate on averages. In the next chapter I look at the various techniques for telling you how spread out the data are.

There's no such thing as an average

Most people reading this book will be familiar with the idea of the average. We use this term in our everyday conversations and you might have come across it in maths lessons at school. Averages are also referred to as measures of **central tendency**. When we do statistical analysis we have to be careful about how we think and write about averages, for two reasons. First, there are several different averages, and they all tell us slightly different things. Second, the meaning we give to the term 'average' in our everyday lives doesn't always match any of these different measures.

My dictionary gives the following meanings for 'average': standard; normal; typical; regular. It defines 'on average' as meaning: usually; ordinarily; generally; for the most part; typically; on the whole. But while these are the meanings we give to the term 'average' in our conversations, the three averages we're going to look at give us quite specific pieces of information that don't quite match up to any of these particular definitions. To avoid confusion, it's often best to refer to the specific average that you're using. In the sections below, we're going to look at the mean, the median and the mode.

What most people 'mean' by average

When most people talk about an average in the mathematical sense, they are probably referring to what's called the arithmetic mean. This is often just shortened to the mean (although, technically, there are other kinds of mean). The arithmetic mean is the most commonly used average (or measure of central tendency), but it's not always the best one to use. The mean is calculated by adding up the values of each case and dividing by the number of cases we have.

Table 3.2 lists the names and ages of 10 people.

If we wanted to calculate the mean age for this group, we would need to do the following calculation (or, more likely, get our computer software to do it for us):

$$\frac{30 + 48 + 29 + 28 + 25 + 22 + 50 + 40 + 30 + 65}{10} = 36.7$$

Table 3.2: Respondents' age in years

Name	Age in years	Name	Age in years
Leo	30	Zion	22
Kareem	48	Cara-Beth	50
Nora	29	Dennis	40
Samarria	28	Ishod	30
Brianna	25	Peggy	65

The answer will be in the same units as the original data on age, so the mean age of the group is 36.7 years old. Before we move on to look at the other two measures of central tendency – and see how these are different – let's look at what the mean tells us, what it doesn't tell us, and some of its advantages and disadvantages.

The first thing you might notice from the answer to the equation is that, although all the respondents rounded their age to a whole year, the mean came out as a decimal. It's often the case that a mean won't reflect an actual value in the dataset and it can also, as is the case here, take on a decimal value when all the cases have values that are whole numbers. Neither of these things is necessarily a problem, but there are circumstances where it's not ideal. We'll look at some of these situations later in this chapter.

As you can see from the equation, one of the characteristics of the mean is that it uses all the data provided in a variable. This might seem like the 'fairest' way to calculate an average, as every single age has been included in the calculation. However, as we shall see, this is sometimes an advantage and sometimes a disadvantage, depending on the distribution of the variable.

To see why including all the cases isn't always a good thing, let's look at the same data again, but with an extra case added:

$$\frac{30 + 48 + 29 + 28 + 25 + 22 + 50 + 40 + 30 + 65 + 118}{11} = 44.1$$

I've added in Kane Tanaka, who was 118 years old at the time of writing (2022). Kane certainly stands out as being quite a lot older than the other 10 people in our group. Because of this, she might be considered what is called an outlier. An outlier 'lies outside' most of the values. In this case you can see that there is quite a large gap in age between Kane, at 118 years old, and the next oldest person, Peggy, at age 65.

Because calculating the mean uses the value from every case, outliers can make the mean a misleading figure. We can see that just by adding Kane to our group, the mean age increased from 36.7 to 44.1. And most of the group – 7 of the 11 people – are aged below that mean. So although the mean represents the group arithmetically, it might not be the best way to convey what the age of the group looks like overall. We'll come back to outliers – and other things that can affect how useful the mean is – later in the chapter.

Thinking back to our common-sense understandings of the 'average', what does the mean tell us? Does it tell us what is 'normal' or 'typical'? Does it tell us what is 'usually' the case or what happens 'generally'?

Well, it doesn't quite do any of these things. It's an arithmetic calculation of the middle or centre of the data (hence 'central tendency'), but this centre isn't necessarily a 'typical' value or what 'usually' happens. It's clearly not usual or typical in the example above, as no actual case has the value of 44.1 years. In fact, the mean is more than four years away from the nearest actual age of the 11 people. So, while the mean is clearly one measure of the 'middle' of the data – and it can be a very useful measure – we need to be careful not to confuse what it really tells us with some of the commonplace meanings we attach to the idea of an 'average'.

A different type of middle

We can think of the mean as the 'arithmetic centre' of the data in a variable, but there is another measure of central tendency that identifies the centre in a different way. The median is calculated by taking the value of the middle case when all the cases are arranged in order of value, from largest to smallest or vice versa. If we look at these same 11 people, we can see that the median age is 30 years old:

$$22, 25, 28, 29, 30, \mathbf{30}, 40, 48, 50, 65, 118$$

The median, at 30, seems like a better summary of the ages of the people group. It's closer to most of the other people's ages than the mean is, and two people are actually 30 years old. In this case, because we have an outlier, the median might be our preferred measure to use.

But let's go back to the original data in Table 3.2 and see what the median would be for those 10 people:

$$22, 25, 28, 29, 30, 30, 40, 48, 50, 65$$

We have a bit of a problem here, because there isn't a middle value in the dataset. When a variable has an odd number of cases, identifying the median is very straightforward. But if you have an even number of cases, things are a little more complicated. To work out the median we have to look at the two middle cases (because there isn't a single middle case). We then have two possibilities. If those cases have the same value – as they do in our example – then the median is simply the value that those two cases share. If they have different values, we calculate the value halfway between (by calculating a mean).

In our example above, things work out quite nicely as the two middle values are both 30, so that would be our median:

$$22, 25, 28, 29, \mathbf{30}, \mathbf{30}, 40, 48, 50, 65$$

But if we had data where things didn't work out so neatly, we'd have to calculate the middle value. The median here would be 29.5 (calculated as 29 + 30/2):

$$22, 25, 28, \mathbf{29}, \mathbf{30}, 30, 40, 48$$

Thinking back to our everyday understanding of 'average', what does the median tell us? I wrote earlier that we can think of the mean as the 'arithmetic middle' of the data. The median also represents the middle of the data, but it is the middle when the values for the cases are placed in numerical order. Again, it's not exactly the 'typical' or 'usual' value, but it is another useful measure that works well in some circumstances. Before we look at when the mean and median work best and when they aren't so good, there is one more measure of central tendency to consider: the mode.

The most common value

The mode is probably the most straightforward average. It's simply the value that occurs most often in a variable. If we look at our original data on age again, we can see that the mode is 30 (which, in this case, also happens to be the median for this variable):

$$22, 25, 28, 29, \mathbf{30}, \mathbf{30}, 40, 48, 50, 65$$

But let's imagine that the data was slightly different and looked like this:

$$22, 25, 28, 29, \mathbf{30}, \mathbf{30}, 40, 48, \mathbf{50}, \mathbf{50}$$

In this dataset there isn't one mode. There are two people aged 30 and two aged 50, so we've got two modes. This isn't necessarily a problem, but it means we can't represent the mode of this variable with a single figure. It's possible to have more than two modes in some datasets or, when no two values are the same, you might have no mode at all. As with the median, sometimes the data isn't ideal for identifying the mode.

One of the modes is right in the centre and one is actually the highest value (and so nowhere near the middle). So the mode isn't really a measure of the 'centre' of the data, even though it's a measure of *central* tendency. It is just the most commonly occurring value, which might not be very representative of the variable at all. Again, what the different averages tell you is quite specific, and it doesn't quite match up with the way we use the term 'average' in our daily lives.

In these examples, we saw why the mean might not always be the best average to use, but we also saw some of the weaknesses of the median and mode. So let's now use some examples to see how useful these three measures are in different circumstances.

Example 1: Marathon runners

Imagine that we wanted to find out the average time it took for the competitors in a marathon to finish running the race. We know that calculating an average is appropriate, because time is a continuous variable: it can take any value and can be divided into sub-units, such as a fraction of a second. But how do we decide which average to use? Thinking about what generally happens in running races can help us with this decision. But we would also need to have some specialist knowledge about marathon finishing times.

Think about what the finish line of a marathon looks like when runners come to the end of the race. You'll notice that people very rarely finish at exactly the same time. Running events are usually taken very seriously, and runners' finishing times are often recorded to the nearest hundredth of a second. This means that almost every finisher will have a slightly different finishing time. This is important in deciding which measure of central tendency will be the most useful, as it rules out the mode. If everyone has a slightly different finishing time, there won't be a mode at all. And if a couple of people just happen to have exactly the same time, this would probably just be a coincidence, and wouldn't tell us anything useful about the overall distribution of finishing times.

This leaves us with two options: the mean and the median. Remember that one of the strengths of the mean is that it uses all the information available to us about our variable. As the mean would be calculated using every single runner's finishing time, it is the most comprehensive measure. Because of this, we would usually choose to use the mean unless we could think of a good reason not to. We saw earlier that having outliers in our data can cause problems for the mean. Are we likely to have outliers in our marathon data? We can probably guess the answer without having to look at the data itself. A marathon is just over 26 miles, which obviously takes quite a long time to run. The current world record is just under two hours, so there aren't going to be many people finishing in a quicker time than that. Also, organised marathons usually involve closing roads and city streets, and the organisers shut down the event after about seven hours, so you couldn't get a finishing time after that. We can be fairly sure, then, that all the finishing times will be between two and seven hours, and there won't be any extreme outliers affecting the calculation of the mean.

Another problem that can affect the mean is if the data are **skewed**. We'll look at the concept of skew in more detail later, but, in simple terms, the distribution of data in a variable (such as a finishing time) is skewed if most of the cases are relatively high or relatively low. If most of the runners finished with times of between two and four hours, but the remaining minority was spread out between four and seven hours, the distribution of the finishing times would be skewed. (In this case they would have what is called a **positive skew**.)

We could see whether marathon finishing times are skewed by looking at our data on a graph called a **histogram**. But as I haven't actually collected any data on this, a quick search on the internet gave me the answer. It turns out that data on marathon finishing times don't tend to be skewed. Most people have middling finishing times, with relatively small numbers getting very fast or very slow times. In fact, marathon finishing times often appear as a 'bell' shape in a histogram, showing that they are normally distributed. (I discuss the **normal distribution** in more detail in the next chapter.)

So, we've established that our data are unlikely to have any extreme outliers or be skewed, and that most – if not all – of the values are likely to be different. In this case, the mean seems to be the most sensible average to use. It uses the most information, and none of the reasons we might avoid it are relevant to our data on marathon finishing times.

Example 2: Earned income

Our second example is earned income, which we identified as a continuous variable earlier in this chapter. Imagine that we want to find out what the average income is for people in a particular country. Again, before we even examine what the data on income look like (or, more technically, how these data are distributed), it's useful to think about what we know already about income.

We know that people's income varies a lot, with some people having very low incomes, perhaps only receiving welfare benefits or working in minimum wage jobs, and some people being paid very large amounts of money. There are many different possible income levels between these two extremes. Even if we rounded up people's income to the nearest dollar, pound or euro, there's plenty of scope for many thousands of different values for any particular person's income. Because of this huge variation, for the same reasons we discussed in relation to marathon finishing times, we can again rule out the mode as the best measure. In fact, in this example the mode is quite likely to be the income of people working full-time and earning the minimum wage. This might be useful information, but it doesn't tell us anything about the rest of the population who earn more than this.

Let's consider our other options: the mean and the median. Because the mean uses all the available information, we should use it unless we have a good reason not to. But, in the case of income, there are two very good reasons not to use it: skew and outliers.

The example of the employee in the USA who earns US$94.6 million, that I discussed earlier, shows us that there can be extreme outliers in data on income. People who earn tens of millions of dollars clearly earn many times the amount that most people do. There are relatively few people who earn many millions of dollars, but their earnings are so high that they exert quite a strong influence on the value of the mean. The mean will always be 'correct', in terms of being the arithmetic 'middle' of the data, but if there are extreme outliers, it may not be the most effective measure to show us what a 'typical' income might look like. Extreme outliers tend to 'pull' the mean towards them and away from the rest of the data. What that means in this case is that the mean average income would be a lot higher than the income of most people.

Another reason for not using the mean is the fact that income data tends to have a skewed distribution: it's usually positively skewed. As I explained earlier, this means that relatively more cases have lower values than higher values. In simple terms, the data is 'bunched up' towards lower incomes and 'stretched out' towards the higher incomes. Figure 3.0 shows an example of positively skewed data on income. (It actually shows household disposable income, rather than earned income, but it has the same kind of skewed distribution, and so the same issues apply.)

You can see that the bars tend to be higher on the left side of the graph, indicating that the most common levels of disposable income are between £15,000 and £40,000. There are people who have much higher levels of disposable income than this, but the shorter heights of the bars to the right side of the graph show that there are many fewer of them.

The two vertical dotted lines on the graph show us the mean and median values for disposable income in this dataset. The median value, at £29,900, is lower than the mean, which is £36,900. Depending on which of these we use, the 'average' level of disposable income looks quite different.

Figure 3.0: A positively skewed distribution

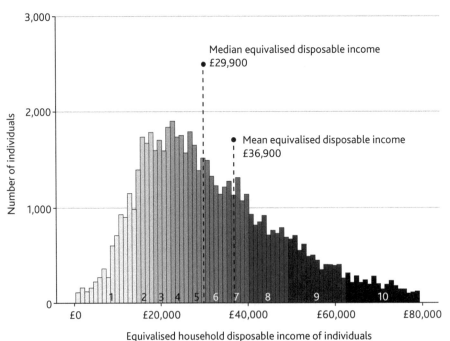

Note: Distribution of UK household disposable income, financial year ending 2020.

Source: ONS (2021)

With skewed data, it's generally recommended to use the median. As always, both values are 'technically' correct, but because they tell us slightly different things, we need to think about what exactly it is we want to find out. Although the mean uses all the data available to us, because the data are skewed, and because there are likely to be outliers, the people earning more in the dataset exert quite a bit of influence over the value of the mean. This ends up in a situation in which most people earn less than the mean, so the mean doesn't really tell us what people 'typically' earn.

While the median doesn't use all the information that the mean does, we know that there will always be the same number of people with values (in this case, income) above the median as there will be with values below the median. In this case, where we are concerned about the effect of skew and outliers on the mean, using the middle value might be a better indication of what is 'typical' in terms of income. We can see in our graph that the median isn't the most common value (and we have already seen why the mode wouldn't work), but it probably gives us the most useful idea of what the 'average' income is.

Example 3: Student flats

Our last example involves a property investor who wants to build some apartments for students. She has decided that, to save money on architects' fees and to speed up construction, she wants to build all the apartments to the same specification, with the same number of bedrooms. Because of this she wants to find out how many bedrooms the 'average' student apartment has. We know that the mean makes use of the most information, so let's look at that measure first and see if there's any reason not to use it.

One of the disadvantages of the mean is that, because it is the result of an arithmetic calculation, it often turns out to be a value that doesn't exist in the dataset. In other words, it's quite likely that no cases in the data share their value with the mean. This wasn't a problem for our marathon finishing times because we can all imagine what, for example, 3 hours 47 minutes and 34 seconds is like, even if no one actually finished in that time. That time gives us a good idea of the 'typical' finishing time, and it would work perfectly well as a target for someone running their first marathon. For these purposes, it doesn't matter whether anyone had ever finished a marathon in that exact time.

If, however, we got information on all the student apartments in a particular city, found out how many bedrooms they all had, and then calculated the mean, we might have a problem. If the mean number of bedrooms was 3.64, that's not very helpful for our property developer. Does she build apartments with three or four bedrooms? You might think that, because the mean is closer to four than three, she should build apartments with four bedrooms. But because the mean is the result of an arithmetic calculation, it's possible to get a mean of 3.64 in a dataset with no four-bedroom apartments at all. You could even get that same mean when there were no apartments with three *or* four bedrooms.

Our developer could build her apartments and find out that no one wanted to rent them!

The median is usually our second choice after the mean, so let's see how useful it would be here. If there are an odd number of cases in our dataset, we would end up with a median value that actually existed in our data: in this example, an actual number of bedrooms. This is useful not only because it would be a whole number – you can't build a fraction of a bedroom – but also because we know that there would be an actual apartment in our city with that number of bedrooms. If there was an even number of cases, however, this might not be the case: if there was no 'true' median but the two middle numbers were three and four, we would face the same problem as we did with the mean: not ending up with a whole number.

But even if we had a true median that was a whole number and represented an actual number of bedrooms in a real apartment, the median might not be the most helpful measure. It's possible for the median to be three and for there to be only one three-bedroom student apartment in the city. The middle value isn't necessarily a popular value.

In this case, the mode would probably be our best bet. As I said earlier, the mode isn't used very often but sometimes it's well suited to a particular variable. There are two reasons why it works well here. First, we don't have much variation in the possible values. The number of bedrooms must be a whole number (unlike disposable income or marathon times, which can be measured to several decimal places). There is also a practical limit to the range of sizes of student apartments: there can't be less than one bedroom (or one room, if we count studio apartments), and there probably won't be many that have more than 10 bedrooms. The mode works best when a variable has only a relatively small number of different values, as it does in this example.

When choosing the best average to use we also have to consider what we're trying to find out. Our property developer really wants to find out what the most popular size of student apartment is, so the mode is ideal because that's exactly what it does.

The only possible issue would be if there were two or more modes. This is unlikely in a large dataset, but it's still possible. It might not matter for our property developer, however, because she is only concerned that the apartments she builds are reasonably popular. Her final decision would probably be influenced by other factors, such as initial costs, availability of land, and so on. It's important to remember that the results of statistical analyses are only the first step in moving towards a conclusion. We always have to think about the wider context before we can decide the implications of these results. This is a topic we return to in the last chapter of this book.

Exercise 3.0 asks you to think about which average you might use with three different variables.

EXERCISE 3.0

Think about the following variables. Without searching on the internet to find out, estimate how the data might be distributed for each of them. Considering this distribution, decide what would be the most appropriate average to use for each variable, and why this would be the case:

a)   Goals in football (soccer) matches.

b)   Views of videos on YouTube.

c)   Points scored by each team in basketball games.

Summary

In this chapter I introduced you to some basic techniques for conducting univariate analysis. We looked at using frequencies and percentages with categorical data, and using averages with continuous and discrete data.

In the next chapter we're going to look at some more techniques for examining the distribution of continuous and discrete variables.

References
Gorard, S. (2021) *How to Make Sense of Statistics*, London: SAGE.

ONS (Office for National Statistics) (2021) 'Average household income, UK: Financial year 2020', www.ons.gov.uk/peoplepopulationandcommunity/personalandhouseholdfinances/incomeandwealth/bulletins/householddisposableincomeandinequality/financialyear2020

Smith, E. (2008) *Using Secondary Data in Educational and Social Research*, Maidenhead: McGraw-Hill.

Sources
Figure 3.0 was based on analysis of 'Average household income, UK: Financial year 2020', www.ons.gov.uk/peoplepopulationandcommunity/personaland householdfinances/incomeandwealth/bulletins/householddisposableincome andinequality/financialyear2020

Table 3.1 was based on an analysis of the Crime Survey for England and Wales, 2011–2012 Teaching dataset:

ONS (Office for National Statistics) (2013) *Crime Survey for England and Wales, 2011–2012: Teaching dataset*, SN 7401, DOI: 10.5255/UKDA-SN-7401-1.

Useful resources

My YouTube SPSS® tutorials covering univariate analysis can be found at: https://youtu.be/5Fdpy7IlNZg

These three chapters provide useful examples of the use (and misuse) of different kinds of averages:

Blastland, M. and Dilnot, A. (2008) *The Tiger That Isn't: Seeing Through a World of Numbers*, London: Profile [Chapter 5: 'Averages: The White Rainbow'].

de Vries, R. (2019) *Critical Statistics: Seeing Beyond the Headlines*, London: Red Globe Press [Chapter 5: 'What Does It Mean to Be Average?'].

Huff, D. (1954) *How to Lie with Statistics*, London: Penguin [Chapter 2: 'The Well-Chosen Average'].

Answers to exercises

Exercise 3.0

a) Football (or soccer, if you're from North America) matches aren't often very high scoring. It's not uncommon for matches to finish with no goals at all, and fairly unusual for any team to score more than three or four goals. Because of this, we could say that there isn't a great deal of variation in the number of goals scored (at least relative to some other sports). Goals only make sense in terms of whole numbers, too, as the idea of 'half a goal' wouldn't make sense. In terms of choosing an average, the mean doesn't look like a great measure, as it often results in a number with decimal places. The median and mode are both contenders, as they usually result in a value that is in the dataset (which, in this case, is a whole number). There's a chance that there wouldn't be a true median, but if we're looking at a large number of games this is unlikely. However, according to FootyStats (https://footystats.org/stats/common-score), the vast majority of games have between 0 and 3 goals. This lack of variation suggests that the mode could be the most useful measure. At the time of writing (2022), the mode was 2 goals.

b) As someone with a YouTube channel I'm very aware that most videos on YouTube don't get viewed that many times. Channels that have many billions of views exist, but they are certainly in the minority. This means that the distribution of views per video is probably positively (or right) skewed (although I couldn't find data on the internet to categorically confirm this). There are also some clear outliers, such as 'Gangnam Style', which had so many views it broke the counter. Because of this, the mean probably isn't the best average to use, as it doesn't work well with skewed data or outliers. There are hundreds of millions of videos (800 million, according to some estimates) with a large variation in the number of views, so the mode wouldn't be the best average to use either. In this case, it looks like the median would be the most suitable average. It also has the advantage that it can often produce a figure that exists in the data (as a whole number).

c) In contrast to football (soccer) matches, basketball games tend to be relatively high scoring, with teams scoring 100+ points on a regular basis. According to data from Basketball-Reference.com (www.basketball-reference.com), the mean number of points scored by a team in National Basketball Association (NBA) games from 1946 to 2017 was around 100. The same data show that the distribution of points in games during this period wasn't far off a perfect normal distribution, so the mean would probably be the best average to use. If having a measure that resulted in a whole point was important, the median would also be a contender, and shouldn't be too far off the mean (because of the normal distribution).

4

What you see is only half the story: why you need more than averages to describe distributions

WHAT IS THIS CHAPTER FOR?

In the last chapter we looked at some basic techniques to analyse a single categorical or continuous variable. In this chapter I present some more techniques for univariate analysis of continuous and discrete variables that complement those covered in the last chapter.

WHAT DOES IT COVER?

In this chapter we go beyond looking at averages and I explain why measures of spread – or 'dispersion' – are just as important. I start with some very basic concepts that you'll already be familiar with, such as minimum and maximum values, and move on to more sophisticated measures. I also show how averages can be used with measures of spread to give us a useful overview of the distribution of a variable. I end by looking at some common types – or shapes – of distribution and explain why you need to know about them.

WHAT WILL YOU LEARN?

- Why averages can be misleading
- How measures of spread can add to our understanding of the distribution of a variable
- Why the shape of a distribution is important and what the most common shapes look like

WHAT CONCEPTS AND TECHNIQUES ARE COVERED?

- Minimum and maximum values
- Range
- Mean deviation and standard deviation
- Normal distribution
- Positively and negatively skewed distributions

What averages can and can't tell us

We've seen how averages (measures of **central tendency**) can help us find out 'typical' or 'middle' values for a variable. We've also seen that each of these measures – the mean, the median and the mode – tells us something slightly different, and which measure is most suitable depends on what the data look like and what you want to find out.

Averages can be a very useful way of summarising one aspect of the distribution of a variable, but it's important to remember that a 'central' or 'typical' value isn't the whole story: it's rare that we'd only be interested in the 'middle' of the data. In the next section we're going to look at another group of statistical techniques that can tell us something else about the distribution of a variable: how the data are spread out.

Measures of spread and what they can tell us

Although we might be interested in finding the average value for a variable, we'll probably also be interested in some other qualities of the distribution. We want to know how our variable 'varies' and we need other measures to tell us about that. In this section we're going to look at some different statistical techniques called measures of spread. The technical name you might come across is measures of dispersion, but dispersion is just another name for spread.

As was the case with some of the statistics we've looked at previously – such as frequencies, percentages and maybe the mean – you'll probably be familiar with some of these measures of spread. You may not even have realised that by using them you were 'doing statistics'. The first few are quite easy to understand, but the last two we look at can be quite tricky.

At the extremes: minimum and maximum values and the range

Two of the simplest measures of spread are the minimum and maximum values. These are just the highest and lowest values for a variable in your dataset. As a teacher, I'm always interested to know the highest mark that has been achieved in a test, and also the lowest mark. Along with other information, this helps me decide if the test is too difficult or too easy. As researchers, we are often interested in the 'extremes': the highest and lowest; the fastest and slowest; the biggest and smallest.

There is another common measure of spread called the range. This is just the distance between the highest and lowest value in our variable. For students' test scores, if the minimum value (the lowest score) was 15 and the maximum value (the highest score) was 85, to calculate the range we simply subtract 15 from 85 to get 70.

Minimum and maximum values, and the range, can be useful starting points when you look at the spread of your variable. But they can't tell us much about how spread out the data are *in general*. This is because they don't provide us with any information about how many cases had values close to the minimum or maximum values: we only know that at least one case had the minimum value and at least one case had the maximum value. So is there anything else that we can do?

Remember that one of the advantages of the arithmetic mean is that it uses all the data from a variable to calculate a 'typical' value for a variable. We saw that although in some circumstances this could actually be a disadvantage, much of the time we could think of the mean as the average that best represented the data in terms of what is 'typical'.

There are also some measures of spread that use the values from every case to calculate a measure of how spread out the data in a variable are *in general*. In the next section we'll look at two of these – the **mean deviation** and the standard deviation – and see how they can be used to help us understand spread.

The mean deviation: the average distance from the average

Unlike minimum and maximum values, which only tell us about the highest and lowest values in a variable, the mean deviation (MD) tells us how spread out the data are *on average*. It's a concept that can be quite hard to grasp at first because it's calculated using two different averages: it measures the average distance from the average. As you might guess from its name, it uses the mean average, and so it measures the mean distance from the mean.

What does this look like in practice? And how can we use this information? Let's look at some examples. We'll use data on age, like we did in Chapter 3, but I've made a little change in the data we used in Table 3.2 just to make the maths easier to follow. I've also put the data in Table 4.0 in order, to make the distribution of ages clearer.

Table 4.0: Respondents' age in years (ordered)

Name	Age in years	Name	Age in years
Zion	22	Leo	33
Brianna	25	Dennis	40
Samarria	28	Kareem	48
Nora	29	Cara-Beth	50
Ishod	30	Peggy	65

Because there are only 10 values in the table, it's quite easy for us to see how the ages are spread out in this very small dataset. But when we're working with datasets with hundreds or thousands of cases, there is far too much information for us to be able to interpret it 'by eye'. Calculating averages and measures of spread provides us with much more precise assessments of the distribution of a variable, and also makes it easier for us to compare the distribution of different variables (something we'll come back to in Chapter 6).

The mean age in this dataset is 37. The minimum value is 22, the maximum value is 65, and the range is 43 (calculated by subtracting 22 from 65). But what would the mean deviation be? And how would we work it out?

To calculate the mean deviation for these ages, you would have to do the following:

1. Calculate the mean for the variable. We've already done this and we know that it's 37.
2. Calculate how far each person's age is above or below the mean. This is the **absolute deviation** of each case from the mean.
3. Add up all of the deviations, ignoring whether they are above or below the mean. You should use positive rather than negative numbers for numbers below the mean. This is what is meant by **absolute numbers**.
4. Divide the total of these absolute deviations by the number of cases, just like when you are calculating a mean average. The result is the mean deviation.

Let's do this for a few cases. You can see the results of this in Table 4.1.

We know that our mean average age is 37. And we know that Zion is 22 years old. So, the absolute deviation of Zion's age from the mean age is $37 - 22 = 15$. Brianna is 25, so that's 12 years away from the mean age ($37 - 25 = 12$). Samarria is 28, so that's 9 years away from the mean age. And so on. We need to do this calculation for all the cases until we have an absolute deviation for each of them.

We now use these absolute deviations to calculate a different type of mean: the mean deviation. This is calculated in the same way as the arithmetic mean we initially calculated. But instead of adding up all the individual ages and dividing the total by the number of people in our dataset, we add up *the distance of each person's age from the mean* and then divide the total by the number of people. This tells us how far, on average, the ages of our cases are spread out (or 'deviate') from the mean. The larger the mean deviation, the more spread out your data are. The smaller the mean deviation, the more closely clustered around the mean they are.

Table 4.1: Respondents' age in years (mean age and mean deviation)

Name	Age in years	Absolute deviation
Zion	22	15
Brianna	25	12
Samarria	28	9
Nora	29	8
Ishod	30	7
Leo	33	4
Dennis	40	3
Kareem	48	11
Cara-Beth	50	13
Peggy	65	28
Total	370	110
	Mean = 37	Mean deviation = 11

Another way of thinking about the mean deviation is a measure of how good the mean would be as a prediction for the value of any of the other cases. The smaller the mean deviation, the more likely it is that the mean would be close to the value of any other case that you might choose. Or, to put it differently, smaller mean deviations suggest that, overall, the mean is a more representative measure of the values in the dataset.

The standard deviation

Even if you've done some statistics before or have read research reports containing the results of statistical analysis, you probably won't have heard of the mean deviation. But you might have come across a similar measure, the standard deviation.

So what is the standard deviation? How is it different from the mean deviation? And why are you more likely to know about the standard deviation than the mean deviation?

The mean deviation (MD) and the standard deviation (SD) are both measures of spread. And they both tell you how much the values of a variable are spread out *in general*. In fact, they measure almost the same thing, and if you compare the MD and SD for any particular variable in a dataset, you'll see that the two measures have very similar values.

Both the MD and the SD have been around for a long time, but the SD became more popular from the early 20th century, and has since been the measure that is commonly used in mainstream statistical analysis. The transition was quite controversial at the time and, according to Gorard (2005), the reasons for preferring the SD may not be relevant for practical research today.

The SD is more difficult to calculate than the MD. This isn't really a problem for doing any actual analysis, as a computer will calculate the SD for you. But it does mean that, unless you're confident with maths, showing you how it's worked out is unlikely to help you understand what the SD is and why it can be useful.

Perhaps the most important difference between the MD and the SD is that the MD has a reasonably straightforward interpretation – the mean distance from the mean – and the SD does not. This is the reason I teach my students about the MD, even if I know lots of them won't use it in practice: it's easier to understand how the MD is calculated and what it means. And, as I explain below, it can be interpreted in almost the same way.

The exact definition of the SD is much more complicated and doesn't have the same kind of 'real-world' interpretation as the MD: any definition of the SD inevitably sounds like a long sentence of mathematical and statistical language. But because the SD is so widely used, you need to know about it. It will be the figure you see in most publications, and it's also connected to other useful statistical techniques that I cover later in this book. As some software packages don't even have an option to calculate the MD (Microsoft Excel does, but IBM SPSS® doesn't), you'll probably have to use the SD if you do any statistical analysis yourself.

So what is the SD? And how is it calculated? You can look up the equation on Wikipedia or in almost any statistics textbook, so I'm not going to show it here, but the technical description is as follows:

> The square root of the arithmetic mean of the squares of the deviations from the arithmetic mean.

That definition probably hasn't helped you work out what it's measuring and why it might be useful, but it's actually not all that different from how the MD is worked out. What I'm going to say now will probably have some statisticians tearing their hair out, but, for all intents and purposes, in real-life situations you can interpret the SD as the average distance from the average. It's not quite correct but it's near enough. The SD will always be a slightly larger value than the MD, but the two figures will be close in relative terms. In the absence of an easy-to-interpret definition of the SD, this 'rough' interpretation works fine.

What's most important is not whether you use the SD or MD, but how these measures can help us understand our data, and to demonstrate this, we're going to look at a real study that got a lot of coverage in the news media. We'll see how paying attention to different measures led to different headlines in different articles that covered the findings.

In late 2021, many news outlets reported the same story. Here are a few of their headlines:

> Dogs can understand more than 200 words and phrases. (T. Whipple, in *The Times*, 7 December 2021)

> Dogs know up to 215 words and phrases, study finds. (C. Magloire, for Sky News, 8 December 2021)

> Clever canines can understand an average of 89 words. (BBC *Newsround*, 8 December 2021)

There are links to these articles at the end of this chapter, and to the original publication by Reeve and Jacques (2022), if you want to read them in full. However, I want to concentrate on the news headlines for the time being. Then we'll look at the academic article where the original research was published, to get some further information and to show how the SD can be useful.

The first thing you might notice about the headlines is that all three quote different figures: 200, 215 and 89. The difference between 200 and 215 isn't that important: one headline just uses a round number. The important difference is these two words: 'up to'. The second headline clearly signals that 215 must refer to the maximum number of words that were understood by a dog in the study. But the first headline could be interpreted as saying that *all* dogs can understand 200 words, which isn't what the study found.

The last headline refers to the average number of words understood by dogs in the study: 89. If you read the full study, you can see that this is the mean average, and the actual value is 88.75. So this might be a better estimate of what any particular dog is likely to understand. The study also tells you that the minimum number of words understood by a dog in the study was 15.

One thing we've learned about the mean is that it doesn't tell us what proportion of cases takes that value or a value close to it. Similarly, we don't know how many dogs had word comprehension levels close to the minimum and maximum values. None of these measures tell us what proportion of dogs could understand around 89 words or how many dogs understand many more or many fewer words. To find this out, we need to use another measure, one that gives us an idea of how representative the mean is, or, to put it another way, lets us know how far out the data are spread out from the mean *in general*. In other words, we need a measure like the MD or SD.

As we might expect from an academic analysis, the authors of this study included the SD in one of their tables: 37.58. Let's round that up to 38 to make things simpler. This means that, roughly, the average distance from the mean average was 38. As the average number of words known was 89 and the average distance from that mean was 38, this tells us that the data were spread out quite a lot. It also tells us that the mean isn't likely to be a great predictor of the number of words known by a particular dog.

This isn't a bad thing, though. Some data are spread out by their very nature. A relatively large SD (or MD) just tells us this. The SD is useful because it's a measure of how far the data are spread out *in general*, in contrast to measures like minimum or maximum values that only tell us where the extremes of the data lie. If this study is correct, the SD simply tells us that there is quite a lot of variation in the number of words that different dogs understand. This might 'typically' be around 89 words, but a lot of dogs understand many more or many fewer words than this.

So the headlines aren't wrong, but they don't give the whole picture. Even though some of the articles mentioned the minimum and maximum values and the mean average, none of them mentioned the SD. This is probably because it's quite a tricky concept, but it is (alongside the MD) the best way of answering the question: how likely is my dog to understand the average number of words?

Even when interpreted as 'the average distance from the average', the SD and MD are still a bit abstract. While we might understand what this means mathematically, it's still difficult to translate into a practical sense of how spread out the data are. Where the SD and MD become really useful is when comparing how spread out the data are in different groups. If we compared the variation in word comprehension between purebreed and crossbreed dogs, the average for each group might be different. But the variation in word comprehension might also be different for the two types of dog, and the SD and MD would be the best way to compare this. We look at these kinds of comparison later, in Chapter 6. In some situations, however, the SD can give us a more intuitive picture of how spread out our data are. We'll look at this next, when we examine the different ways in which data are commonly distributed, and how one of these distributions relates to the SD.

The shapes of distributions

We've seen how we can use statistical measures to summarise the distribution of a variable. However, there are other – more direct – ways of finding out what the distribution of our data looks like. And the simplest is to just to look at the data on a graph. We can use something called a histogram to do this. We saw one of these earlier, Figure 3.0 in Chapter 3, when we looked at the distribution of income.

There are an infinite number of ways that the data in a variable can be distributed. The advantage of looking at a histogram is that it gives you an (almost) direct view of that distribution. It can also tell you if the 'shape' of your data looks like some of the common ways in which data are distributed, some of which have names. If you can recognise that your variable is distributed in a particular way, you can then just refer to the name of this distribution rather than having to show a graph when you're writing about it. You'll also see these different types of distribution mentioned in research reports, so it's useful to be familiar with their names, even if you're not going to do any analysis of your own.

One of the most commonly occurring distributions is what is called the **normal distribution** or **Gaussian distribution**. I mentioned the normal distribution earlier when we were looking at averages. But what does this term mean? And why is it important?

The normal distribution

Figure 4.0 shows data on around 8,000 high schools in California. Each of the cases in this dataset represents an individual school. (Remember that even though our cases are often people, this isn't always the case.) Figure 4.0 is a histogram, like the one we saw in Chapter 3 that showed data on income. Each of the bars covers a range of values, in this example representing the average years of teaching experience for the teachers in every school in the dataset.

You can see that the bars make up a shape a bit like a 'bell'. This shows that they are what we call 'normally distributed'. The black line on the graph shows what the data would look like if they followed the perfect mathematical normal distribution. We can see that the bars showing our data don't quite match this line, so our data aren't perfectly normally distributed – but they are pretty close.

At this point you might be wondering where this 'normal distribution' came from and why we're interested in it. There are two answers to this: one mathematical and one from the world around us. In the mathematical world, the normal distribution is a concept that exists in theory, a bit like a perfect circle.

But the normal distribution doesn't only exist as a mathematical idea; we can also see it in data from the natural and social worlds. The birth weight of babies

Figure 4.0: A normally distributed variable

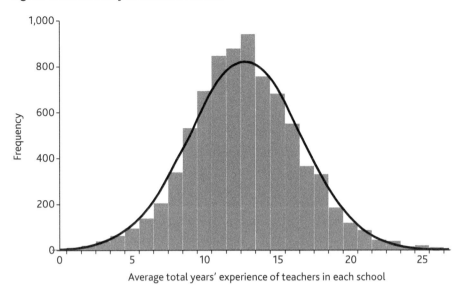

is normally distributed, as are adults' heights and their shoe sizes. So are the retirement ages of players in the National Football League (NFL) in the USA and daily changes in stock market prices. The normal distribution is interesting to us not because of its origins in mathematics, but because variables that we're interested in might be normally distributed.

The normal distribution and the standard deviation

There is *one* part of the mathematics of the normal distribution that's useful to us, however. Normally distributed data has a special relationship with the standard deviation and one that can be helpful to know about when we're looking at the distribution of a variable. You will always find this relationship in normally distributed data, regardless of the variable you are looking at. But it's *only* the case in normally distributed data – it's not true for variables that have other kinds of distributions (which we look at in more detail later).

Figure 4.1 shows this relationship. You might recognise the bell-shaped curve of the normal distribution that we saw in Figure 4.0, but the rest of the graph probably won't make much sense until I've explained what it means.

It just happens to be the case that, if – and only if – the data for a variable are normally distributed, the following things are true:

a) About two-thirds of all the cases will have values between one standard deviation below the mean and one standard deviation above the mean.

b) Around 95% of all the cases will have values between two standard deviations below the mean and two standard deviations above the mean.

c) Nearly all the cases – more than 99% – will have values between three standard deviations below the mean and three standard deviations above the mean.

When I first explain this relationship to my students, they usually have two questions: Why is this the case? And how is this information helpful?

The answer to the first question is quite straightforward. The relationship between the normal distribution and the standard deviation is just a mathematical law. Going back to our example of a perfect circle, you might remember from maths at school that the area of a circle is always πr^2: the radius of the circle, multiplied by itself, and then multiplied by *pi* (3.14159...).

This formula always works, whatever the size of a circle. The same is true for the relationship between the normal distribution and the standard deviation shown in Figure 4.1. Whatever your variable is, whatever the value of the mean and standard deviation, the relationships (a) to (c) described above will always be true if your data for that variable are normally distributed. You can use this information both to help you understand the distribution of a variable and to communicate that distribution to others.

A simple example will help show how we can use this information. Imagine I measure the height of all the students in my class and the average (mean) height is 160 cm. I also calculate the SD and it is 20 cm. I create a histogram and it shows me that the data I have collected on the height of my students are normally distributed. Because the data are normally distributed, we can apply the rules (a), (b) and (c) listed earlier and shown in Figure 4.1.

It's useful at this point to think about the SD not just as approximately 'the average distance from the average', but as a unit of measurement in itself. As in

Figure 4.1: The normal distribution and the standard deviation

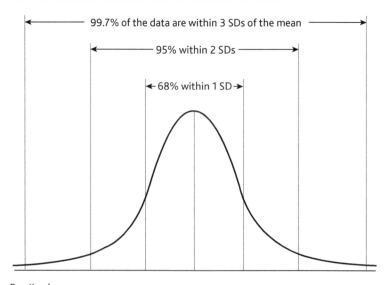

Source: Dan Kernler

this case our SD happens to be 20 (and as we are measuring height in centimetres, our SD is actually 20 cm), let's think of each SD as a unit of 20 cm.

Rule (a) says that around two-thirds (or 68.3%, to be exact) of all cases have values between one SD below and one SD above the mean. In our example of students' heights we start with the following figures: mean = 160 cm; SD = 20 cm. Because our data are normally distributed, it will be the case that approximately two-thirds of students will have heights that are between 160 cm minus 20 cm and 160 cm plus 20 cm. If we do the maths we can see that two-thirds of students would have heights of between 140 cm (160 cm − 20 cm) and 180 cm (160 cm + 20 cm).

Rule (b) states that around 95% of all cases would have values between two SDs below and two SDs above the mean. Our mean is still 160 cm and our SD is still 20 cm. To find out the range of heights that will apply to 95% of students, we need to do a similar calculation. But this time, instead of adding one SD to the mean to find the upper end of that range and taking one SD from the mean to find the lower limit, we need to add two SDs and subtract two SDs. For our variable – students' height – we know that the SD is 20 cm. Two SDs is 20 cm × 2 = 40 cm. We can take this away from the mean – which is still 160 cm – using the following calculation: 160 cm − 40 cm = 120 cm. The calculation for the upper end of the range is just as simple: 160 cm + 40 cm = 200 cm. This tells us that 95% of students' heights would fall between 120 cm and 200 cm.

The calculation for rule (c) is very similar, apart from the fact that you need to subtract and add three SDs, and it gives the range for roughly 99% of all students' heights.

We now know these mathematical rules that always apply to normally distributed data. It doesn't matter what your variable is – it could be marathon finishing times, scores on a test or the height of students – if the data are normally distributed, these rules apply. And it doesn't matter what your mean and SD are: you just use them to calculate the different ranges that correspond with different proportions of cases. But how do we use this information?

Much of what we do in statistical analysis is about working out what our data look like and communicating it to others. When we're talking to people who understand some basic statistical concepts, just telling them the mean and the SD will provide them with a reasonable understanding of the distribution of a variable. If our data are normally distributed, telling them this will further increase their understanding of this distribution. And, as most people who have studied statistics learn about the relationship between the mean and SD in normally distributed data, these three pieces of information can be combined to give quite a comprehensive picture of a variable.

You might notice that I'm not being particularly precise when choosing the figures that correspond to the proportions of cases that fall within one, two and three SDs. I've written 'two-thirds', when the actual number to one decimal place is 68.3%. I've written 95% instead of 95.5% and 99% instead of 99.7%. This is because the very precise percentages in Figure 4.1 only apply to the perfect theoretical normal distribution. This distribution doesn't exist in practice, and it's common to hear people talk about 'approximately normally distributed data'. In reality, data will never be perfectly normally distributed and is likely to look something like the histogram in Figure 4.0. Because 'real-life' data won't be perfectly normally distributed, the precise percentages in Figure 4.1 won't be completely accurate. That's why it's unnecessary to be so precise: the actual figures will be slightly different, but we know that they will be somewhere close.

If your data aren't normally distributed, you won't be able to do the type of calculation that I did earlier. You can't calculate the proportion of cases within one, two or three SDs below or above the mean when your variables aren't normally distributed. But that's okay. It's useful when you can do these calculations, but it's not a problem if your data won't allow this. And even if your variable is normally distributed, you don't have to do these calculations unless you think that the answer would be useful. Statistical packages don't tend to calculate them by default, but they're easy to do with a calculator. These calculations can help you think about how the data for a variable is spread out, but they're not always crucial parts of your analysis.

> ## Box 4.0: How 'normal' is the normal distribution?
>
> In some ways it's unfortunate that the Gaussian distribution has become known as the 'normal distribution', as the word 'normal' suggests that this is something that we should expect or aspire to. In fact, it's not a 'problem' if the data for a variable are not normally distributed, if they are skewed, or if they have a completely differently shaped distribution. The data are what they are, and our job is to find out what they look like and to report it.
>
> It's true that, if your data are normally distributed, they will have a special relationship with the SD, and this can help you communicate things about what your data look like. It's also true that it's useful to know about the shape of the distribution of your variable before deciding which average would be the best one to use. It's even true that some statistical procedures work best with normally distributed data or shouldn't be used in other situations.
>
> However, some people have argued that there is too much emphasis placed on the normal distribution, and this had led to misconceptions about its importance (Bruce, 2018) as well as misguided ideas about when normally distributed data is required (Williams et al, 2013). While it's important to pay attention to the distribution of your data, nothing has 'gone wrong' if the data in your variable isn't normally distributed.

Skewed distributions

Apart from the normal distribution, there are other common ways in which data from a variable are distributed, and some of these also have names. It can be useful to know about these distributions because the way in which a variable is distributed can affect the kind of statistical measures that are most appropriate. It's also handy to know the names of these distributions, as it makes it quicker and easier to tell other people what your data look like.

A key idea relating to the shape of distributions is **skew**. We looked at this idea briefly when we were discussing the median (because the median works better than the mean with skewed distributions). Whereas the normal distribution is a symmetrical bell–like shape, skewed distributions are not symmetrical: the left and the right side don't look the same. They look like 'wonky' versions of the normal distribution.

The distribution of people's disposable income we saw in the last chapter in Figure 3.0 wasn't symmetrical; more of the cases were over on the left side of the graph. This is because there is a relatively large number of people with a small amount of disposable income in comparison to the smaller number who have a lot of disposable income. This kind of distribution is called **positively skewed** or 'right skewed'. The distribution of house prices tends to be positively skewed, as is the number of points scored by individual players in basketball games.

Figure 4.2 shows data on the same Californian schools we saw in Figure 4.0. The variable we're interested in this time is the number of students in each school. We can immediately see that the bars in the histogram form a different shape to the one in Figure 4.0. Although there are some similarities – the bars

Figure 4.2: A positively skewed distribution

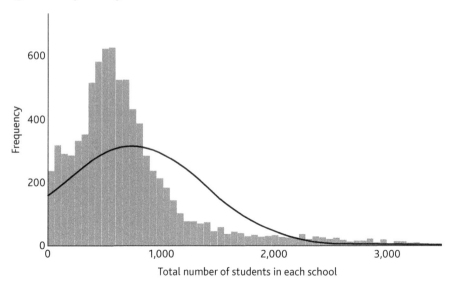

rise to form a peak and then fall – the most obvious difference is the lack of symmetry. Like the histogram on income we saw in Chapter 3 (Figure 3.0), the cases are clustered towards the left side of the graph. This means that most of the schools have less than 1,000 students, even though there are a small number of schools with much larger numbers of students. As with income, the data here are positively skewed.

You can recognise a positively skewed distribution by looking for two distinguishing characteristics. As well as cases being bunched up towards the left side of the histogram, there will be a long 'tail' of cases stretching towards the right side of the graph. This 'tail' on the right side is why this kind of distribution is sometimes referred to as 'skewed to the right'.

Another type of skew is **negative skew** or left skew. This is when the asymmetry of the distribution is in the other direction: most of the cases are over on the right side of the histogram and there is a long 'tail' of cases on the left. The distribution of the age of retirement is negatively skewed, because most people don't retire until relatively late in their lives. A sporting example of negative skew is the distance of long jumps performed by athletes in events such as the Olympics. Most of the jumps are clustered towards longer lengths, with very few athletes jumping shorter distances.

As I've already noted, the distribution of your variable is important because it can have implications for choosing the most appropriate statistical techniques. You can see in Figure 4.3 that, in skewed distributions, the three measures of central tendency can produce quite different values and could give different impressions about where the 'centre' of the data are or what might be a 'typical' value. The example of disposable income, which was positively skewed, showed us that the median was usually a more useful measure than the mean with skewed data.

Apart from affecting the kind of analyses you can do, the shape of the distribution of a variable helps you get a feel for what the data for that variable 'look like'. This is why I always recommend looking at a histogram for each of your continuous and discrete variables, as well as producing measures of central

Figure 4.3: Normally distributed and skewed data and their relationship with the mean, median and mode

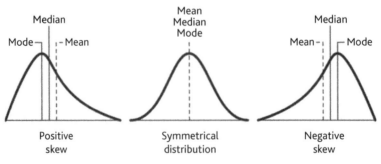

Source: Diva Jain

tendency and spread. Looking at the data on a graph can help you think about the variable – not necessarily in terms of precise figures, but in terms of where in the distribution most of the cases lie, and what this means for a specific variable. In relation to the example of disposable income, the positively skewed distribution means that most people have income levels at the lower end of the range: they don't have that much money to spend. But that distribution also shows us that there are a small number of people with very large amounts of disposable income. These are both important findings when thinking about issues such as poverty and economic inequality.

Knowing the names of common distributions also helps you communicate about your data more concisely. There are many other, less common, distributions, and I have only covered the main ones here. If you don't think that the distribution of a variable fits one of these types, you can always show exactly what it looks like with a histogram. It's quite convenient, however, to be able to use terms such as 'normally distributed', or 'positively skewed' and 'negatively skewed' when they are appropriate, as it saves you having to use a graph to make your point.

Summary

In this chapter we've seen that there's quite a bit more you can do with continuous and discrete data when it comes to univariate analysis. As we saw in Chapter 3, although averages can be a good starting point, looking at how the data are spread out can not only give you more information about how a variable is distributed, but also help you decide which average to use.

In the next chapter we start to look at how to examine the relationships between variables. We look at the relationship between two categorical variables first, and go on to discuss techniques for continuous and discrete variables in the chapters that follow.

References

BBC *Newsround* (2021) 'Clever canines can understand an average of 89 words', 8 December, www.bbc.co.uk/newsround/59580613.amp

Bruce, P. (2018) '3 myths about the normal distribution', Elder Research Blog, 27 July, www.elderresearch.com/blog/3-myths-about-the-normal-distribution

Gorard, S. (2005) 'Revisiting a 90-year-old debate: The advantages of the mean deviation', *British Journal of Educational Studies*, 53(4): 417–30. https://doi.org/10.1111/j.1467-8527.2005.00304.x

Magloire, C. (2021) 'Dogs know up to 215 words and phrases, study finds', Sky News, 8 December, https://news.sky.com/story/whos-a-clever-boy-dogs-know-up-to-215-words-and-phrases-study-finds-12489835

Reeve, C. and Jacques, S. (2022) 'Responses to spoken words by domestic dogs: A new instrument for use with dog owners', *Applied Animal Behaviour Science*, 246(2022): 105513, https://doi.org/10.1016/j.applanim.2021.105513

Whipple, T. (2021) 'Dogs can understand more than 200 words and phrases', *The Times*, 7 December, www.thetimes.co.uk/article/dogs-can-understand-more-than-200-words-and-phrases-w36fqpgvl

Williams, M.N., Grajales, C.A.G. and Kurkiewicz, D. (2013) 'Assumptions of multiple regression: Correcting two misconceptions', *Practical Assessment, Research, and Evaluation*, 18, Article 11, https://doi.org/10.7275/55hn-wk47

Sources

Figures 4.0 and 4.2 were created using data from the California Department of Education 2006 Adequate Yearly Progress (AYP) data files, www.cde.ca.gov/re/pr/aypdatafiles.asp

Figure 4.1: Dan Kernler, https://commons.wikimedia.org/wiki/File:Empirical_Rule.PNG; https://creativecommons.org/licenses/by-sa/4.0/legalcode

Figure 4.3: Diva Jain, https://commons.wikimedia.org/wiki/File:Relationship_between_mean_and_median_under_different_skewness.png; https://creativecommons.org/licenses/by-sa/4.0/legalcode

Useful resources

My SPSS® video covering univariate analysis can be found at: https://youtu.be/5Fdpy7IlNZg

5

How the tables turn: examining relationships between categorical variables

WHAT IS THIS CHAPTER FOR?

In the previous two chapters we looked at examining variables individually – what is called univariate analysis. We saw that there are different techniques you can use, depending on whether a variable is categorical or continuous. In this chapter we start to explore ways to find out about the relationships between two different variables – bivariate analysis. As most variables in the social world are categorical, we start by looking at relationships between two categorical variables.

WHAT DOES IT COVER?

After briefly outlining the different types of bivariate analysis, I focus on a technique called cross-tabulation and show the different ways it can be used, and the different kinds of statistics that can be used to help determine the nature of the relationship between the two variables. I discuss the advantages and disadvantages of the different ways of using cross-tabulation, and show how to avoid some common pitfalls.

WHAT WILL YOU LEARN?

- What cross-tabulation is and why you've probably already done it
- How cross-tabulation is different – and similar – depending on the number of categories in your variables
- How percentages can help you make sense of differences between groups
- Why running percentages along rows and columns gives you different answers (to different questions)
- What expected counts are, where they come from, and how they can be useful

WHAT CONCEPTS AND TECHNIQUES ARE COVERED?

- Groups, sub-groups and totals
- Observed counts and expected counts
- Percentages (within and between groups)

We're finally looking at relationships!

In the previous chapters we looked at some key ideas and concepts, and covered some basic techniques to analyse individual variables one at a time. In this chapter and Chapters 6, 7 and 8 we look at different ways to examine relationships between two variables. This kind of analysis is called bivariate analysis as, instead of looking at just one variable, we'll look at the relationship between two of them (as 'uni' means one and 'bi' means two).

When we looked at univariate analysis in previous chapters, we saw that different techniques were needed for categorical and continuous (or discrete) variables. This is also the case when we're looking at the relationship between two variables. But because we have two variables – and each one of them could be a categorical variable or a continuous variable – things are a little bit more complicated. With univariate analysis we only had to decide whether our variable was continuous or categorical: we basically had two options. For bivariate analysis we have to make a two-stage decision.

To choose the most appropriate bivariate analysis, we have to do two things:

1. Work out whether each of our two variables is categorical or continuous.
2. Choose the appropriate bivariate technique for the combination of categorical or continuous variables that we have.

If you've read Chapter 2, you'll already know how to work out whether your variable is continuous or discrete. (If you don't know how to do this, and you haven't read Chapter 2, this would be a good time to do so.) Once you've done this, you'll be left with three possible combinations of your two variables:

• categorical and categorical
• categorical and continuous
• continuous and continuous.

Table 5.0 shows these combinations alongside the appropriate bivariate analyses for each one. In this chapter, we're going to cover the first combination: two categorical variables. In the chapters that follow, we'll look at the other two combinations and the bivariate analyses that are used for these.

Table 5.0: Combinations of variables and the appropriate bivariate analyses

Combination of variables	Bivariate technique(s)
Categorical and categorical	Cross-tabulation
Categorical and continuous	Comparing distributions
Continuous and continuous	Correlation and regression

Categorical variables are everywhere

As I discussed earlier in the book, most variables in the social world are categorical. Categorical variables such as social class, race and ethnicity, gender, religious affiliation, marital status, employment status, and so on, are of interest to researchers from a wide range of disciplinary backgrounds. And many variables specific to areas such as education, health, work and employment, consumption, family and household, leisure, crime and the media are also categorical.

Because of this, it's important to be familiar with techniques that you can use to examine the relationship between two categorical variables. The technique we're going to look at – cross-tabulation – is one of the most commonly used bivariate analyses. In principle, it's a very simple technique, and one that you're probably familiar with, as it essentially involves creating a table of groups and **sub-groups**. You might have already conducted a cross-tabulation without even realising it. As with some of the other techniques we've covered in previous chapters, if you've done it before, you probably didn't think of it as 'doing statistics'.

Let's start with the simplest example possible, which is looking at the relationship between two categorical variables that only have two categories each. I'll show you some examples with variables with more than two categories later. Before we look at cross-tabulation in detail, it might be useful to try to answer the questions in Exercise 5.0 for a little revision about the differences between categorical and continuous variables.

EXERCISE 5.0

Look at the following variables from the Labour Force Survey (LFS) teaching dataset:

- Ethnicity
- Religion
- Gross hourly pay
- Number of children aged 0–4 years
- Age when completed full-time education

a) Can cross-tabulation be used appropriately to analyse the relationship between any two of these variables? If so, which variables?

b) Why are only those pairs of variables suitable for cross-tabulation?

Looking at the relationship between two variables with two categories

For the first example, I'm going to use data from the National Survey of Sexual Attitudes and Lifestyles (Natsal) 2010–12 teaching dataset. This dataset is open access and can be downloaded from the UK Data Service. We're going to look at whether people who drink alcohol are more likely to smoke tobacco than those who don't drink alcohol. Table 5.1 shows us the result of cross-tabulating the variables 'Drink alcohol' and 'Smoke tobacco'.

Our table of results provides us with several useful pieces of information. First, in the bottom right cell it shows us the total number of cases in our analysis: 15,155. We can also see, along the bottom row, how many of these people currently smoke tobacco (N = 4,223). The far-right column also breaks down the cases into those who drink alcohol (N = 12,333) and those who don't (N = 2,822). However, you could have produced all this information simply by conducting some univariate analysis and doing frequency counts for each of the two variables separately.

Table 5.1: A cross-tabulation of two variables with two categories each (frequencies only)

		Smoke tobacco		
		Yes	No	Total
	Yes	3,552	8,781	12,333
Drink alcohol	No	671	2,151	2,822
	Total	4,223	10,932	15,155

Cross-tabulating the two variables provides more information by telling us how many cases are in each sub-group. As there are four different possible combinations of answers to the two questions, there are four different sub-groups in our table:

- drink alcohol and smoke tobacco
- drink alcohol but don't smoke tobacco
- don't drink alcohol but smoke tobacco
- don't drink alcohol and don't smoke tobacco.

We now have the number of people who fall into each of these four groups. We can see, for example, that of the 15,155 people in the survey, 3,552 both drink alcohol and smoke tobacco. We can also see that 8,781 people drink alcohol but don't smoke tobacco. The table also shows us that 671 people smoke tobacco but don't drink alcohol and that 2,151 neither smoke tobacco nor drink alcohol. But what does that tell us about the relationship between drinking alcohol and smoking tobacco? Are people who drink alcohol more or less likely to also smoke tobacco?

How percentages can help

You may have already worked out an idea of the relationship between the two variables just by looking at the data in Table 5.1. But as this table only includes the number of cases in each group or sub-group – what are called the frequencies or counts – it's not always easy to work out what's going on. Luckily, we can make the table easier to interpret by using percentages to make the results simpler to understand.

Table 5.2 shows the same data as Table 5.1 but expressed as percentages rather than frequencies. Percentages can help us understand the patterns in the data more clearly, but we must be careful to interpret them correctly. Let's see what we can learn from the data in this table.

Table 5.2: A cross-tabulation of two variables with two categories each (percentages by rows only)

		Smoke tobacco		
		Yes	No	Total
	Yes	28.8%	71.2%	100.0%
Drink alcohol	No	23.8%	76.2%	100.0%
	Total	27.9%	72.1%	100.0%

If we look at the bottom row of Table 5.2, we can see that most respondents don't smoke tobacco – just over 72% of them said that they didn't. But we probably knew that already from our univariate analyses. What we really want to find out about is the relationship between drinking alcohol and smoking tobacco.

We can see that 28.8% of respondents who drink alcohol *also* smoke tobacco. We can also see that a slightly smaller proportion (23.8%) of those who *don't* drink alcohol *do* smoke tobacco. So if we divide people up according to whether they drink alcohol or not, we can see that drinkers are slightly more likely to smoke than non-drinkers.

Table 5.3 shows the same data, again using percentages rather than frequencies. However, if you look closely, you'll see that the percentages are different to those shown in Table 5.2. The figures in both tables are all correctly calculated percentages, so why are they different?

Table 5.3: A cross-tabulation of two variables with two categories each (percentages by columns only)

		Smoke tobacco		
		Yes	No	Total
	Yes	84.1%	80.3%	81.4%
Drink alcohol	No	15.9%	19.7%	18.6%
	Total	100.0%	100.0%	100.0%

By carefully comparing the tables we can see why the percentages in the cells are different. In Table 5.2, the percentages are calculated along the rows and in Table 5.3 they are calculated down the columns. Because of this they each tell us something slightly different. We can think of each table as providing answers to different questions.

So what exactly does each table tell us? This is much easier to see if we look at a row or column in isolation:

Top row only

		Smoke tobacco		
		Yes	No	Total
Drink alcohol	Yes	28.8%	71.2%	100.0%

The top row of Table 5.2 shows data only for the participants who reported drinking alcohol. We can see that nearly 29% of these people smoke tobacco and just over 71% do not. This shows the proportion of drinkers who smoke and the proportion of drinkers who don't smoke. To calculate these proportions, the respondents who drink alcohol were treated as a separate group and were divided into those who smoke and those who don't.

The same was done to calculate the percentages in the second row. The percentages of smokers and non-smokers were calculated for *only* those respondents who reported not drinking alcohol. When we look at the second row of the table in isolation, we can see that of the people who didn't drink alcohol, nearly 24% smoked and just over 76% didn't smoke:

Second row only

		Smoke tobacco		
		Yes	No	Total
Drink alcohol	No	23.8%	76.2%	100.0%

For the data in Table 5.2, the respondents were first separated into two groups: those who reported drinking alcohol and those who reported not drinking alcohol. The percentages of smokers and non-smokers were then calculated separately, first for drinkers and then for non-drinkers. But the percentages in Table 5.3 were calculated differently. Again, this is easier to see if we concentrate on one part of the table at a time:

First column only

		Smoke tobacco
		Yes
	Yes	84.1%
Drink alcohol	No	15.9%
	Total	100.0%

Instead of separating out respondents into drinkers and non-drinkers and then calculating the percentage of each group who smoke, the percentages in Table 5.3 were calculated by separating out the respondents into smokers and non-smokers, and then calculating the proportion of each group that drinks alcohol. Although, at first, this might seem to be the same as what was done in Table 5.2, it is actually different and produces different outcomes.

In Table 5.2 we saw that the percentage of alcohol drinkers who also smoked is 23.8%. But the data in Table 5.3 tell us that the percentage of smokers who also drink alcohol is 84.1%. So why are these two figures so different and what do they tell us?

The explanation for the difference is that the two tables provide answers to two different questions:

> Table 5.2: What proportion of alcohol drinkers also smoke tobacco?
> Table 5.3: What proportion of tobacco smokers also drink alcohol?

These proportions are different because the groups that we use for the calculations are different. The percentages in the first row of Table 5.2 are calculated using only the respondents who reported drinking alcohol. The percentages in the first column of Table 5.3 are calculated using only the respondents who reported smoking tobacco.

If we look back at Table 5.1 we can see that the frequency (or count) of cases in the sub-group that both drink alcohol and smoke tobacco is 3,552. This number is used in the calculations of percentages in both Table 5.2 and Table 5.3. But in Table 5.2 it has been divided by 12,333 – the number of respondents who drink alcohol. In Table 5.3 it has been divided by 4,223 – the number of respondents who smoke tobacco. This is why the percentages in the two tables are different: they represent the percentage of the same sub-group (those who drink and smoke) within different groups (everyone who drinks vs everyone who smokes).

Which way do I run the percentages?

My students often find it difficult to decide which way to run the percentages in their tables. It's important to remember that the percentages calculated by the software you are using will always be correct – they'll just be an answer to a particular question. You must decide the question you want to answer before you can work out which way to run the percentages. For example, do you want to know the proportion of drinkers who smoke, or the proportion of smokers who drink? The answer to this question will depend on exactly what you're trying to find out.

An example I use with my students comes from the Crime Survey for England and Wales (CSEW) 2011–12 teaching dataset. I ask them to find out whether full-time university and college students are more or less likely than the rest of the population to have experienced crime in the last year. They go on to produce results that look like either those in Table 5.4 or Table 5.5.

Table 5.4: The relationship between being a student and experience of crime, example 1

		Full-time student at university or college		
		Yes	No	Total
Experienced crime in the past year	Yes	3.6%	96.4%	100.0%
	No	2.6%	97.4%	100.0%
	Total	2.8%	97.2%	100.0%

Some of my students will end up with Table 5.4 and try to interpret the results. They might conclude that students are less likely to be victims of crime because only 3.6% of those who experienced crime were students. Sometimes this is their final answer but, occasionally, they will go on to notice that only 2.6% of those who had no experience of crime were students. This leaves them confused and unable to give a good answer to my question. Occasionally they'll try to argue that students are both *more* and *less* likely to be victims of crime (which obviously can't be true!)

The reason these students were confused is because they were running the percentages the wrong way to answer my question. Table 5.4 provides the answer to a different question: what proportion of participants who experienced crime were students? (It also provides the answer to another question: what proportion of participants who didn't experience crime were students?) But as we know that most participants in this survey weren't students – only 2.8% were, according to the total on the bottom row of the table – it's not surprising (and not very interesting) to find out that they were the minority of those who experienced crime and the minority of those that didn't.

Table 5.5 shows the results of the analysis that answer my original question. Here, the participants were divided into students and non-students, and the percentages of those who had and hadn't experienced crime were calculated for students separately from non-students. We can see from these data that 28.5% of students had experienced crime in the past year compared to only 22.3% of non-students. So students were more likely to experience crime than non-students. Running the percentages this way provides all the information needed to answer my question.

Table 5.5: The relationship between being a student and experience of crime, example 2

		Full-time student at university or college		
		Yes	No	Total
Experienced crime in the past year	Yes	28.5%	22.3%	22.5%
	No	71.5%	77.7%	77.5%
	Total	100.0%	100.0%	100.0%

Percentages *and* frequencies

In Tables 5.2 to 5.5 I only included percentages. I did this to make it easier to focus on the figures I was explaining. However, when presenting results in a research report, percentages should usually be accompanied by frequencies, as can be seen in Table 5.6:

Table 5.6: A cross-tabulation of two variables with two categories each (frequencies and percentages by rows)

		Smoke tobacco		
		Yes	No	Total
Drink alcohol	Yes	3,552 28.8%	8,781 71.2%	12,333 100.0%
	No	671 23.8%	2,151 76.2%	2,822 100.0%
	Total	4,223 27.9%	10,932 72.1%	15,155 100.0%

Including frequencies means that whoever reads the table can see the actual number of cases in each group and sub-group, as well as the total number of cases in the dataset. Percentages are sometimes used to disguise very small numbers of cases, and it's important to be transparent about how many cases are in the analysis.

Box 5.0: How do I choose which variable should be on the rows and which should be on the columns of a cross-tabulation?

When you carry out a cross-tabulation, you need to choose which of your variables will run along the rows and which will run down the columns of your table. Whatever software you use to do your analysis, it will require you to make this choice.

The good news is that this choice won't make any difference to your results. Your table will look different depending on your choice, but it won't affect the frequencies in each sub-group. What is important, however, is that if you use percentages, you choose to run the percentages in a way that matches the question you want to answer. This match – between the position of the variable in the table and the direction in which you run the percentages – is what really matters.

A different way of looking at the data: observed counts and expected counts

So far, we've looked at using frequencies (sometimes called **observed counts**) and percentages when cross-tabulating variables. We've seen that you need to run the percentages in the appropriate direction to answer a particular question, and making this decision can require a bit of thought.

Using frequencies and percentages is the most common approach when cross-tabulating categorical variables. However, there is another way of examining the relationship between the variables that uses the data in the table in a slightly different way.

Table 5.7 shows the same data we have been using to look at the relationship between drinking alcohol and smoking tobacco. You might have noticed that the numbers at the top of the four cells in the middle of the table are the same as in Tables 5.1 and 5.6. These are the frequencies in each sub-group. For example, 3,552 of the people in the study both drink alcohol and smoke tobacco.

Table 5.7: A cross-tabulation of two variables with two categories each (observed counts and expected counts)

		Smoke tobacco		
		Yes	No	Total
Drink alcohol	Yes	3,552 (3,437)	8,781 (8,896)	12,333
	No	671 (786)	2,151 (2,036)	2,822
	Total	4,223	10,932	15,155

As I explained earlier in this chapter, the term frequency just refers to the number of cases in a particular group or sub-group. They are also referred to as counts – because you count up the number of cases – and are sometimes described as observed counts. The term 'observed' is used because these are the cases you actually have – and can see – in your dataset.

It might seem unnecessary to introduce a third term for what is essentially the same thing. We already know these numbers as frequencies and counts, so why make things more complicated? One reason is that – like frequencies and percentages – you will come across these words in the wider literature and when using software packages, so it's important to know what they mean. But a more important reason, in terms of cross-tabulation, is to distinguish observed counts from **expected counts**.

Expected counts are the numbers in brackets (parentheses) in the cells representing the four sub-groups in Table 5.7. But what are expected counts? Where do they come from? And how can we use them to help us understand the relationship between these two variables?

Just like the word 'normal' in the **normal distribution**, the term 'expected' can be a bit misleading in the context of expected counts. It doesn't mean what we are expecting to see in our results (after all, we might all have different expectations about what we'd find out from the same analysis). It means what we would expect to see in our data *if there was no relationship between the two variables*.

But what does 'no relationship' mean? And what would it look like in the context of a cross-tabulation?

There are two ways that we can think about this. No relationship between the two variables that we've been looking at would mean you are no more likely to smoke tobacco if you drink alcohol (and vice versa). Or, to put it another way, knowing whether someone drinks alcohol wouldn't be useful in helping you try to predict whether they smoke tobacco. Another way of thinking about this idea is that, if there was no relationship between the two variables, the cases would be shared out 'fairly' between the four sub-groups in the table. Expected counts show you what the data would look like if the cases were actually shared out 'fairly' in this way.

But how do we know what a fair share of cases would look like? And how are these expected counts calculated?

Calculating expected counts

Expected counts are calculated using the totals of the different groups in each variable. The totals in the final column of Table 5.8 show that 12,333 of our participants drink alcohol and 2,822 don't. We can see by looking at Table 5.3 that this means that 81.4% of our participants are drinkers. The bottom row of Table 5.8 also shows that 4,223 of our participants smoke tobacco and that 10,932 don't, meaning that 27.9% are smokers (as can be seen in Table 5.2):

Table 5.8: A cross-tabulation of two variables with two categories each (expected counts and totals only*)

		Smoke tobacco		
		Yes	No	Total
	Yes	(3,437)	(8,896)	12,333
Drink alcohol	No	(786)	(2,036)	2,822
	Total	4,223	10,932	15,155

Note: *Expected counts have been rounded to whole numbers.

Knowing that 81.4% of our participants drink alcohol and that 27.9% smoke tobacco gives us the basic information to work out what proportion would both drink alcohol and smoke tobacco if there was no relationship between the two activities. If the cases are fairly shared out, 27.9% of 81.4% of all 15,155 cases should be people who both drink and smoke.

The simplest way to work out this number is to use the following formula:

$$(4,223/15,155) \times 12,333 = 3,437$$

You could also work it out by calculating 27.9% of 15,155 and then calculating 81.4% of the result. This is a bit more complicated, and because the decimals have been rounded up and down it doesn't work out at exactly the same figure, but it would be close enough for the purposes of analysis. *Remember that you don't have to do any of these calculations yourself* – the computer software package you are using will do these for you. You just need to select the option, or type the command, to include expected counts in your results.

You'll notice that 3,437 is the number in brackets in the cell in Table 5.8 that contains the expected count of those who both drink alcohol and smoke tobacco. In Table 5.9, we focus on this cell and look at how you can use the observed count and the expected count to examine the relationship between these two variables.

Table 5.9: Observed counts and expected counts for participants who drink alcohol and smoke tobacco

		Smoke tobacco
		Yes
Drink alcohol	Yes	3,552 (3,437)

In the bottom right cell of Table 5.9 we can see two figures. The figure 3,552 is the number of participants in the study who both drink alcohol and smoke tobacco. We've seen this figure before in some of the other tables in this chapter, and we know that it is the 'frequency' or 'observed count'. Below this figure, in brackets, is the 'expected count' that we've just calculated. Remember that the expected count is what the data would look like if there was no relationship between the variables. In our current example, that would be the number we'd see if there was no relationship between drinking alcohol and smoking tobacco.

Because the observed count – what is actually in our data – is different from the expected count – what the data would look like if there was no relationship – we can conclude that there *is* some kind of relationship between drinking alcohol and smoking tobacco. But what kind of relationship is it? And how do expected counts help us work this out?

When comparing the observed counts with the expected counts, we need to see whether the observed count is higher or lower than the expected count. In Table 5.9 the observed count is higher than the expected count. This means that there are more people who both drink and smoke in our study than we would expect there to be if there was no relationship between drinking and smoking. So, we can conclude from this that people who drink alcohol are more likely to smoke tobacco than those who don't drink alcohol, and vice versa.

Table 5.10 shows the observed counts and expected counts for all four sub-groups. We can see that the observed count for those who don't drink alcohol

Table 5.10: A cross-tabulation of two variables with two categories each (observed counts and expected counts)

		Smoke tobacco	
		Yes	No
Drink alcohol	Yes	3,552 (3,437)	8,781 (8,896)
	No	671 (786)	2,151 (2,036)

and don't smoke tobacco is larger than the expected count. This means that those who *don't* drink alcohol are also more likely *not* to smoke tobacco. This makes sense given what we learned from our interpretation of Table 5.9: if people who drink are more likely to smoke, then people who don't drink will be less likely to smoke.

We can also see that for both the other two sub-groups – those that smoke but don't drink and those who drink but don't smoke – the observed counts are smaller than the expected counts. This also fits in with our other findings: not doing one of these activities makes the other less likely. In summary, we could say that there is a **positive association** between drinking and smoking: if you do one of them, you're more likely to do the other.

A simple example of expected counts

If you know how to interpret observed and expected counts, it's not essential to understand exactly how they're worked out. A computer software package will generate them for you, and the important thing is that you know what your results mean. But understanding where they come from does help some people better understand what they mean, so I always show my students how expected counts are calculated. Starting with very simple examples makes the idea of expected counts much easier to understand.

Imagine that the data we have on people's smoking and drinking behaviours wasn't like that in the tables we have already examined but instead, looked like the data in Table 5.11. You can see that there are 100 cases in total. Looking at the totals in the column on the far right, you can also see that 50 of these 100 people drink alcohol and 50 of them don't drink. The totals on the bottom row show that 50 participants smoke tobacco and the other 50 don't smoke.

Table 5.11: An imaginary simple example of expected counts

		Smoke tobacco		
		Yes	No	Total
	Yes	(25)		50
Drink alcohol	No			50
	Total	50	50	100

You'll see that I haven't put any observed counts in the cells representing the four sub-groups. These aren't important for this example, so I've left them out to keep things simple. I have, however, put an expected count in the drink/smoke sub-group. You'll see that this expected count is 25. Without doing any calculations, can you see where this number came from?

Because I've used very simple numbers in this example, it's much easier to see the logic of expected counts. If we know that half (50/100) of our participants drink alcohol and also that half (50/100) of our participants smoke tobacco, we can use those proportions to think about what a 'fair' or 'even' distribution of cases would look like. If there was no relationship between drinking and smoking, we would expect *half* of *half* of all our participants to both drink and smoke. Half of 100 is 50, and half of 50 is 25, which – as we can see in Table 5.11 – is our expected count for this sub-group.

In the case of this very simple example, the expected counts would also be 25 in the other three sub-groups (because each one would be half of half of 100). It's very unlikely that the expected counts would all be the same with real data – I designed this example to be as simple as possible! While you would use the same logic and calculations, you'd usually be using different numbers for each cell, like the data shown in Table 5.8. But if you can understand where the expected count of 25 came from in Table 5.11, you understand the logic of how expected counts are worked out. The numbers are usually more difficult to work with, but the logic and maths is just the same.

Variables with more than two categories

In the examples of cross-tabulation I have used so far, all the categorical variables have only had two categories each. But many of the variables we are interested in have more than two categories. In the tables below I've shown another analysis from the National Survey of Sexual Attitudes and Lifestyles (Natsal). Like the previous analysis, it examines the relationship between drinking alcohol and smoking, but this time I have used variables that divide participants into more than two, simple 'Yes' and 'No' categories. Smoking is divided up into four categories, from 'Non-smoker' to 'Heavy smoker', and drinking alcohol is divided up into three categories, from 'None' to 'More than recommended'.

I've run the analysis in two different ways. Table 5.12 shows a cross-tabulation with frequencies (observed counts) and percentages run down the columns, for each smoking status. Table 5.13 shows the same analysis, with both observed counts and expected counts.

As you can see, the only difference between these analyses and the ones we saw earlier is that the tables are bigger. This makes them slightly more difficult to interpret, simply because more numbers are involved. If you're using percentages, you still need to decide which way to run them, and this needs to match the question you are asking. In Table 5.12 the percentages are run down the columns, and show the proportion of each group of smoker 'types' (from 'Non-smoker' to 'Heavy smoker') that fall into each category of alcohol consumption.

Table 5.12: A cross-tabulation with frequencies and column percentages

		Current smoking status				
		Non-smoker	Ex-smoker	Light smoker	Heavy smoker	Total
Alcohol consumption per week	None	2,475 32.5%	786 24.1%	646 23.6%	468 32.1%	4,375 29.0%
	Not more than recommended	4,628 60.7%	2,154 65.9%	1,696 61.8%	728 49.9%	9,206 61.0%
	More than recommended	521 6.8%	327 10.0%	401 14.6%	263 18.0%	1,512 10.0%
	Total	7,624 100%	3,267 100.0%	2,743 100.0%	1,459 100.0%	15,093 100.0%

Table 5.13 shows the same data but with observed counts (frequencies) and expected counts. We can do exactly the same thing as we did before, in terms of interpreting the results, by comparing the observed counts with the expected counts in any particular cell. Using expected counts can be useful when cross-tabulating variables with a large number of categories, because you can draw a conclusion from each cell at a time, without having to refer to, and digest, the figures in a whole row or column.

The variables in Table 5.13 have only three categories for alcohol consumption and four categories for smoking status, resulting in 12 sub-categories. Some variables, such as social class or ethnicity, have many more categories, and tables of more than 20 categories are not uncommon. In analyses involving variables with many categories, using observed and expected counts can be a useful alternative to using frequencies and percentages. However, you should be careful to make sure that your conclusions match the analysis you are using, as the two different techniques produce subtly different types of information.

Table 5.13: A cross-tabulation with observed and expected counts*

		Current smoking status				
		Non-smoker	Ex-smoker	Light smoker	Heavy smoker	Total
Alcohol consumption per week	None	2,475 (2,210)	786 (947)	646 (795)	468 (423)	4,375
	Not more than recommended	4,628 (4,650)	2,154 (1,993)	1,696 (1,673)	728 (890)	9,206
	More than recommended	521 (764)	327 (327)	401 (275)	263 (146)	1,512
	Total	7,624	3,267	2,743	1,459	15,093

Note: *Expected counts have been rounded to whole numbers.

Summary

This is the first chapter in the book where we have looked at the relationship between two variables. All the techniques covered in this chapter can only be used with categorical data (whether this is **nominal** or **ordinal**).

In the next chapter we'll look at what you can do when one of your variables is categorical and the other is either continuous or discrete.

Sources

Exercise 5.0 uses variables from the following dataset:

ONS (Office for National Statistics), University of Manchester, CMIST (Cathie Marsh Institute for Social Research), UK Data Service (2019) *Quarterly Labour Force Survey, July–September 2018: Teaching dataset* [data collection], ONS [original data producer(s)], SN: 8499, DOI: 10.5255/UKDA-SN-8499-1

Tables 5.1 to 5.3 and 5.6 to 5.13 were based on analysis of the British National Survey of Sexual Attitudes and Lifestyles, 2010–2012 Teaching dataset:

University of Manchester, CMIST (Cathie Marsh Institute for Social Research), UK Data Service (2021) *National Survey of Sexual Attitudes and Lifestyles, 2010–2012: Teaching dataset* [data collection], University College London, Centre for Sexual Health and HIV Research [original data producer(s)], SN: 8735, DOI: 10.5255/UKDA-SN-8735-1

Tables 5.4 and 5.5 were based on analyses of the Crime Survey for England and Wales, 2011–2012 Teaching dataset:

ONS (Office for National Statistics), University of Manchester, Cathie Marsh Centre for Census and Survey Research, UK Data Service (2013) *Crime Survey for England and Wales, 2011–2012: Teaching dataset* [data collection], UK Data Service, SN: 7401, DOI: 10.5255/UKDA-SN-7401-1

Useful resources

I have made four videos on how to conduct cross-tabulation using SPSS®. These can be found here:

Introducing cross-tabulation: https://youtu.be/ZOGwysV9ZQY
Using percentages in cross-tabulation: https://youtu.be/PyDj4RHrmnI
Combining percentages and frequency counts in cross-tabulations: https://youtu.be/ByluYl5LncQ
Observed and expected counts in cross-tabulations: https://youtu.be/ybnFUiwO210

Hans Zeisel wrote a very useful chapter about deciding which way to run percentages in a cross-tabulation. Unfortunately, having run to six editions, his book is now out of print, but your library might have a copy:

Zeisel, H. (1985) *Say it with Figures* (6th edn), New York: Harper & Row [Chapter 3: 'In Which Direction Should Percents Be Run?'].

Answers to exercises

Exercise 5.0
a) The only pair of variables that can be appropriately analysed using cross-tabulation is ethnicity and religion.

b) This pair of variables can be analysed using cross-tabulation because they are both categorical. None of the other variables in the list are categorical, so they cannot be used in a cross-tabulation.

6

What does it all *mean*? Comparing distributions between groups

WHAT IS THIS CHAPTER FOR?

In the last chapter we looked at how to analyse the relationship between two categorical variables using cross-tabulation. In this chapter we'll cover the techniques you'll need when one of your variables is categorical, but the other is continuous or discrete.

WHAT DOES IT COVER?

We focus on a technique that is often referred to as 'comparing means'. I explain why the mean is not always the appropriate average to compare, and show how comparing the measures of spread of different groups, combined with comparing the averages, provides a more complete understanding of the differences in the distribution of a variable between two groups.

WHAT WILL YOU LEARN?

- How comparing averages can help us see differences in the distribution of a continuous (or discrete) variable between different groups
- How to know which average to use in different circumstances
- Why it's important to compare measures of spread as well as averages, and what the different measures of spread can tell us
- How the mean and the standard deviation can be combined to give a single measure of the difference between two groups

WHAT CONCEPTS AND TECHNIQUES ARE COVERED?

- Comparing means and medians
- Comparing standard deviations and other measures of spread
- Using means and standard deviations to calculate effect sizes

In previous chapters, we looked at a range of techniques to analyse one variable at a time (univariate analysis) and one technique to analyse the relationship between two variables: cross-tabulation. If you remember, cross-tabulation is only appropriate if you have two categorical variables. If any of your variables are continuous or discrete, you need to use a different method of analysis. In this chapter we're going to look at techniques we can use to analyse the relationship between one categorical variable and another variable that is either continuous or discrete.

Continuous or discrete variables are less common than categorical variables in many areas of the social sciences. However, it's likely that there will be a few continuous or discrete variables in most datasets. Variables relating to time, money or space are commonly continuous, and variables that involve counting – the number of people in a household, for example – are often discrete.

You might want to see if, or how, the distribution of one of these continuous or discrete variables varies between groups. For example, you could compare the salaries of men and women. This analysis would involve a continuous variable (salary) and a categorical variable (gender). We know that we couldn't use cross-tabulation for this analysis, because it only works with two categorical variables. So how could we analyse a relationship between a categorical and a continuous variable?

Analysing the relationship between a categorical and a continuous variable

When I'm teaching my students how to analyse the relationship between a categorical and a continuous variable, I set them a challenge. I get them to discuss, in small groups, how they would do this if they had to invent a technique themselves. My class used to be filled by students studying either criminology or sociology, so I would ask them the following question:

> How could I work out whether sociology or criminology students did better on last year's exam?

My students usually identify certain information as important. They recognise, for example, that the highest mark and the lowest mark from students studying each subject could be useful. But they also realise that this only tells them about the most and least successful students, and not about most students. They usually mull over the idea of adding up all the scores from one group and comparing them with the total scores from the other group. But they often sense that this wouldn't be fair, because there are usually different numbers of students studying each subject.

In some years a group of students will get very excited because they think they've come up with a solution. Why don't we calculate an average for each group, and see which average is higher? Surely that will tell us which group has done better? And that's what statisticians do. The foundation of the technique we're going to cover in this chapter is something that some of my students worked out how to do on their own!

Comparing means vs comparing distributions

This technique is widely known as 'comparing means'. This description makes sense in terms of what is at its core – after all, my students correctly identified working out the average for each group and then comparing them as a good way of finding out which group of students did better in the exam. However, I don't really like the term 'comparing means' for two reasons.

First, as we saw in Chapter 3, the mean isn't always the most appropriate average to use. If the distribution of your continuous variable is **skewed**, the median is usually a better measure of **central tendency**. So, in certain situations, it might be best to compare medians (or even modes) rather than comparing means. Second, as we saw in Chapter 4, as well as looking at averages, it's also important to look at how the data for a continuous variable are spread out. This isn't only true when you're doing univariate analysis; it's also the case when you're comparing the distribution of a continuous variable between different groups. As well as comparing means or medians, it's also useful to compare minimum and maximum values, ranges and standard deviations. For this reason, I prefer to describe this kind of analysis as 'comparing distributions'.

For the examples below, I'm going to use data from the 2018 Labour Force Survey (LFS) teaching dataset from the UK Data Service. The LFS collects data on issues relating to work and employment from a large sample of people aged 16 and over. As with most of the datasets used in this book, these data are open access and you can download them yourself if you want. I've provided more details about this dataset at the end of the chapter.

We're going to look at whether people who were born in the UK work longer or shorter hours than people who were born outside the UK. This is a nice, simple example to start with as our categorical variable – where someone was born – has only two categories: born in the UK or born outside the UK. Because participants in the LFS could only specify the number of hours they worked each week *to the nearest hour*, the data on working hours is discrete rather than continuous. However, as I discussed in Chapter 2, we can usually use the same statistical techniques with discrete and continuous data. In this case, it's fine to compare the distribution of a discrete variable between two groups because fractions of a working hour make sense in theory. The results of the analysis are shown in Table 6.0.

So what do these results tell us? If we start by looking at the first column of numbers in the table we can see that the total number of cases in our dataset is 40,084. Of those, 33,866 were born in the UK and 6,218 were born outside the UK. We might have guessed that most of the workers in the UK were born in the UK, so it's not surprising that these groups are different sizes. In terms of conducting our analyses, it doesn't matter that these groups are different sizes, and this won't affect the kind of conclusions that we can make. We would only

Table 6.0: Comparing the distribution of two groups (number of cases and mean only)

	Working hours	
Born in the UK	N	Mean
Yes	33,866	36.55
No	6,218	37.37
Total	40,084	36.68

need to be concerned if the *absolute* size of one of our groups was very small, which is something that can cause problems in some statistical analyses.

The column on the right side of the table shows us the mean average working hours for everyone in the dataset and the means for those who were born in the UK and for those who were not. The overall mean is 36.68 hours. The mean for workers born in the UK is 36.55 and the mean for those born outside the UK is 37.37. We can see from this that workers born outside the UK work nearly one hour a week longer, on average, than workers who were born in the UK.

However, as I said earlier, the mean might not be the best average to use. It's usually fine when the data are **normally distributed** and there are no extreme **outliers**, and it does have the advantage of using data from every single case. As we would expect the mean and the median (and usually the mode) to have very similar values when the data are normally distributed, it might not make much difference which measure we used. Although, as we shall see, there are situations in which the mean isn't the best average to compare.

Table 6.1 shows not only the number of cases in each group and the means, but also the medians. There are two things worth noting about the medians. First, they are all whole numbers. This is because the median often represents an actual value from the dataset, and in this dataset participants had to state their working hours to the nearest whole hour. (If you remember, the median is the value of the middle case when all the cases are put in order, from the lowest to the highest value.) Second, all three medians are slightly higher than the mean averages. But why is this the case? And what does it tell us about the distribution of this variable?

Table 6.1: Comparing the distribution of two groups (number of cases, mean and median)

Born in the UK	Working hours		
	N	Mean	Median
Yes	33,866	36.55	38
No	6,218	37.37	40
Total	40,084	36.68	38

Figure 6.0 is a **histogram** showing the distribution of hours worked in a usual week. We would usually have looked at this when we were doing our exploratory univariate analysis, so by the time we did any bivariate analysis we would already know what the distribution of this variable looked like. Examining the way that a continuous or discrete variable is distributed is important, because it can help us decide whether the mean or the median is the best measure to compare between the two groups.

We can see that the data in Figure 6.0 aren't quite normally distributed. Whereas the bars on the right side fit quite neatly with the black line that shows the perfect normal distribution, on the left side some bars aren't quite high enough to reach the line and other bars are a little higher than the line. The distribution looks a little bit **negatively skewed**, which explains why the means

Figure 6.0: Histogram showing the distribution of hours worked in a usual week

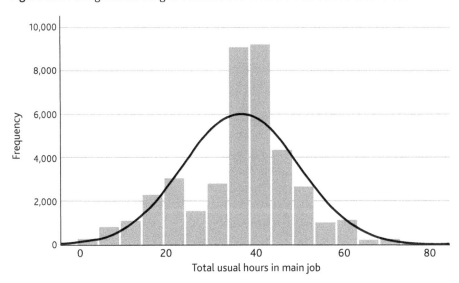

are smaller than the medians. Given that there isn't a great deal of difference between the mean and median values, it's not a crucial decision in this case, as the overall conclusion wouldn't change whichever measure we used (but the median does have the advantage of providing a value that actually exists in the data). However, as we shall see, in other cases the means and medians can tell very different stories. This is just one illustration of why exploratory univariate analyses are important, and shows why you should bear these results in mind when you conduct further analyses.

Once we have compared the averages of the two groups – using either the mean or the median – it's useful to go on to look at some **measures of spread**. Table 6.2 shows four measures of spread (or 'dispersion'): the standard deviation (SD); the minimum value; the maximum value; and the range.

Let's start with the simplest measures: minimum and maximum values. You can see from Table 6.2 that there is no difference in the minimum and maximum working hours of those who were born in the UK and those who weren't. However, before we conclude that there is really no difference between the groups in this respect, we need to think carefully about how the data might have been collected.

Table 6.2: Comparing the distribution of two groups (number of cases, standard deviation, minimum and maximum values, and range)

	Working hours				
Born in the UK	N	SD	Minimum	Maximum	Range
Yes	33,866	13.04	1	97	97
No	6,218	12.66	1	97	97
Total	40,084	12.99	1	97	97

The minimum value is quite easy to explain. As the cases were all people who work, the minimum number of hours that could be reported was 1. And as there are many thousands of people in each group, it's not surprising that at least one person in each group worked for only 1 hour a week. One of the limitations of minimum (and maximum) values is that they don't give us any idea of *how many* cases took that value, although the histogram in Figure 6.0 suggests that, among the cases as a whole, not many people worked 5 hours or less.

There are several plausible explanations for the maximum values. The simplest is that the maximum number of hours worked by anyone in each group was 97. This is what the data show at face value, but there are some other possibilities. It could also be that these figures are just the result of the way the data were collected or recorded. It's possible that either participants in the research were prevented from providing a value higher than 97, or that values of higher than 97 were recoded before the data was released.

Figure 6.1 shows the original question from the 2018 LFS. This was very easy to find with a quick Google search, and there's a link to the document at the end of this chapter. We can see that the researchers collecting the data combined any responses over 97 hours into a single category of '97 or more'. So, because of the way that these data were collected, we can't draw any conclusions about whether the maximum number of hours worked by those born in the UK is different from the maximum number of hours worked by those who were born elsewhere. We should also bear in mind that this may also have had an impact on the mean values for each group, but it is unlikely to have affected the median (which is another good reason to compare the medians rather than the means). But, more generally, this shows that we need to be careful when interpreting statistical outputs, and that we should always be mindful of how the data have been collected and recorded.

There is one more measure of spread that we haven't discussed yet: the standard deviation (SD). We looked at the standard deviation – and the closely related **mean deviation** (MD) – in Chapter 4. As I noted in that chapter, the SD doesn't have a straightforward interpretation, and even though it's pretty close to being the average distance of all the **data points** from the mean (which

Figure 6.1: Question on working hours from the 2018 Labour Force Survey (LFS)

TOTUS1 How many hours per week do you usually work in your (main) job/business (please exclude meal breaks)?	UK EQ FORCED

    97 = 97 or more
    99 = don't know or refusal

ONS ✓   GOV ✓   EUL ✓

Applies to those not doing overtime or working for own/relative's business
IF (EVEROT=2) or (OWNBUS=1) OR (RELBUS=1)

Source: ONS (2018, p 73)

is actually what the MD tells you), this can still be a fairly abstract idea when you're looking at one variable on its own.

It's easier to understand how useful the SD can be once we start comparing the distribution of a variable between different groups. This is because it can be a useful measure of whether the distribution of a variable is more spread out for one group than another, and what the difference in spread is between those two groups.

We can see from Table 6.2 that the overall SD of working hours – shown in the 'Total' row – is 12.99. But the SD for those born in the UK is a bit higher, at 13.04, and the SD for those born outside the UK is lower, at 12.66. This tells us that there is slightly more variation in the working hours of those who were born in the UK than there is among those who were born outside the UK.

As I explained in Chapter 4, the advantage of the SD over measures such as the minimum and maximum values and the range is that, like the mean, it is calculated using data from every case. Because of this, it is more representative of what is happening in your data – or in a particular group in your dataset. It's a measure of the overall spread of the data, not just a measure of what the data look like at the extremes.

Before we move on, it's important to note that limiting the upper value of working hours to 97 will have affected both the mean and the SD. However, given that it also affected the maximum value and range, the SD is a better measure of the overall spread of the data in each group.

Exercise 6.0 will help you practice working out when comparing the distributions of different groups is the most appropriate strategy for analysing the relationship between two variables.

EXERCISE 6.0

Consider the same variables from the Labour Force Survey (LFS) teaching dataset, as we did in the last chapter:

- Ethnicity
- Religion
- Gross hourly pay
- Number of children aged 0–4 years
- Age when completed full-time education

a) Can comparing distributions be used appropriately to analyse the relationship between any two of these variables? If so, which variables?

b) Why are only those pairs of variables suitable for comparing distributions?

c) In each pair, which would be the dependent and which would be the independent variable?

Bringing everything together

So how do we combine all the information that we've looked at so far and draw some conclusions about the differences in distribution between the two groups?

Table 6.3 shows all the measures of distribution that we have discussed. Because of the way the data have been collected, the minimum and maximum values and the range don't tell us as much as we'd like, but we can still conclude that there are workers from both groups who work only few hours a week and those who work 97 hours or more (which is a very long working week).

Table 6.3: Comparing the distribution of two groups (measures of central tendency and spread)

| | Working hours | | | | | |
Born in the UK	Mean	Median	SD	Minimum	Maximum	Range
Yes	36.55	38	13.04	1	97	97
No	37.37	40	12.66	1	97	97
Total	36.68	38	12.99	1	97	97

Given the slightly skewed distribution of working hours and considering the issues with data collection discussed above, the medians are probably the most useful averages to compare. We can see that the median number of working hours for workers born in the UK is 38 and the median for those born outside the UK is 40. This suggests a slightly larger difference than we get from comparing the means, but the direction of the relationship is the same using either measure, and the overall conclusion would be that, on average, those born outside the UK work only slightly more hours than those born in the UK.

The SDs give us an idea of how spread out the data on working hours are for each group. This is important because it tells us how much working hours vary *within* each group. Or, to put it another way, how similar – or different – the people in each group are in terms of how many hours they work.

The SDs in each group are quite similar. Workers born in the UK had a slightly higher SD than those born outside the UK. This means that there is marginally more variation in working hours for the former group compared to the latter. Another way of thinking about this is in terms of how close people's working hours are to the mean number of working hours. People who are born outside the UK are a little bit more likely to have working hours that are close to the mean than those born in the UK.

Calculating an effect size

As we've seen, communicating the findings of statistical analyses often involves presenting more than one measure and explaining what story these figures tell us overall. However, in the case of the analysis we have just done – comparing the distributions of a continuous or discrete variable between two groups – there is a technique that we can use to combine some of these statistics into an overall measure of the difference between the two groups. There are several different techniques, all based on the same principles, that can calculate what is called a **standardised mean difference effect size**. The one that we are going to use is called 'Cohen's *d*'.

What all these techniques have in common is that they combine the means we calculated for each group with the SD for the variable as a whole to create a single figure that summarises how different the two groups are in terms of the distribution of a variable. For our example, this provides a measure of how different the working hours of those born in the UK are compared to those of people born outside the UK.

The formula for calculating Cohen's *d* is as follows:

$$(\text{Group 1 mean} - \text{Group 2 mean})/\text{overall SD}$$

For our example above, it doesn't really matter which group is 'Group 1' and which group is 'Group 2'. When calculating effect sizes that are only intended to describe the differences between groups, I usually subtract the smaller mean from the larger mean, so that the result is a positive number. But when calculating Cohen's *d*, we do need to be sure to use the SD for the variable as a whole (although the type of SD used does vary between different versions of the standardised mean difference effect size).

If we designate those born outside the UK as Group 1 and those born in the UK as Group 2, using the figures in Table 6.3, our calculation would be as follows:

$$(37.37 - 36.55)/12.99 = 0.06$$

The answer, our **effect size**, is very close to zero and suggests that there isn't much difference between the two groups. As is the case with most statistical results, there aren't any hard and fast rules about what a 'large' difference would be. This depends on the area of study, what would be expected based on previous findings, and many other factors. However, it is safe to say that this result means that the two groups are very similar in terms of their hours of work.

If we compare the two histograms for the two groups, shown in Figures 6.2 and 6.3, we can see that the shape of the two distributions is very similar. If we laid them on top of each other, almost all of the area of the bars in both charts would overlap. This is basically what effect sizes like Cohen's *d* do – they give us an idea of how much the distributions of the two groups overlap.

In summary, we can say that whether someone was born in the UK or not makes only a small difference to the number of hours they work. Those born outside the UK work slightly more hours, and there is slightly less variation in working hours in this group compared to those who were born in the UK, but we haven't found a great deal of difference between the two groups.

Figure 6.2: Histogram for Group 1

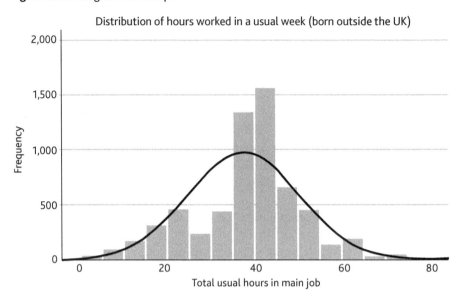

Distribution of hours worked in a usual week (born outside the UK)

Figure 6.3: Histogram for Group 2

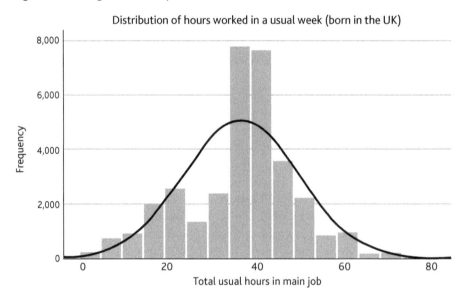

Distribution of hours worked in a usual week (born in the UK)

Students are sometimes disappointed when they find no difference between groups, or a very weak relationship between variables. They often think that this means that they haven't found anything out or that the analysis has 'failed' in some way. This couldn't be further from the truth. Finding out that there is very little difference between groups or that a relationship is weak can be very important. This is especially the case if you were expecting a difference or relationship and are surprised by the result.

Box 6.0: A brief history of the 'effect size'

The term effect size is used in relation to many different statistical outputs. Cohen's *d* is one example of a family of measures called 'standardised mean difference' effect sizes. These are based around the difference between the means in two different groups, with this difference being 'standardised' by dividing by a standard deviation. These measures are often used to analyse the data in studies using experimental designs, with one mean coming from a group that received a new treatment (the experimental group) and one group that received a conventional treatment or no treatment at all (the **placebo** group). However, they are also used to describe the differences between groups in non-experimental research. Other standardised mean difference effect sizes include Glass's *delta* and Hedges' *g*. I have used Cohen's *d* here because it is the simplest measure, and is well suited to describing the differences between two groups.

A different example

Before moving on to look at comparing the means of more than one group, we'll look at a different analysis from the same LFS dataset. This time we'll compare the hourly wages of men and women. We can see from the results shown in Table 6.4 that, unlike with our previous example, there are some noticeable differences between the groups. As we are familiar with these outputs from the last example, I won't go over them in so much detail.

The first thing you might notice is that there are fewer cases (9,478) than the previous analysis (that included 40,084). This may because people find it relatively easy to provide an estimate of the number of hours they work each week but may not know exactly how much they earn an hour if they are paid a yearly salary. If this analysis was part of a real research project, it would be important to do some extra research into the LFS to work out why there is a low response rate for this question, and what the implications might be for your findings.

Unlike with our previous example, where we wouldn't expect the groups to be of equal sizes, we might expect there to be a similar number of male and female participants. We can see from the data in Table 6.4 that we haven't quite got equal numbers in both groups, but the proportions aren't far off. But we don't need the numbers to be equally balanced – or even in proportion to the wider population – to do the analysis. Any calculations we are doing take into account the number of cases in each group, so any comparisons will be fair ones.

Table 6.4: Comparing the distribution of hourly wages between men and women

				Hourly wage			
	N	Mean	Median	SD	Minimum	Maximum	Range
Men	4,468	16.67	13.45	12.62	0.38	349.46	349.08
Women	5,010	13.25	10.94	8.13	0.56	128.50	127.94
Total	9,478	14.86	12.03	10.63	0.38	349.46	349.08

In the next column of the table we can see the means. Here there is a noticeable difference between men and women, with men earning an average of £16.67 an hour and women taking home only £13.25 per hour. There is a slightly smaller difference between the medians, but the difference is still in favour of men.

Again, medians might be the best measure, as a histogram I produced told me not only that the data are **positively skewed** (as is often the case with the distribution of income), but also that there were some outliers: people who earned very high amounts per hour. Regardless of the average used, however, the general story is of men being paid more than women.

In this example the minimum and maximum values, and the range, tell us quite a lot. The highest hourly rate for men (£349.46) is approaching three times the highest rate for women (£128.50). The minimum values are rather odd, being less than a pound. As the lowest legal minimum wage (for apprentices) in 2018 was £3.70, no one should have been earning less than that. However, many people work for 'cash in hand', and as surveys such as the LFS are very good at collecting data on people and activities that may not appear in official records, it is likely that some of the lower rates of pay reflect work that takes place 'off the record'. However, the ranges do appear to show that there is greater variation in men's pay than women's pay, at least at the extremes.

Compared to the range, the SD provides a much better idea of the *general* spread of hourly pay in each group. We can see that men's pay varies more than women's pay by a considerable amount. This means that not only is women's pay lower on average, but that it is generally closer to the female average than men's pay is to the male average.

If we calculate an effect size (Cohen's *d*) using the formula we used previously and inputting the data from Table 6.4 we get a result of 0.32 in favour of men. This is a much more substantial difference than we saw in the last example, and suggests that there is a considerable difference between the amount men and women are paid.

What effect sizes look like

Figure 6.4 shows what different effect sizes look like in terms of how much overlap there would be between the two groups if the histograms of their distributions were laid over each other. Think of the curves in the diagrams as tracing the tops of the bars in a histogram for each group. The horizontal black line at the top of each graph shows the distance between the means of the two groups. (The numbers on the axis are arbitrary and just used for illustration.) Our effect size of 0.32 would look like something in-between the first two graphs. Although, as I mentioned earlier, there are no hard and fast rules about what counts as a 'large' effect, an effect size of 0.32 in differences in pay between groups would be considered reasonably large in most social science disciplines. And going back to the figures in Table 6.4, a £2 to £3 difference in hourly wages can make a large difference in terms of quality of life and the ability to balance a household budget.

Figure 6.4: Visualisation of different effect sizes calculated using Cohen's *d*

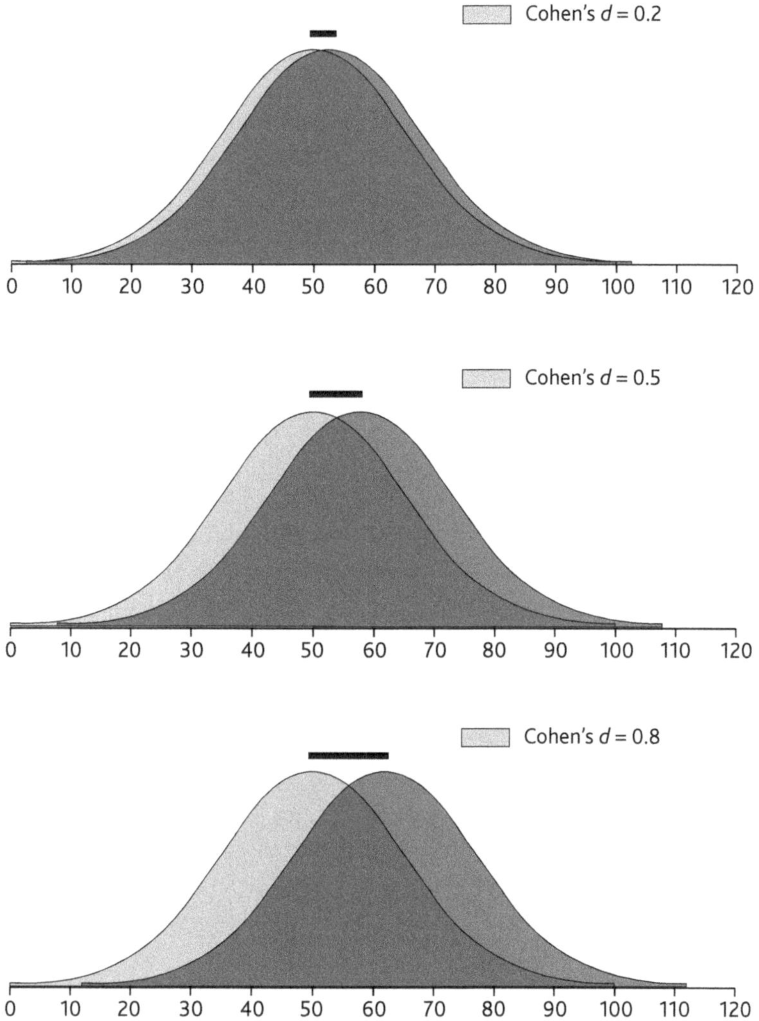

Source: Martin Héroux

Box 6.1: Cohen's *d*, the normal distribution and standardisation

You might have noticed that, in Figure 6.4, the graph showing effect sizes has distributions that appear to be perfectly normally distributed. Strictly speaking, Cohen's *d* and other similar standardised mean difference effect sizes assume that the data in each group are normally distributed. Because these effect sizes are standardised, the amount of overlap between the two groups can be calculated for any particular effect size. This overlap would always be the same, for any stated effect size, regardless of the variable you are using or the scale you used to measure that variable (a Cohen's *d* of 0.5 will always mean 67% overlap in the groups, for example).

However, this is only true if the continuous variable in your analysis is normally distributed for both groups. If you use Cohen's *d* or other similar measures with data that aren't normally distributed, the overlap between the two groups won't be quite the same as the figure you read in a textbook. You can still use this type of effect size with data that aren't normally distributed – they are still an indicator of the size of the effect – but you should bear in mind that the results won't necessarily have all the properties of, or be directly comparable with, effect sizes calculated with variables that are normally distributed.

Comparing distributions of more than two groups

So far, we've looked at two examples comparing the distribution between groups of a continuous or a discrete variable. In both of those examples, the categorical variable (sometimes referred to as the **grouping variable** in these kinds of analysis) had only two categories. But, as we saw in Chapter 5, many of the categorical variables we are interested in have more than two categories. This isn't a problem, as we can still compare the distribution of a continuous variable between more than two groups. The only difference is that our tables become larger and, as I will explain later, we can't calculate an effect size like Cohen's *d* (at least not to compare more than two groups at once).

I conducted another analysis using the same LFS data, this time looking at the relationship between hourly wages and ethnicity. The results of the analysis are presented in Table 6.5. We can interpret the results in the same way as we did for the previous two examples. As usual, we also need to look for any issues in the data that might affect our analyses, and in this example these are different to those that arose in our previous analyses.

If we start with the means, we can see that there are some quite stark differences between the ethnic groups. LFS participants in the Bangladeshi ethnic group had the lowest mean hourly wage of £9.82, while those in the Chinese group earned nearly twice as much on average, with a mean of £18.79. The overall mean was £14.86, with quite a few groups having values close to this figure.

Table 6.5: Comparing the distribution of hourly wages between several groups

Ethnicity	N	Mean	Median	SD	Minimum	Maximum	Range
				Hourly wage			
White	8,496	14.89	12.03	10.46	0.38	349.46	349.08
Mixed/Multiple ethnic groups	117	15.17	12.33	9.55	2.25	57.70	55.45
Indian	230	16.40	12.13	18.63	1.73	259.63	257.90
Pakistani	99	13.24	10.10	10.62	0.85	91.11	90.26
Bangladeshi	28	9.82	7.76	5.17	1.44	21.26	19.82
Chinese	58	18.79	15.67	12.70	3.75	61.50	57.75
Other Asian	99	13.04	10.02	8.53	1.60	48.58	46.98
Black/African/Caribbean/ Black British	238	13.56	11.87	7.30	3.35	60.00	56.65
Other ethnic group	108	13.88	11.30	8.16	3.89	40.06	36.17
Total	9,473	14.86	12.03	10.63	0.38	349.46	349.08

As we already know that the distribution of hourly wages in our LFS data has a positively skewed distribution, and we also know that there are outliers, the median is the most useful measure to compare. As you can see in Table 6.6, while all the groups have a lower median than their mean, the order of the groups is slightly different depending on the average that we use. The choice of average to use doesn't only affect our estimates of how much different groups are paid; in this case, it also changes the relative position of some of the groups in terms of the highest and lowest wages. This underlines how important these decisions can be, and why we should always pay attention to how the data for a continuous or a discrete variable are distributed. (It also shows why 'comparing means' isn't a very useful description of this kind of analysis.)

Moving on to the measures of spread, we can interpret the data in the same way as in our previous examples. We've already highlighted some issues with the minimum values for this variable, so we won't pay much attention to those

Table 6.6: Order of ethnic groups' hourly wages using different averages

	Mean	Median
1.	Chinese	Chinese
2.	Indian	Mixed/Multiple ethnic groups
3.	Mixed/Multiple ethnic groups	Indian
4.	White	White
5.	Other ethnic group	Black/African/Caribbean/Black British
6.	Black/African/Caribbean/Black British	Other ethnic group
7.	Pakistani	Pakistani
8.	Other Asian	Other Asian
9.	Bangladeshi	Bangladeshi

figures. However, the maximum values are interesting because they vary so much. They range from £21.26 per hour in the Bangladeshi group to £349.46 in the White group. It's worth pointing out that the £349.46 figure is an outlier, as is the £259.63 for the Indian group, but even ignoring these two figures there is considerable variation between the other groups. It's also interesting that the groups with the highest medians didn't always have the highest maximum values. The Chinese group, for example, had the highest median hourly pay, at £15.67. But the maximum value for this group was £61.50, much lower than three other groups.

There is also variation in the SD. There is a general pattern of higher SDs among the highest paid groups, but the order of variation doesn't strictly follow the order of pay (measured by either the mean or median). The greatest variation – by some distance – is among the Indian group and the least variation is in the Bangladeshi group. Although outliers affect the SD in a similar manner to the mean, the SD is still a useful indicator of the overall spread of the values.

Now that we've looked at the averages and measures of spread, let's look at the number of cases in each of the groups. This is something that you would have done in your exploratory univariate analysis (see Chapter 3), but it's important to take forward what you've learned from univariate analysis to inform the bivariate analysis that you do later. The most important point here is that the number of cases in some of the ethnic groups is quite small. The Bangladeshi group stands out, with only 28 cases, but the Chinese group is also quite small, with 58 cases. This is important because, notably, these are the lowest and highest paid groups.

The reason we need to look out for small groups is because small numbers are **volatile**. This is an idea that is mentioned throughout this book and relates to a central principle of statistical analysis: the relative size of different groups isn't usually important, but small numbers of cases in any group can be a problem. This is because a group with a small number of cases is much more sensitive to any changes in the data than a large group. This means that whether a case is included in any particular analysis (or in a study in the first place) can have a relatively large impact on what the results might be.

To show you what this means in practice I've compared two groups from our dataset: Bangladeshi and Black/African/Caribbean/Black British. The first group has only 28 cases, whereas the second group has more than eight times that number, at 238. I removed the individuals with the three lowest hourly wages from each of the groups. You can see the difference this made in Table 6.7.

Unsurprisingly, removing the three cases with the lowest wages from the smaller group made more difference to the average for that group than taking the three lowest paid cases from the larger group did for that group's average. The mean for the Bangladeshi group rose from £9.82 per hour to £10.61 per hour (a change of £0.79) while the mean for the Black/African/Caribbean/Black British group only rose from £13.56 to £13.69 (a change of £0.13). Because both the changes were less than a pound, it might seem at first that the difference in changes between the two groups isn't important. But the difference in relative terms is actually very large: the effect on the Bangladeshi group was

Table 6.7: How the volatility of small numbers can affect the results of statistical analyses

| | | Hourly wage | | | | | |
Ethnicity	N	Mean	Median	SD	Minimum	Maximum	Range
Bangladeshi	28	9.82	7.76	5.17	1.44	21.26	19.82
Bangladeshi less 3 cases	25	10.61	8.00	4.88	6.35	21.26	14.91
Black/African/Caribbean/ Black British	238	13.56	11.87	7.30	3.35	60.00	56.65
Black/African/Caribbean/ Black British less 3 cases	235	13.69	11.95	7.26	4.26	60.00	55.74
Total	9,473	14.86	12.03	10.63	0.38	349.46	349.08

six times greater. And because we are often interested in relative differences, and in change, this could have an impact on the conclusions we make.

The other important consideration is what we're measuring. The change that removing these cases made to the previous difference between the two groups might only be £0.66, but the variable is hourly pay. In a 37-hour week, this translates to a difference of £24.42, and over a year it would be £1,267.20. And this difference has been created by only three people in each group being excluded from the analysis. Non-response, drop-out and **missing data** are common in research and aren't usually random: losing data at one end of a distribution isn't an unlikely scenario. In terms of this example, people being paid cash in hand may be reluctant to provide information about their earnings because of possible implications for tax or benefits. And at the other end of the scale, high earners may be unwilling to divulge information about some sources of income because of a desire to avoid taxes. It's important to avoid conducting analyses with small groups, if at all possible, in order to reduce the volatility associated with small numbers. It may be necessary, in some circumstances, to collapse two or more categories into a single group, or even to completely exclude very small groups from your analysis.

(Some readers might have noticed that in this example the median values were impacted much less by the removal of these three cases than were the mean values. While median values can be less volatile than mean values, this isn't always the case – it will depend on the distribution of the data – so they shouldn't be seen as a universal solution when small numbers of cases.)

Effect sizes with more than two groups

We saw earlier that standardised mean difference effect sizes, such as Cohen's *d*, could be a useful way of summarising, in a single figure, the difference in the distribution of a variable between two groups. But in our latest example we have more than two groups. So can we still use this type of effect size? The answer is yes, and no.

This type of effect size can only be used with two groups, so you would have to choose two groups to compare to use this technique. In addition, you couldn't just use the data from Table 6.5 to do the calculation. The means from each of the two groups would be fine, but the 'total' SD in that table is for all the groups combined. The SD that you would need for the calculation would be the combined SD for only the two groups you were comparing. This figure can be generated relatively easily in most statistical software packages, but it's important that you remember to do this.

Summary

In this chapter we've seen how you can analyse the relationship between one categorical variable and one continuous or discrete variable. All the examples have used real datasets, and I've highlighted some of the issues that can arise when you're using real data. I also emphasised the importance of doing more than just 'comparing means', and using the various measures of central tendency and spread to tell you about the differences between groups. We also saw that, in certain circumstances, standardised mean difference effect sizes could be a useful way of summarising the different distributions of a variable between two groups.

In the next two chapters we look at techniques for analysing the relationship between two continuous or discrete variables.

References
ONS (Office for National Statistics) (2018) *Labour Force Survey, User Guide: Volume 2 – LFS Questionnaire 2018*, Version 1, May, www.ons.gov.uk/file?uri=/employmentandlabourmarket/peopleinwork/employmentandemployeetypes/methodologies/labourforcesurveyuserguidance/lfsvolume2jm18.pdf

Sources
Tables 6.0 to 6.7 and Figures 6.0, 6.2 and 6.3 were created by analysing data from the following dataset:

ONS (Office for National Statistics), University of Manchester, CMIST (Cathie Marsh Institute for Social Research), UK Data Service (2019) *Quarterly Labour Force Survey, July–September 2018: Teaching dataset* [data collection], ONS [original data producer(s)], SN: 8499, DOI: 10.5255/UKDA-SN-8499-1

Figure 6.4: Martin Héroux, https://scientificallysound.org/2017/07/27/cohens-d-how-interpretation (used with the author's permission).

Useful resources
My YouTube SPSS® tutorials covering the techniques discussed in this chapter can be found here:

Comparing means: https://youtu.be/vw8pRKYTY7k
Comparing means – interpretation of results: https://youtu.be/1mMRpfeWkVM

Answers to exercises

Exercise 6.0

a) The following combinations of variables are suitable for comparing distributions:

Dependent variable	Independent variable
Gross hourly pay	Ethnicity
Gross hourly pay	Religion
Number of children aged 0–4 years	Ethnicity
Number of children aged 0–4 years	Religion
Age when completed full-time education	Ethnicity
Age when completed full-time education	Religion

b) Each pair of variables has one categorical variable and one continuous (or discrete) variable.

c) The dependent variables are all continuous or discrete and the independent variables are categorical.

7

You're so predictable: using correlations

WHAT IS THIS CHAPTER FOR?

In this chapter I introduce some techniques for bivariate analysis, called correlations, which measure the predictability of a relationship. I explain how these techniques work, the situations in which they can be used, and how the results should be interpreted. Although I concentrate on techniques that can be used with continuous or discrete variables, I briefly introduce some techniques for other kinds of data. The concepts in this chapter are central to understanding regression analysis, which is covered next, in Chapter 8.

WHAT DOES IT COVER?

I focus on the idea of correlation, and look at the Pearson correlation coefficient in particular. I also cover other types of correlation, such as Spearman's *rho*, that are used when your variables are not continuous or discrete. I discuss the importance of using scatterplots to examine relationships visually, and of thinking about what a relationship might look like before you conduct any analysis.

WHAT WILL YOU LEARN?

- When you can and can't use different kinds of correlational analysis
- The strengths and weaknesses of correlation techniques
- How to interpret the results of correlation

WHAT CONCEPTS AND TECHNIQUES ARE COVERED?

- Positive and negative relationships
- Linear and non-linear relationships
- Strength of relationship
- Predictability
- Line of best fit
- Pearson's *r*
- Spearman's *rho*

You've probably heard the word 'correlation' before. And it's likely that you've heard it used incorrectly. Journalists, politicians and even academics often use this term to refer to any kind of link between two different things. But, as I noted in

Chapter 1, this word has a very specific meaning, and in this chapter you'll learn exactly what correlation is and how this type of analysis can be useful to you.

A correlation is a very useful way of describing a relationship between two variables, because it provides a measure of how much variation in one variable is *matched* by variation in the other: it tells you about the predictability of that relationship. We'll look at exactly what this means later in this chapter and discuss when you can – and can't – use correlations.

There are many different methods for establishing the level of correlation between two variables, but we'll start with one of the most commonly used measures, the Pearson correlation coefficient (often called Pearson's *r*). It's called 'Pearson' after its inventor, Karl Pearson, and is best suited to analysing the relationship between two continuous variables, although it can also usually be used with discrete data. You shouldn't use this technique with categorical data of any kind, though. There are correlation coefficients that can be calculated for certain types of categorical data, and we'll discuss some of these later in this chapter.

What is a correlation?

If I wanted to look at the relationship between the time my students spent studying and how well they did in an assessment, I could use a correlation to do this. The result – a correlation coefficient – would tell me how closely the amount of time students spent studying was related to the mark they achieved.

As with any study, there are things I'd have to think about when collecting the data. I'd have to be careful how I measured 'studying', and only count studying that was relevant to my course. If I was asking students to report their time studying, I might suspect that some of them wouldn't be completely honest about this. But putting these issues aside, the data I collected would be suitable for calculating Pearson's correlation coefficient because both variables are the appropriate **level of measurement**.

As we saw in Chapter 2, time spent studying is a continuous variable. My students could record the time they spent studying using a stopwatch or timers on their phones. I probably wouldn't need them to record this to the exact second, but the fact that time *can* be meaningfully divided up into smaller and smaller units on a continuum – and we have accurate ways of measuring this – means that the variable is continuous and so is the appropriate level of measurement for Pearson's correlation.

As I mark my students' assignments out of 100%, 'assignment mark' isn't truly continuous. For one thing, it's 'bounded', because it can't be higher than 100 or lower than zero. But, more importantly, I usually only give marks in percentages as whole numbers. Technically, this means that this variable is discrete. But these scores share some characteristics with continuous data, as it would make sense in theory to give someone a mark of 55.4% (and students sometimes end up with such a figure when a mean average mark is calculated from two or more marks). The only reason I don't tend to mark in fractions of a per cent is because I don't believe I can differentiate students' performance that accurately. So, even though this variable is discrete rather than continuous, it still meets the requirements for Pearson's correlation.

Now that we've checked that our two variables are suitable for analysis using Pearson's correlation, we could go ahead and calculate this statistic, which would always be a figure between −1 and +1. But before we look at the results of this calculation in detail, it's worth thinking some more about what we're really doing when we use correlations.

Visualising correlation

So how does correlation work? A good way to understand correlation is to think about it visually. If I entered each of my students' assessment results into a spreadsheet, alongside the number of hours they had spent studying for our class, I would have two columns of numbers. For each student I would have a percentage between 0 and 100 for their assessment score and a value representing the number of hours (or minutes, seconds, and so on) they had studied. I could create a **scatterplot** like the one in Figure 7.0, in which every dot represented a student with a particular assessment score and a particular number of hours of study.

A correlation coefficient works out the extent to which variation in one variable *matches* variation in another. This is quite a difficult idea to understand at first, so it can be easier to visualise by thinking about it in terms of how close the points on a scatterplot are to a straight line. As well as plotting the points on the graph, I asked the software package to draw what is called a **line of best fit** through these **data points** to help you see this. The closer the data points are to a straight line, the easier it would be to predict values of one variable just by knowing the values of the other variable – in this case, to predict a student's mark in a test from the time they spent studying.

Figure 7.0: The relationship between hours studied and assessment score

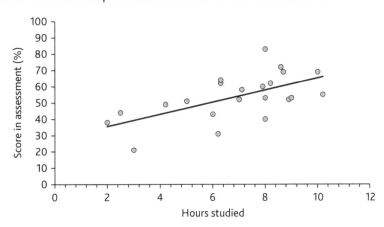

Although I have drawn a graph to present the idea of a correlation, when you ask the computer software to calculate a correlation, it only uses maths to calculate the correlation coefficient. The value of Pearson's correlation for the data shown in Figure 7.0 is +0.61. The result of the calculations for Pearson's correlation is called Pearson's r, so we would say that $r=0.61$. I'll discuss what this means, and how you interpret Pearson's r, in the next section. But before reading any further, you might want to try answer the questions in Exercise 7.0. I've written a detailed discussion of the answers to these questions at the end of the chapter.

EXERCISE 7.0

Look at the scatterplot in Figure 7.0. Remember that each of the dots on the graph represents a different student. You can trace a line from each point straight down to see how long they studied for, and straight across to the left to see what mark they got in the assessment.

Try to answer the following questions:

a) How would you describe, in everyday language, the relationship between how long a student spent studying and the mark they got?

b) How accurately, in general terms, do you think you'd be able to predict a student's mark if you only knew how long they studied for?

c) Thinking about your answers to questions (a) and (b), do you think it's worthwhile to spend a lot of time studying for an assessment?

If we used the correct technical terms, we'd say that there is a **positive relationship** between the two variables: students who study for longer tend to get better marks in their assessment. However, it's not a perfect relationship: some students studied for longer than others but ended up getting a lower mark.

So why do we need to calculate a correlation coefficient at all? Wouldn't it be easier just to draw a scatterplot like the one in Figure 7.0? Couldn't we just look at this scatterplot and then describe what we see?

It *is* usually a good idea to have a look at your data on a graph or chart, and this is something we'll return to at various points in the book. However, in some cases, scatterplots won't show you a clear picture of a relationship for the following reasons.

Both scatterplots and correlation coefficients can give you useful information. But a correlation coefficient can often tell you things that you wouldn't be able to work out by simply looking at a scatterplot. Because a correlation is calculated mathematically, it gives you a precise figure that is understood universally and can be used to make comparisons between the strengths of different relationships.

You can, of course, compare scatterplots from different analyses, but unless the relationships they show are very similar or very different, it can be difficult to describe what they have in common and what distinguishes them from each other. This is partly because, in some situations, statistical analyses are better at identifying relationships than the human eye and brain, and partly because of the kind of data we use in social research and the relationships that we tend to discover.

Many of the relationships in social research aren't very strong and so can be difficult to see on a scatterplot. Although, as we will see in Chapter 9, the human brain is very good at picking out certain kinds of visual patterns, the relationship between two variables shown in a scatterplot is often very difficult to see clearly. But correlational analysis works out the relationship between two variables mathematically, and so it can identify (and quantify) relationships that would otherwise be very difficult – if not impossible – to detect by eye.

It's also the case that we sometimes analyse datasets that contain a very large number of cases. There are lots of useful datasets that contain many thousands of cases, and sometimes even several million cases. When variables from very large datasets are plotted against each other on a scatterplot, you often just end up with a big 'blotch' on your graph. This is because there are so many points on the graph – each representing a single case – that, however small they are made, many will overlap with each other and obscure the relationship between the two variables. In these situations, a scatterplot provides you with very little useful information about the strength, or even the direction, of a relationship.

Figure 7.1 shows a weak correlation in a dataset with several thousand cases. As you can see, it would be impossible to work out the strength of the relationship just by eye. However, a correlation coefficient (in this case, $r=0.085$) can give a

Figure 7.1: A weak correlation in a large dataset ($r=0.085$)

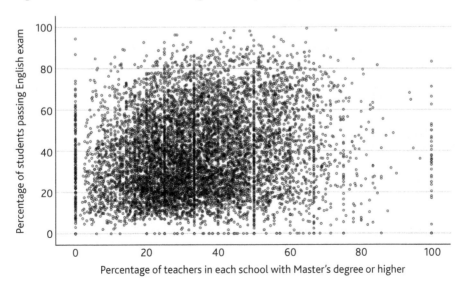

precise idea of this. In the next section, I explain how to interpret correlation coefficients such as this one.

Negative and positive correlations, and what they can tell you

You might be able to work out the direction of a relationship by looking at a scatterplot like the one in Figure 7.0 but, in cases like that shown in Figure 7.1, even the direction of the relationship can be difficult to see. It's very hard to estimate exactly how strong a particular relationship is just by looking at a scatterplot, and it's also quite challenging to communicate to others exactly what you've seen. But a correlation coefficient can tell you, and those reading your research, both the direction of a relationship and exactly how closely two variables are related.

You can compare one correlation coefficient with another because it's what's called a standardised measure. We've seen standardised measures before – the standard deviation is an example of one. But you don't need to worry too much about what this means: for the moment it's enough to say that a correlation of +0.61, for example, means exactly the same whether you are looking at the relationship between age and income or the relationship between coffee consumption and blood pressure. It doesn't matter that these two pairs of variables are very different to each other, and it wouldn't matter what unit of measurement we used: a correlation of +0.61 always means the same thing in terms of how closely two things are related. In terms of the strength and direction of a relationship, a Pearson's correlation coefficient means the same to a physicist as it does to an archaeologist, a geographer or a sociologist.

The plus sign in front of the 0.61 means it's a positive correlation. In a positive correlation one variable tends to go up as the other rises, and vice versa. In the example shown in Figure 7.0, this means that students' scores in their assessments tend to be higher if they spend more time studying. The figure of 0.61 refers to how closely the variation in one variable matches the variation in the other. It's a measure of how *predictable* the relationship between the two variables is.

The minus and plus signs are very important. The plus sign isn't always shown in the output of most statistical packages, or in research reports, so if a correlation coefficient doesn't have a minus sign, you can usually assume that it's positive. I've included them here in the text just to make things easier. We've already looked at a positive relationship so we'll now see how negative correlations are different. In a **negative relationship**, larger values for one variable are associated with smaller values for the other. There might, for example, be a negative relationship between time students spend playing video games and the amount of time they spend studying in the library: students who spend more time playing video games would tend to spend less time studying in the library (see Figure 7.2).

Pearson's *r* always takes a value between −1.0 and +1.0. A correlation of +1.0 or −1.0 is a perfect correlation and means that the variation in one variable matches the variation in another variable *exactly*. Using our example, this

Figure 7.2: A negative relationship

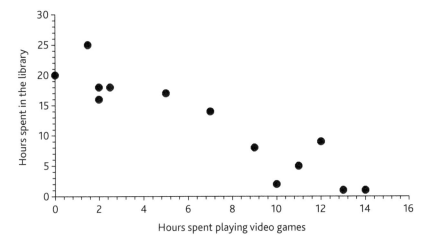

would mean that you could precisely predict a student's assessment score by using only information about how long they had studied (and vice versa). In a perfect correlation, all the points on a scatterplot lie on a perfectly straight line (see Figure 7.3). In contrast, a correlation coefficient of zero would mean that there was no relationship at all between the two variables. The scatterplot for a correlation of zero would just look like a random scattering of data points.

It's important to remember that a correlation of −1 is *just as strong* as a correlation of +1; the only difference is the direction of the relationship. Both relationships would show as a perfect straight line on a scatterplot, but they would

Figure 7.3: A perfect linear relationship

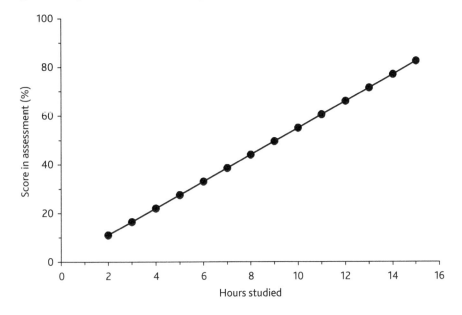

be sloping in different directions. On a conventionally formatted graph, where the **x-axis** and **y-axis** meet at zero on the bottom left, the line representing a positive correlation would slope upwards from left to right and the line representing a negative relationship would slope downwards from left to right.

Correlations of zero, +1 or −1 are very rare in practice. It's much more likely that you will get a figure in between these points, and so usually correlations are stated to one or two decimal places. You'll find various guidelines in textbooks stating what constitutes a 'strong', 'medium' or 'weak' correlation, but these definitions are arbitrary and not always useful in practice. For now, the most important point to remember is that correlations have a maximum value of +1 or −1 and a minimum value of zero.

Non-linear relationships

One of the limitations of the Pearson's correlation coefficient is that it's only suited to identifying linear relationships. Linear relationships, as the name suggests, are relationships that can be best described on a graph by using a straight line. Both Figures 7.0 and 7.3 show linear relationships between the number of hours a student has spent studying for an assessment and the score they achieved in that assessment. Both datasets are completely fictional, but I've used them here to show some features of a linear relationships. In Figure 7.3, the line that I've asked the software to draw on the graph, called the line of best fit, goes through all the data points (represented by the circles). This is because it is a perfect linear relationship. This means that you could perfectly predict how well a student had done in their assessment using only data on how long they spent studying. However, in reality, data are more likely to look like what we see in Figure 7.0. In these data, the amount of time spent studying isn't a perfect predictor of how well a student did in their assessment. However, the relationship is still roughly a linear one: it seems to be the case that, on average, assessment scores increase with time spent studying at approximately the same rate.

There are plenty of reasons to suspect that, if we actually examined real data, the relationship between how many hours students spend studying and the mark they achieve in their assessment might not be linear. First, there is the issue of the assignment being marked out of 100 – however many hours you study, you can't score more than 100%. The dependent variable has what's called a 'ceiling', so there is a limit to the highest mark you can attain. Having this kind of 'ceiling' for only one of the variables can lead to relationships becoming non-linear.

There's also the issue of what are called 'diminishing returns'. Not every hour that you study is likely to have the same value in terms of increasing your mark. The difference between having done no study at all and having done two hours study is likely to be quite large in terms of your ability to take the test. But the difference between having done 50 hours of study and 52 hours of study is unlikely to make as much difference to your outcome.

Before we draw any conclusions from the results of correlational analysis, it's important for us think about these kinds of issues and to consider whether we would *expect* the relationship we are examining to be linear. If the relationship is not linear, but we calculate a Pearson's correlation coefficient anyway, we run the risk of misinterpreting the relationship between the two variables. To see how that might happen, and how it could be misleading, let's look at some examples of non–linear relationships.

Anscombe's quartet is a famous, and very useful, illustration of this problem. The 'quartet' refers to the four different scatterplots shown in Figure 7.4. They were created by Francis Anscombe and published in 1973.

Figure 7.4: Anscombe's quartet

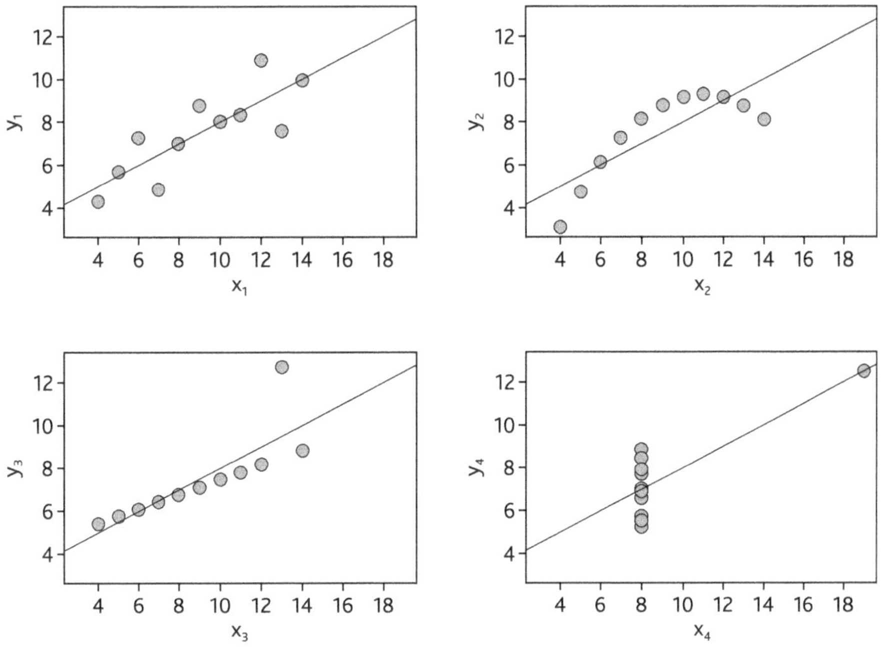

Source: Schutz/Anscombe

As you can see, these scatterplots show four very different relationships between four pairs of variables. But you wouldn't guess this if you just looked at the statistics. The means of the x values are all the same, as are the means of the y values. Variation from the mean is also similar for all the x variables as well as for all the y variables. However, most importantly for our current discussion, the Pearson's correlation coefficient for all four pairs of variables is 0.816. If you had simply calculated correlation coefficients without first conducting some exploratory univariate analyses and then creating some scatterplots, you might have mistakenly concluded that the relationships between the variables in all four datasets were identical.

Before going on to look at the lessons we can learn from Anscombe's quartet, it's worth looking at each of the four scatterplots and trying to work out what is going on in each one. I've written Exercise 7.1 to help you with this. The answers are at the end of the chapter.

EXERCISE 7.1

Look carefully at the four scatterplots in Figure 7.4.

a) How well does the line in each graph represent the pattern in the data?

b) How would you describe the pattern taken by the data in each graph?

We've seen that Pearson correlation coefficients can provide very specific information about both the direction and the predictability of a relationship. However, as Anscombe demonstrated, if you aren't sure that the relationship is a linear one, then these coefficients can be misleading. And if you have a lot of cases, or there is only a weak relationship between the variables, you may not be able to see whether the relationship is linear by looking at a scatterplot. So what should you do when you have two continuous or discrete variables you want to analyse? You might find the following guidelines helpful:

a) Always think about the nature of the relationship first. Have you read anything that has provided useful information about the relationship? What does your everyday understanding of the world suggest? Based on what you already know, does it make sense that this relationship would be linear?

b) Examine the relationship visually by creating a scatterplot. If you have a hunch about what shape the relationship might be, you can look for evidence of this in the scatterplot. However, this may not be very helpful if you have lots of cases and/or the relationship is weak.

c) If, after completing tasks (a) and (b) from Exercise 7.1 you still believe that the relationship is likely to be linear, you can go ahead and calculate a Pearson's correlation coefficient. But always bear in mind when interpreting your results that, unless you have clearly verified this on a scatterplot, there's still a chance that the relationship isn't linear.

Interpreting predictability: turning r into r-squared

I wrote earlier in this chapter that lots of textbooks provide guidelines about what counts as a 'strong' or 'weak' correlation. But I also warned you that these guidelines are fairly arbitrary and it can be quite challenging to communicate exactly what a particular correlation coefficient means to people who are unfamiliar with statistics. One of the problems with Pearson's r is interpreting it in 'real-world' terms. We know that a correlation of $r=0.85$ is stronger than one of $r=0.61$, but what do either of these actually mean?

A measure that is very important in the next chapter, where we discuss regression analysis, is called **r-squared** (r^2). This measure is, quite literally, r, squared: Pearson's r multiplied by itself. Its technical name is the **coefficient of determination**, but you probably won't hear many people call it that. Although it's simple to calculate – you can turn Pearson's r into r-squared just by multiplying r by r – it's actually very useful. This is because it has a much more intuitive meaning than Pearson's r.

R-squared is intuitive because it can be interpreted in terms of percentages. It describes the *percentage* of variation in one variable that is matched by variation in the other variable. If we took the two figures above, $r=0.85$ and $r=0.61$, we can turn these into r-squared values just by using a calculator:

$$0.85 \times 0.85 = 0.723$$
$$0.61 \times 0.61 = 0.372$$

Our first r-squared value is just over 0.72. That would mean that around 72% of the variation in one of our variables is matched by variation in the other variable. So, if we were looking at the relationship between caffeine intake and blood pressure, this would mean that 72% of the variation in blood pressure was matched by variation in caffeine intake (and vice versa). We must remember, however, that neither Pearson's r nor r-squared tell us whether changes in people's blood pressure *causes* them to increase their caffeine consumption or the other way around (although you might want to think about which possibility would be mostly likely, and why you think this would be the case).

Our second r-squared is just over 0.37 and can be interpreted in the same way. If you remember, 0.61 was the Pearson's r value in the relationship between time spent studying and score on a test, shown in the scatterplot in Figure 7.0. The r-squared value of 0.372 tells us that around 37% of the variation in test scores was matched by the variation in time spent studying. (In this example, you should be able to easily guess which variable is likely to have led to change in the other.)

You might remember from your school maths lessons that if you multiply a negative number by a negative number (or 'square' it) you always end up with a positive number. If, for example, you multiply minus 2 by minus 2, you get plus 4. Because of this, an r-squared value is always positive, even for a negative correlation. This makes sense because it measures the percentage of the variation in one variable that is matched by the variation in another variable, and this cannot be less than zero (that is, no match at all).

R-squared is a very useful measure, and it's one we'll discuss more in the next chapter. If you conduct a Pearson's correlation in a software package, you'll always get a value for r, but an r-squared value may not be automatically calculated for you. This isn't really a problem, however, as it's easy to calculate r-squared yourself once you have the value for Pearson's r.

Correlations for ordinal data and non-linear relationships

So far, the only correlation coefficient we've looked at is Pearson's *r*. I've concentrated on this particular measure for two reasons: it's one of the most commonly used correlation coefficient, and it's also central to the technique of regression analysis that we'll be discussing in the next chapter. However, there are other correlation coefficients that can be used in different situations.

Spearman's *rho* correlation coefficient (also called Spearman's rank) can be used when one or more of your variables is **ordinal** rather than continuous or discrete. When a variable is ordinal, it works by considering the rank of a case – where it is in relation to the other cases – rather than its absolute value. Spearman's coefficient can be used with the following types of variable pairs:

• One ordinal variable and one continuous/discrete variable
• Two ordinal variables
• Two continuous/discrete variables

An example of a relationship of the first type would be a student's month of birth in the school year and their performance in a test, marked as a percentage score. This is an area of research that has gained a great deal of attention in recent years. Imagine that data were available on a student's date of birth, but only for the month in which they were born. (This might be for issues of confidentiality, for example, to prevent individuals being identified.)

In the dataset, students would be ranked according to how near, or far away, their month of birth was from the start of the school year. The other variable would be a percentage score in the test for each student. Spearman's *rho* would be the most appropriate correlation to use here, as one variable would be ordinal and the other would be discrete.

You might wonder why the month of birth variable in this example must be ordinal. Couldn't we just give those students who were born in the first month of the school year a score of zero and the other students a value based on how many months later they were born? Wouldn't this create discrete data that would be suitable for analysis with Pearson's *r*?

We could do this, but we would be misrepresenting the true level of measurement for this variable. As we don't know exactly when in each month students were born, we can't really count the number of whole months they are away from the beginning of the school year, so we can only create an ordinal measure. For example, a student born on the 1st of October was born almost a month before a student born on the 31st of October but would be in the same category ('October'). In contrast, a student born on the 30th of September would be born only one day before the student whose birthday was on the 1st of October, but they would be in a different category ('September'). So the categories aren't providing a true measurement of the amount of time from the beginning of the school year that students were born. They are not 'equal interval' data so they can only provide us with an indicator of order. To get discrete data we would need to have their date of birth (and for true continuous data, we would need their time of birth, too!).

If we were looking at the same issue but could only get data on a student's month of birth and their academic performance measured as a rank – from the highest attaining student to the lowest – we could still use Spearman's *rho*. We would have two ordinal-level variables, which meets the criteria for this kind of analysis.

The requirements for using Spearman's *rho* are a bit more forgiving than for Pearson's *r*, but there are still some rules about the distribution of the data. Although the relationship doesn't have to be linear, it does have to be what's called **monotonic**. This means that, overall, the relationship between the variables must be going in roughly the same direction. So if students' attainment tends to increase in line with a later month of birth, this relationship doesn't have to be linear, but this trend can't change to decreasing with later months of birth part-way through the school year.

In Figure 7.5 the graphs A and B show monotonic relationships. You can see that the lines are by no means straight – and so the relationship between the two variables is not linear – but the slopes don't change their angle to the extent where the direction of the relationship would change from positive to negative. Graph C, however, is non-monotonic because, depending on the value of the variables, the relationship changes from positive to negative. While Spearman's *rho* would be fine to use with the relationships shown in graphs A and B, it wouldn't be suitable for the relationship in graph C.

Figure 7.5: Monotonic and non-monotonic relationships

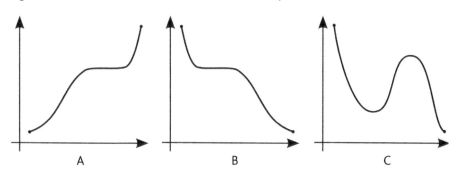

A   B   C

Source: Oleg Alexandrov

You'll notice that in the list I made of situations where Spearman's *rho can* be used, I included the example of a pair of continuous or discrete variables. You'd usually use Pearson's *r* for this, but in some circumstances Spearman's *rho* can be better. If you have two continuous or discrete variables, and your scatterplot indicates (or your thinking suggests) that the relationship *is not linear*, but it is monotonic, then Spearman's *rho* would be the better measure to use. If the two variables shown in Figure 7.6 were both continuous or discrete, that would meet one of the requirements for using Pearson's coefficient. But, as you can see, the relationship is not linear – it follows a curve that rises from left to right – it is **curvilinear**. Pearson's *r* won't accurately describe non-linear relationships, so it wouldn't be the best technique to use in this case. However, this relationship *is* monotonic, and Spearman's *rho* would work well with these two variables.

Figure 7.6: A scatterplot showing a monotonic relationship

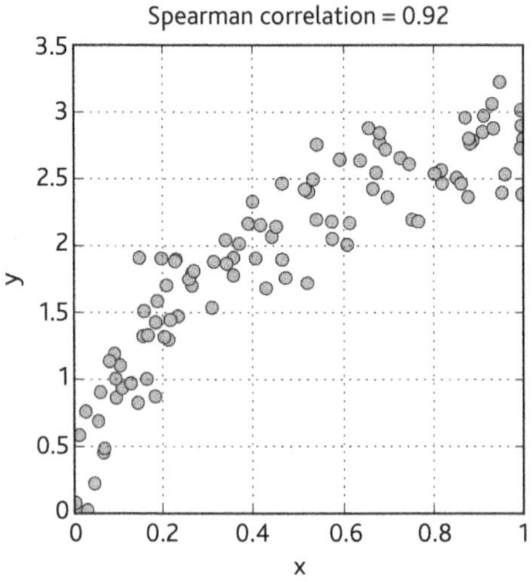

Source: Skbkekas

It's also the case that Spearman's *rho* is less sensitive to **outliers**. In Figure 7.4, you can see an outlier in the scatterplot showing the relationship between y_3 and x_3. This outlier would affect the result of Pearson's *r* much more than it would for Spearman's *rho*, and so Spearman's *rho* might have been a better option (but the result would then not take the same value as in the other graphs in Anscombe's quartet).

There is another correlation coefficient that is similar to Spearman's *rho*, which can also be used with ordinal or continuous/discrete variables: Kendall's *tau*. There have been lengthy arguments between statisticians about which is better, and when, but there seems to be agreement that Kendall's *tau* is better than Spearman's *rho* when there are lots of 'ties' in the rank order.

Continuing the example we used, perhaps we're also interested in possible links between educational attainment and birth order. We might suspect that there are differences between the attainment of first-born children and those born second, third, and so on. As there are going to be lots of 'ties' because there will be many children who are born first, second or third, in this kind of analysis Kendall's *tau* will be the best one to use.

Summary

Many different correlation coefficients have been devised by statisticians, and it's not possible to cover them all here. I've focused on the ones that are used most often by social researchers and also those that I think are the most useful. The coefficients that we've looked at in this chapter are all measures of how predictable values of one variable are from the values of another variable. And they all tell you the direction of the relationship: whether it is positive or negative. They also all produce values between +1.0 (a perfect positive relationship) and −1.0 (a perfect negative relationship). Because of this they can all be interpreted in roughly the same way (but Spearman's *rho* and Kendall's *tau* don't have the equivalent of an 'r-squared').

In the next chapter we look at regression analysis. Many different types of regression analysis have been developed by statisticians, but the type we're going to look at is called **ordinary least squares** (OLS) regression. OLS regression uses Pearson's *r* but provides you with more information than a simple bivariate correlation. While the correlation coefficients we've looked at in this chapter are only measures of the predictability and direction of a relationship, regression analysis tells you how much – on average – one variable changes when the other one changes. Regression analysis also allows you to analyse the relationship between a dependent (outcome) variable and more than one independent (explanatory) variable in a single analysis: what is known as **multi-variable analysis**.

References

Anscombe, F.J. (1973) 'Graphs in statistical analysis', *The American Statistician*, 27(1): 17–21.

Sources

Figure 7.1 was based on analysis of the California Department of Education 2006 Adequate Yearly Progress (AYP) data files: www.cde.ca.gov/re/pr/ayp.asp

Figures 7.4 and 7.7 to 7.10 are based on Anscombe's work, but have been recreated by Schutz: https://en.wikipedia.org/wiki/File:Anscombe%27s_quartet_3.svg

Anscombe.svg: Schutz (label using subscripts): Avenue, https://commons.wikimedia.org/wiki/File:Anscombe's_quartet_3.svg, 'Anscombe's quartet 3', https://creativecommons.org/licenses/by-sa/3.0/legalcode

Figure 7.5: Oleg Alexandrov, https://commons.wikimedia.org/wiki/File:Monotonicity_example1.svg, 'Monotonicity example1.svg', marked as public domain, more details on Wikimedia Commons: https://commons.wikimedia.org/wiki/Template:PD-self

Figure 7.6: Skbkekas, https://commons.wikimedia.org/wiki/File:Spearman_fig5.svg, 'Spearman fig5.svg', https://creativecommons.org/licenses/by-sa/3.0/legalcode

Useful resources

My YouTube SPSS® tutorial that covers correlation and regression can be found at: https://youtu.be/4bwRtnjQxw0

Answers to exercises

Exercise 7.0

a) The general trend is that students' scores in the assessment go up the more they study. You can see this because the data points go from the bottom left of the scatterplot to the top right. This is reflected in the slope of the line. There is a positive relationship between how long students study for and the mark they get in the assessment.

b) You wouldn't be able to predict every student's mark accurately if you only knew how long they studied for. This is because there isn't a perfect relationship between hours studied and assessment score. If you tried to do this for every student, you would be more accurate for some students than for others. The line on the graph is called a 'line of best fit' and represents the mathematical 'best guess' for all the cases combined. If you look closely, you'll see that one data point sits almost exactly on this line. If you used the line to predict the values of one variable from the values of the other, you'd get very close for this case.

c) Because there isn't a perfect relationship between the two variables, studying for a longer time won't guarantee you a higher mark. However, it would seem a sensible strategy because students who studied longer usually got higher marks. But you'd expect a teacher to tell you that!

Exercise 7.1

Looking at each of the scatterplots one at a time, we can judge how well the straight line drawn through the data points summarises the relationship between the two variables. Remember that a correlation coefficient calculates how closely variation in one variable matches variation in the other based on a linear (or straight line) relationship. For the graph shown in Figure 7.7, the line isn't too bad. It cuts right through some data points but misses other ones by a little bit, and there aren't any data points that are really far from the line. You can see that it's generally the case that as the value of y_1 goes up, x_1 also goes up, and so there must be a positive relationship between the two variables. If you tried to predict y_1 with only information about x_1, your estimate usually wouldn't be too far off.

Figure 7.7: A linear relationship

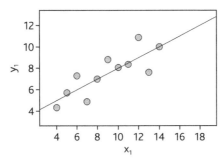

Source: Schutz/Anscombe

There is clearly something else going on in the graph in Figure 7.8. It's obvious that the relationship between y_2 and x_2 isn't linear; the data in the bottom left of the graph start to go up in what looks like a straight line, but then peak and change direction to make an arc. This is what's called a curvilinear relationship. What this means is that the relationship between y_2 and x_2 changes as their values change. What starts as a positive relationship, when the values of y_2 and x_2 are between around 4 and 8, flattens off and then becomes a negative relationship when the values for each variable become larger.

Because the relationship between y_2 and x_2 isn't linear, it's not surprising that the straight line drawn on the graph doesn't fit the data points very well. Although the figure produced by calculating Pearson's coefficient ($r=0.816$) suggests a strong correlation between the two variables, this figure is based on a linear relationship and so provides a misleading account of the relationship.

Figure 7.8: A curvilinear relationship

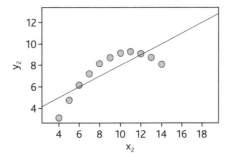

Source: Schutz/Anscombe

In Figure 7.9, you can see that the relationship between y_3 and x_3 is, for the most part, a perfectly straight line. But the line doesn't go through all the points, and has a slightly steeper angle than the line made by most of the data points. This

Figure 7.9: An outlier

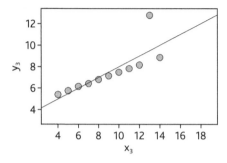

Source: Schutz/Anscombe

is because one of the data points is out of step with the others and has a much larger y_3 value than you'd expect given the overall trend. This is what's called an outlier, and it's the reason why the relationship isn't a perfect correlation. This single data point is the only thing stopping us from being able to perfectly predict values of y_3 by only using information about x_3 (or vice versa). As we'll see when we discuss regression analysis in the next chapter, this outlier has also influenced the slope of the line of best fit, and this would affect our ability to predict how much y_3 changes when x_3 changes. It's not unusual to have outliers in a dataset, so this is quite a common situation to come across.

The last scatterplot, shown in Figure 7.10, has a more unusual problem. The values for x_4 are the same for all but one of the data points. For 10 of the cases, the value of x_4 doesn't change regardless of the value of y_4. But there is also an outlier. This outlier has a different effect than in the previous example, and this effect is much more serious in terms of the impact it has on interpreting the data. While the relationship in Figure 7.9 is a positive one with a single case disrupting an otherwise perfect trend, in Figure 7.10 the value of x_4 is the same (**constant**) for all but one of the cases, regardless of the value y_4 takes. The correlation coefficient doesn't give us the whole story in either case, but it is potentially misleading in its description of the relationship between y_4 and x_4.

Figure 7.10: Many constants and one outlier

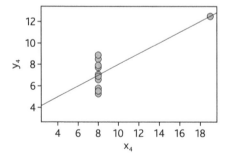

Source: Schutz/Anscombe

8

Where do we draw the line? How regression analysis can tell you more than correlation

WHAT IS THIS CHAPTER FOR?

In the last chapter I introduced the idea of a correlation and showed you some of the techniques for carrying out correlation analysis with different types of data. In this chapter I introduce a technique that is similar to correlation but provides you with more information: regression analysis. Regression analysis is important to know about as it forms the building blocks for many other types of statistical techniques.

WHAT DOES IT COVER?

We start by revisiting Pearson's correlation that we covered in the last chapter. I show you the differences and similarities between correlation analysis and regression analysis, and explain what extra information regression analysis provides. I discuss the assumptions underlying regression analysis and how to check whether your data meet these. I also show you how to use the results of a regression analysis to make predictions, and end the chapter by briefly describing some of the more advanced forms of regression analysis that you can learn once you understand the basics.

WHAT WILL YOU LEARN?

You will learn about the following concepts:

- Line of best fit
- The regression line equation
- Predicted and observed values
- Residuals

You will learn to interpret the following outputs of regression analysis:

- R-squared
- Unstandardised coefficient
- Intercept

What is regression analysis and how is it useful?

Regression analysis is a common statistical technique that is widely used in many different subject areas and academic disciplines. You'll see that it shares quite a lot with **correlation** analysis, but regression analysis can tell us more about the relationships between the variables that we're interested in. It's a very useful technique to understand because it forms the basis for many other methods of analysis (particularly those that fall under the category of 'statistical modelling'), and if you go on to do more advanced statistics, a good understanding of regression analysis will be very helpful.

I'm going to focus on the most basic form of regression analysis, what is called **ordinary least squares** (OLS) regression. I'm also going to restrict my detailed discussions to bivariate analysis: looking at the relationship between two variables. At the end of the chapter I briefly discuss more advanced forms of regression analysis.

How is regression analysis different to correlation analysis?

Before we look at regression analysis in detail, it's worth reminding ourselves of what correlation can tell us and what it can't tell us. If you haven't read the previous chapter that focused on correlation, it might be worth doing so before you start this one.

Correlation is very useful, but it's important to remember that it is primarily a measure of the predictability of the relationship between two variables. It provides us with information about how close the relationship between our variables is to a straight line. Although correlation analysis is conducted entirely through mathematical calculation, it helps to think of how our data would look on a **scatterplot** (and it's good practice to look at your data graphically when you're doing correlation or regression analysis). The closer the **data points** are to a straight line, the stronger the correlation, and the easier it would be to predict values of one variable using just data from the other variable. The further out the data points are spread, the weaker the correlation, and the harder it would be to make such predictions with any accuracy.

The results of a correlation analysis will also tell you the direction of the relationship. Correlation coefficients – the results of correlation analysis – are either positive or negative numbers and tell us whether high values in one variable tend to be associated with high values in the other variable (a **positive** correlation), or whether high values in one variable are associated with low values in the other variable (a **negative** correlation).

Although correlation analysis tells us how close our data is to a straight-line relationship, it doesn't tell us anything else about that line. Crucially, it doesn't tell us anything about the slope of that line: how steeply it rises or falls. The slope of the line tells us the *extent* to which values of the dependent variable tend to get larger or smaller as the independent variable gets larger (or, to put it another way, how much the dependent variable changes when the independent variable changes). Regression analysis, however, does give us this information.

We might, for example, want to look at the relationship between how long people have been doing a job (their experience) and how much they are paid. A correlation analysis will tell us how variation in a worker's experience matches variation in their pay (or, to put it another way, how well we can predict a worker's pay from their experience). This is indicated by the strength of the correlation. It will also tell us whether people with more experience tend to have higher or lower pay. We can see this by looking at whether the correlation coefficient is a positive or negative number. But correlation analysis won't tell us how much more (or less) workers tend to earn with each extra year of experience. In contrast, a regression analysis of the same relationship would provide all the information that a correlation does, but it would also tell us how much pay changes with experience. It can do this because, unlike correlation, it produces statistics about the **line of best fit**.

What is a line of best fit?

Even if you've never heard the term, you may have drawn a line of best fit before. If, at school, you plotted some points on a graph and then took a ruler and drew a line that ran roughly down the middle of them, you were drawing a line of best fit. In fact, you were actually doing a regression analysis (see Berk, 2004).

When we conduct regression analysis, we usually calculate the line of best fit mathematically (by getting a computer to crunch the numbers for us) rather than drawing it 'by eye'. This makes sure that our line is completely accurate (which is hard with just a ruler and a pencil). But we're essentially doing the same thing: drawing a line through the 'middle' of all the points on a graph. And this is the essence of regression analysis. Although you need to learn how to interpret the results and know about things such as assumptions, regression is really just about drawing straight lines. It's a very important statistical technique, but in its basic form, it's quite straightforward.

Before we start regression analysis: assumptions

In the last paragraph I mentioned the word 'assumptions'. We've come across this idea before, mainly in relation to the types of data that can be used with different statistical techniques. An assumption for calculating a mean, for example, is that you have continuous or discrete data.

As with all the statistical techniques I've covered in this book, regression can only be used with certain types of data. The requirements for the most basic form of regression analysis are similar to Pearson's correlation, but there are some additional ones. As with Pearson's correlation, both variables must be continuous or discrete (the numbers used have to have equal intervals between them throughout). And, just like Pearson's correlation, the relationship you are examining must be linear (that is, it follows a straight line).

However, unlike correlation analysis, for regression analysis you have to specify a dependent and an independent variable. I discussed this briefly in the last chapter, but as it's more important for regression analysis than for correlations, we'll look into it in a bit more detail here.

Dependent and independent variables

Working out which is your dependent variable and which is your independent variable isn't often a problem, but it can sometimes be tricky. As I noted in Chapter 1, when I first discuss the idea of dependent and independent variables, some people find it easier to think in terms of outcome variables and explanatory variables. If you can't work out which is your dependent variable, it's useful to think about what the outcome is, and what variables might explain that outcome. The outcome is your dependent variable, and explanatory variables are all independent variables.

Another way of thinking about it is that your dependent variable *depends* on your independent variables. The values of your dependent variable will vary because of changes in your independent variables: they are dependent on them.

Box 8.0: Regression assumptions and more advanced analyses

Although I have specified that regression analysis assumes that both variables are continuous (or discrete) and that the relationship is linear, these assumptions only hold for the most basic form of regression. It's possible to get around these limitations and conduct regression analysis with categorical variables (both dependent and independent) and with relationships that aren't linear. However, to do this you need to learn more advanced techniques that I don't have the space to cover in this book. If you're interested in the possibilities offered by these types of analyses, I suggest that you first read Miles and Shevlin's (2001) book on regression analysis and then look at Roger Tarling's (2009) text that covers many common types of statistical modelling.

Let's start with an easy example that we looked at in the last chapter: how long students spend studying and the mark they get in the exam they were preparing for. In this example, the exam mark is an outcome that might be explained by how long someone spent studying. Your exam mark might *depend* – at least to some extent – on how long you studied. So, in this case, exam marks are the dependent (outcome) variable and the time spent studying is an independent (explanatory) variable.

This is an easy example because one event clearly follows the other: you spend time studying *before* the exam takes places. It wouldn't make sense for the amount of time you spent studying before the exam to depend on the mark that you later achieved. But, as I discussed in Chapter 1, there are pairs of variables where it's not so clear which is the dependent and which is the independent variable (and sometimes, where it's not possible to know).

The results of a correlation analysis don't change depending on which variable you define as the dependent and which you define as the independent variable because they are only telling you about the predictability and direction of the relationship. But this isn't the case with regression analysis, because it's also telling you about how much one variable changes when the other changes, and your results won't make any sense if you get your dependent and independent variables the wrong way around.

How does regression analysis work?

I've already explained that regression analysis involves calculating a line of best fit through your data. It's often easier to think about regression in visual terms – as a line on a scatterplot – than in mathematical terms, so we'll do this with our current example.

If we're going to conduct a regression analysis using marks in an exam as our dependent variable and hours spent studying for that exam as our independent variable, we'll have two pieces of relevant information for each student: their mark in the exam and the time they spent studying. If we created a scatterplot there would a data point (the dot on the scatterplot) for each student, which would indicate the mark they got (on the **y-axis**) and the hours they spent studying (on the **x-axis**). (The y-axis is always used for the dependent variable and the x-axis for the independent variable.) A regression analysis produces a line of best fit that runs down the middle of these data points. This line of best fit is calculated mathematically and is based on two important statistics, the unstandardised coefficient and the **intercept**, both of which I explain in detail below.

What information does regression analysis give you?

The two most important statistics that regression analysis produces are the **r-squared** and the unstandardised coefficient. It gives you other information, too, but I'm going to concentrate on these two measures for most of this chapter.

Box 8.1: Why is it called OLS regression?

You will often see the type of regression analysis I focus on in this chapter referred to as OLS, or ordinary least squares, regression. You don't need to know what OLS means in order to successfully carry out a regression analysis, but I'm going to provide an explanation just in case you are curious.

OLS refers to the way in which the line of best fit is worked out mathematically. The 'least' bit refers to the distance between the line of best fit and all the data points relating to the variables included in the analysis. The line of best fit – by definition – sits where these distances (**residuals**) are the smallest.

The 'squares' refers to something that is done when calculating these differences. For mathematical reasons, the distances above and below are squared, just as they are when a standard deviation is calculated.

It's called 'ordinary' to differentiate it from other kinds of least squares analysis: it's the most basic form of least squares analysis and was the first to be proposed, but other types of least squares analysis have been subsequently developed, and so the original type has come to be known as 'ordinary' least squares.

We saw in the last chapter that Pearson's correlation produced a statistic called r. We also saw that squaring this figure (multiplying it by itself) produced r-squared, and that this statistic has a more intuitive interpretation than r. Regression is very similar to Pearson's correlation and produces some of the same information. When you conduct regression analysis, most software packages will calculate an r-squared value, which – just like Pearson's r – is an indicator of the predictability of the relationship between the dependent variable and the independent variable. R-squared can be any value between 0 and 1 (but no lower or higher). You might remember how to interpret the r-squared from the previous chapter, but we'll look at in more detail in the next section.

With regression analysis we also get two figures relating to the line of best fit. The most useful of these is called the 'unstandardised coefficient'. This is also known as the 'slope', as it is based on the angle of the line of best fit and tells us how steep this is. The unstandardised coefficient can be interpreted as the amount of change in the dependent variable with one unit change in the independent variable. For example, it might tell you how much, on average, students' exam scores increased with every extra hour they studied. Unlike r-squared, the unstandardised coefficient can be any numeric value, in theory at least. We'll see what this means in practice, when I use an example to illustrate this statistic. The other statistic we get is the intercept, which I discuss later in this chapter.

The difference between r-squared and the unstandardised coefficient

It's important not to confuse the unstandardised coefficient with the Pearson correlation coefficient (r) or the r-squared statistic. Although r and r-squared are both coefficients, they measure the predictability of the relationship between the two variables. The unstandardised coefficient (often called the 'b' coefficient) isn't about predictability but about how much the values of one variable change when the values of the other variable change. Depending on what your variables are, you might interpret this as the 'effect' of the independent variable on the dependent variable. In terms of our example, this is how much, on average, students' marks change for every extra hour they spend studying.

Figures 8.0 and 8.1 illustrate the difference between correlation (measured by r and r-squared) and slope (measured by the unstandardised coefficient). Each figure has data from three different scatterplots and the results of a regression analysis for Pearson's r, r-squared and the unstandardised coefficient (labelled as 'b'). Unlike for most of the examples in this book, these graphs haven't been produced using one of the teaching datasets, so they don't represent the relationships between any particular variables; the important thing to focus on is what the data look like in the scatterplots.

In Figure 8.0, you can see that data points in some scatterplots are more spread out than in others. In scatterplot A the data points all form a perfectly straight line. This is reflected in the r and r-squared values, which indicate a perfect correlation of 1.0. In scatterplot B the points are a bit more spread out, and so the r and r-squared values are a bit lower, at 0.8 and 0.64. The data points in scatterplot C are spread out further still, and so the corresponding r and r-squared values are even lower (at 0.4 and 0.16).

Figure 8.0: Different correlations, same slope

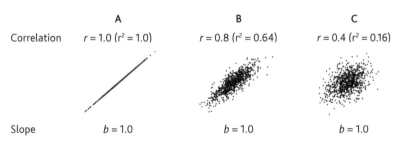

	A	B	C
Correlation	$r = 1.0$ ($r^2 = 1.0$)	$r = 0.8$ ($r^2 = 0.64$)	$r = 0.4$ ($r^2 = 0.16$)
Slope	$b = 1.0$	$b = 1.0$	$b = 1.0$

Source: Denis Boigelot

The different values of r and r-squared for scatterplots A, B and C reflect the different degrees of predictability in the relationship between the two variables. The relationship in scatterplot A is perfectly predictable. The relationship shown in scatterplot B is slightly less predictable, and that shown in scatterplot C is even less predictable.

However, if we look at the unstandardised (*b*) coefficients for the slope, we can see that they are the same (*b*=1.0) for each of the three scatterplots. This means that the line of best fit for all three scatterplots would look very much like the line that the points form in scatterplot A. Although each of the three scatterplots shows relationships with different levels of predictability, they all have the same slope. Or, to put it another way, the average size of the effect of the independent variable on the dependent variable is the same for each of the three relationships.

In each of the three scatterplots shown in Figure 8.1 all the data points form a perfectly straight line. This is reflected in in the *r* and r-squared values, which are 1.0 for D, E and F. This means that, in each case, the values of the dependent variable are perfectly predictable from the values of the independent variable (and vice versa). But, unlike the three scatterplots A, B and C in Figure 8.0, the three scatterplots in Figure 8.1 have different slopes (1.0, 0.5 and 0.25). This means that, in each one, the size of the 'effect' of the independent variable on the dependent variable would be different. It is largest in D, smaller in E, and even smaller in F.

Figure 8.1: Same correlation, different slopes

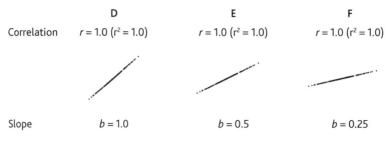

	D	E	F
Correlation	$r = 1.0$ ($r^2 = 1.0$)	$r = 1.0$ ($r^2 = 1.0$)	$r = 1.0$ ($r^2 = 1.0$)
Slope	$b = 1.0$	$b = 0.5$	$b = 0.25$

Source: Denis Boigelot

I hope these examples have helped clarify the difference between the predictability of a relationship and the 'effect' of the independent variable on the dependent variable. Both are important pieces of information, but they tell us different things. In the next section I discuss the results of some regression analysis with real data, so you can see how they are applied in practice.

An example of regression analysis: the relationship between income and expenditure

I'm going to use the example of the relationship between weekly income and weekly expenditure to show you how regression analysis works. I use scatterplots to show you what the data looks like visually, and then report the results of a regression analysis and explain how these figures relate to what you see on the graphs.

Figure 8.2 shows the relationship between household income and expenditure, using data from the publicly available 2013 Living Costs and Food Survey (LCF). While this might not seem to be the most exciting relationship to investigate – you would probably guess that households with higher levels of income tend to spend more – it makes for a good example because it meets the assumptions of regression analysis in that both variables are continuous and the relationship is linear. The fact that the relationship is sufficiently strong to be seen on a scatterplot is also useful.

Each of the data points in Figure 8.2 represents a household. For every household, you can read off an approximate value for the weekly income and weekly expenditure. You can see from the scatterplot that the relationship between income and expenditure is not perfectly predictable. Some people spend only a fraction of what they earn and others spend more money than they have coming in. The cases represented by dots towards the bottom right of the graph spent only a fraction of their income, whereas the expenditure of those in the top left of the graph exceeds their weekly income. However, as we might expect, in general, households that have higher incomes tend to have higher expenditure.

Figure 8.2: A linear relationship shown on a scatterplot

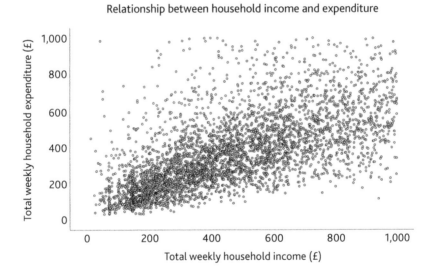

Relationship between household income and expenditure

Although there is a fairly wide spread of dots on the scatterplot, you can see that they tend to cluster together and form a line running from the bottom left of the graph to the middle of the right edge. You could probably draw a line through this with a ruler 'by eye' to give a rough estimate of how much, on average, expenditure increases with household income. Figure 8.3 shows what that line looks like when it's calculated mathematically, using regression analysis.

Figure 8.3: A line of best fit shown on a scatterplot

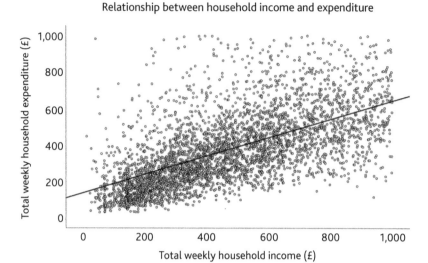

Relationship between household income and expenditure

Interpreting regression results: r-squared

Now that we've seen what regression looks like on a scatterplot, I'm going to look at the statistical information it provides us with in a little more detail. I'll use the data on income and expenditure to illustrate how these statistics can help us understand the relationship between these two variables.

Table 8.0 shows the results from the regression analysis that produced the line of best fit shown in Figure 8.3. Any suitable software package will produce these results for you. As we know, both Pearson's r and r-squared are measures of the predictability of the relationship. In terms of a scatterplot like the one in Figure 8.3, they tell us how close the data points are to a straight line. Pearson's r is rarely reported when the results of regression analyses are written up, but I've included it here to show how it relates to r-squared: they are just the same information expressed in different ways.

Pearson's r value for this relationship is 0.62. This would usually be considered to be a reasonably strong correlation. With correlations of this size or larger, it's often possible to see the relationship on a scatterplot, as is the case in Figure 8.3. However, with weaker correlations – which are very common in social research – it can be difficult to make judgements about a relationship using only a scatterplot. As we saw in the last chapter, if there are many thousands of cases, as there are in some large datasets, it can be even more difficult to see the

Table 8.0: The results of a regression analysis

Pearson's r	R-squared	Unstandardised coefficient	Intercept
0.62	0.38	0.50	137.79

nature of a relationship. This is one of the reasons, alongside accuracy, that we need to use maths to work out the line of best fit.

You'll notice that in Table 8.0 the r-squared value is much smaller than Pearson's *r*. Pearson's *r* must be a value between −1.0 and +1.0 and, because squaring a number always results in a positive number, r-squared will always be somewhere between 0.0 and 1.0. Unless Pearson's *r* is −1.0 or +1.0 (which is very rare), the r-squared will always be smaller. However, as I explained in the previous chapter, when discussing correlations, r-squared has a much more intuitive interpretation than Pearson's *r*.

Box 8.2: Correlation, causation and dependent and independent variables

One of the first things you're usually taught when you learn statistics is that 'correlation doesn't mean causation'. In fact, this phrase has almost become a cliché in statistics teaching. There's a good reason why statistics teachers have traditionally given this warning: a correlation between two things doesn't necessarily mean that one variable caused the change in the other. It could be that the correlation is a complete coincidence, or that one of the variables is serving as an indicator for something else, which might be the true cause of change in the other variable.

However, there are problems with being too cautious about making causal connections between variables. As soon as we label one variable as dependent and one as independent (or as an outcome and explanatory), we are saying that one variable *depends* on the other variable. Just by doing this we are using causal language! We could just do correlation analysis and only discuss the predictability of a relationship, thereby avoiding suggesting any kind of causal link. But if we're doing regression – where we have to specify a dependent and an independent variable – we are already implying that one variable has an effect on the other one. This is less of a problem with some relationships, such as that between time spent studying before an exam and the score in that exam that follows. Because one thing happens before the other, we have a good theoretical basis for thinking that change in one thing has led to change in the other, and not the other way round. However, for other relationships this may be less clear.

So we need to think carefully about the relationships we examine and consider whether we have a good theoretical basis for thinking that a relationship might be causal. Statistics can't tell us this on their own – we must use our knowledge of how the world works to make this decision, and sometimes it's not easy.

This is a very controversial, but important, issue that has been particularly topical in the past decade or so. I have provided a suggestion for further reading on this topic at the end of the chapter.

As you can see from Table 8.0, the r-squared for this analysis is 0.38. While there isn't a way of easily translating Pearson's *r* value into something more intuitive, the r-squared has a nice easy interpretation. R-squared values can be converted into percentages that describe the amount of variation in one variable that is matched by variation in the other. This ranges from 0% with an r-squared of 0.00 to 100% with an r-squared of 1.00. Our r-squared for the relationship between income and expenditure is 0.38, so that means that 38% of the variation in a household's expenditure is matched by variation in their income (and vice versa). Another way of describing the r-squared is as a measure of **explanatory power**. We might say that 38% of the variation in household expenditure is *explained* by the variation in household income (the *explanatory* variable).

The r-squared gives us a measure of the predictability of the relationship that we're examining. In terms of our scatterplot, it describes how close the data points are to a straight line. If we had an r-squared of 1.0 (which would mean we also had a Pearson's *r* of either −1.0 or +1.0), all of our data points would sit on a perfectly straight line. This means that household expenditure would be perfectly predictable from household income: for any particular income, our line of best fit would show the corresponding expenditure for that household.

Pearson's *r* and r-squared aren't affected by which variable in a pair is classified as the dependent variable and which is classified as the independent variable (as they're still just measuring a bivariate correlation). Swapping the independent and dependent variables wouldn't change the value of either statistic. However, for the statistics we are going to discuss next, you would almost always get different values depending on which variable was the dependent one. As I warned earlier, before you start a regression analysis you need to be clear about your dependent and independent variable.

Interpreting regression results: the unstandardised coefficient

One of the limitations of correlation analysis is that it only tells us whether our relationship is positive or negative and how predictable it is. What it doesn't tell us, in relation to our current example, is how much more households with higher incomes spend compared to those with lower incomes. Regression analysis provides this information in the form of the unstandardised (*b*) coefficient.

As you can see in Table 8.0, the unstandardised coefficient for our analysis is 0.50. So what does this mean?

In technical terms, the unstandardised coefficient shows how much the dependent variable changes when the independent variable increases by 1. For this information to be useful we need to know what units were used to measure both of our variables. Both of our variables – household expenditure and household income – are measured in UK pounds sterling. So a unit change in our independent variable is £1.00. Our unstandardised coefficient tells us that for every extra £1.00 in household income we can expect, on average, household expenditure to go up by £0.50. If one household has £10 more in income than another household, on average they would spend £5 more. And if a household has £100 more income than another household, they would spend £50 more, on average.

Our regression analysis has not only told us how predictable our relationship is – like a correlation analysis would do – it has also told us how much one variable changes when the other changes. This is the central difference between the two techniques, and a very important one.

Taking regression analysis further: the intercept, the regression equation and making predictions

If you're just doing a bivariate regression analysis and want to find out how predictable the relationship is, and how much the dependent variable changes when the independent variable changes, then the r-squared and the unstandardised coefficient are the main things you need to know.

However, regression analysis provides some additional information, and if you want to do more with regression analysis in the future, there are also some other concepts that are useful to understand. In this last section, I explore some of these measures and concepts, and look at more of what regression can do. It's not essential reading if you're only interested in the basics, but it might be interesting if you think you might take things further at some point.

Interpreting the results of regression analysis: the intercept

As I wrote earlier, in addition to the r-squared and unstandardised coefficient, regression analysis also produces a value called the intercept (or the **constant**). This is the value of the dependent variable (in our example above, that's weekly expenditure) when the independent variable (household income) is zero.

The intercept can sometimes be a useful figure on its own, but it doesn't always make sense. In my example from earlier, looking at how much difference studying makes to students' exam results, it could be valuable information. As a teacher, I might be interested in how well students did, on average, when they hadn't spent any time (that is, they had spent zero hours) studying for an exam. But if you were looking at the relationship between children's height and weight, as surveys such as the National Child Development Study (NCDS) have done for many years, the intercept would represent a child's weight when their height was zero. This wouldn't make sense, as all children have a height above zero, however young they are. And in the example we looked at in Table 8.0, it's unlikely that any of the households had a typical weekly income of zero, so knowing the expenditure of a household with no income probably isn't very useful.

Using the unstandardised coefficient and intercept to make predictions

So is the intercept useless information when it doesn't make sense for the independent variable to be zero? It's certainly true that the intercept isn't often discussed when the results of regression analysis are reported. Most discussions concentrate on the unstandardised coefficients and the r-squared.

However, you do need the intercept if you're going to use your regression analysis to make predictions, even in cases where it doesn't make sense for the independent variable to equal zero. And you also need to know how the intercept and unstandardised coefficient fit into the equation for the regression line (the line of best fit). This is a useful equation to be familiar with, as it can help you understand regression more fully, and seeing how it can be used to make predictions is a good way of introducing you to it.

In our Living Costs and Food Survey (LCF) dataset we have information on many different households, each with a particular income and expenditure. Our regression analysis uses this information to calculate the average relationship between income and expenditure. As you can see from the scatterplot in Figure 8.3, the line of best fit isn't quite right most of the time – if it was, all the data points would sit right on the line – but it's a useful summary of what's happening in general.

If we think of our regression line as a 'model' of the relationship between household income and expenditure, we can use it to make predictions (or estimations) for hypothetical examples that we don't actually have data for. So, for example, I know from looking at the dataset that none of the households had an income of exactly £300. But, by using the information from our regression analysis, I can estimate the expenditure of a household with an income of £300.

The problem with doing this is that our statistical model – which is how we're now thinking about our regression analysis – doesn't have much predictive power. If you remember, the r-squared is 0.38, which means that only 38% of the variation in expenditure can be explained by variation in income. That 38% is a long way from the 100% that we'd need to make perfect predictions. So you might not be confident to make predictions from this analysis if they had serious consequences, but let's see how we would do it, so that I can show you how it works and how the intercept and unstandardised coefficient fit into the equation for the regression line.

Before we look at the equation in detail, you might want to try to answer the questions in Exercise 8.0, to make sure that you're clear about the concepts of dependent variables, independent variables and the intercept. As usual, the answers are at the end of the chapter.

EXERCISE 8.0

Try to answer the following questions:

a) In the example I used from the National Child Development Study, why would a child's weight be the dependent variable and their height be the independent variable?

b) Can you think of any relationships where the intercept would be useful information on its own? What about relationships where it would only be useful as part of an equation used to make predictions?

The equation for the regression line

To make predictions using the results of a regression analysis you need to input the correct figures into the equation for the regression line. This equation is the one that is used for any straight-line relationship, and you may have come across it when you studied maths at school.

The equation looks like this:

$$y = a + bx$$

In this equation the letters represent the following:

y is the dependent variable
a is the intercept
b is the unstandardised coefficient
x is the independent variable

If we replace the letters in the equation with what they stand for, we get the following:

$$\text{dependent variable} = \text{intercept}$$
$$+ \, (\text{unstandardised coefficient} * \text{independent variable})$$

And if we put in the information from our regression analysis (see Table 8.0), we get:

$$\text{household expenditure} = £137.79 + (£0.50 * \text{household income})$$

So, to make a prediction for a household with an income of £300, this is what the calculation would look like:

$$£287.79 = £137.79 + (£0.50 * £300)$$

Given the information produced by our regression analysis, the best estimate we could make for an income of £300 is an expenditure of £287.79. Because our r-squared is quite low, it's unlikely to be a very accurate prediction, but it's one that is representative of the relationship in our data.

Observed values, predicted values and residuals

To demonstrate how inaccurate predictions made using the regression line equation can be when you don't have a very high r-squared, we can use values from the dataset to test a prediction. This will introduce you to the concepts of **observed values**, **predicted values** and **residuals**, which are important to understand if you go on to do more advanced analyses.

We can see this when we use the regression equation to make a prediction for a case that we already have data on. One of the cases in the LCF has a household income of £400.08. If we input this into our regression line equation, we get the following:

$$£337.83 = £137.79 + (£0.50 * £400.08)$$

Our model predicts that a household with an income of £400.08 would have an expenditure of £337.83. However, the actual expenditure of this household was £451.88, so our prediction based on the regression line is quite far out. The difference between our predicted value (£337.83) and the actual 'observed' value (£451.88) is called the residual. The residual for this case would be the difference between the two figures (£114.05).

The line of best fit is calculated to minimise the total of the residuals. But unless you have a perfectly predictable model, there will always be some residuals. The double-headed arrow in Figure 8.4 shows the residual for one of the data points in the scatterplot showing the relationship between household income and household expenditure. Every single data point on the graph would also have a residual showing the distance between the value predicted for the dependent variable by the regression line, and the actual dependent variable value for that case.

Residuals aren't only important as indicators of the predictability of your regression model (the smaller the residuals overall, the more predictive power the model has); they are also useful for various purposes in more advanced analyses. Understanding what they are, and why they are important, is helpful if you plan to do more advanced statistical modelling in the future. The same can be said for the regression line equation: you don't need to know about it to conduct regression analysis, but knowing how the equation relates to the line of best fit you see on a scatterplot gives you a better overall idea of how regression analysis works.

Figure 8.4: A residual

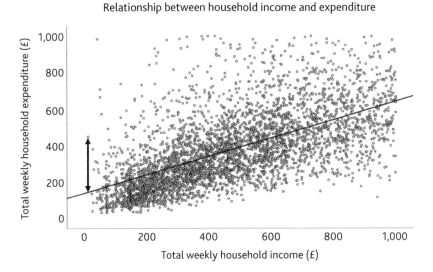

Relationship between household income and expenditure

Doing more with regression analysis: multiple regression and logistic regression

One of the reasons that regression analysis is such an important method of analysis to understand is because it is the basis for many more advanced techniques that are usually described as types of statistical modelling. In this chapter we've concentrated on bivariate regression analysis, but OLS regression analysis can be conducted with more than one independent variable using a technique called multiple regression analysis. Including more than one independent variable in a single analysis can increase the predictive power of our statistical models, and sometimes help us estimate the effects of independent variables on our dependent variable more accurately. Multiple regression analysis is used very widely in social research, and is much easier to learn if you have a good understanding of the basic concepts involved in bivariate regression.

One of the limitations of OLS regression analysis is that it assumes that both (or all) of your variables are continuous or discrete. As we have seen, lots of variables that we're interested in as social researchers are categorical, which might seem to pose a problem for conducting regression analysis. However, a technique called logistic regression allows you to use categorical variables as your dependent variables, and there are workarounds to allow you to include categorical variables as independent variables in most types of regression analysis and to model relationships that aren't linear. I briefly discuss this issue in Box 8.0, where I recommend some texts that may be useful if you want to find out more about any of these methods of analysis.

Summary

In this chapter we've seen how regression analysis can provide you with more information than a correlation analysis. As well as giving you information on the predictability of the relationship between two variables, as is the case with correlation analysis, regression analysis is useful because it also produces an estimate of the effect of the independent variable on your dependent variable. Bivariate OLS regression analysis is the basis on which many more types of statistical modelling are based, and is a vital building block in your understanding if you plan to pursue statistical analysis further.

This is the last chapter dealing with statistical analysis itself. The next chapter looks at how to display data in tables and visually, using graphs and charts. Chapter 10, the final chapter, then provides you with guidance on how to write up your results.

References

Berk, R.A. (2004) *Regression Analysis: A Constructive Critique*, Thousand Oaks, CA: SAGE.

Sources

Figures 8.0 and 8.1 were created by Denis Boigelot and modified by me:

Denis Boigelot, original uploader was Imagecreator, https://commons.wikimedia.org/wiki/File:Correlation_examples2.svg, 'Correlation examples2.svg', cropped image by Patrick White, https://creativecommons.org/publicdomain/zero/1.0/legalcode

Figures 8.2, 8.3 and 8.4 were based on my analyses of the Living Costs and Food Survey, 2013: Unrestricted access teaching dataset:

University of Manchester, CMIST (Cathie Marsh Institute for Social Research), UK Data Service, ONS (Office for National Statistics) (2019) *Living Costs and Food Survey, 2013: Unrestricted access teaching dataset* [data collection], 2nd edn, ONS [original data producer(s)], SN: 7932, DOI: 10.5255/UKDA-SN-7932-2. Contains public sector information licensed under the Open Government Licence v2.0.

Useful resources

My YouTube SPSS® tutorial on correlation also covers bivariate regression analysis and can be found at: https://youtu.be/4bwRtnjQxw0

Jeremy Miles and Mark Shevlin's text is, in my view, the best introduction to multiple regression analysis. Even after having attended several courses on regression analysis, it substantially increased my understanding and clarified some key concepts. I still use many of their ideas in my teaching:

Miles, J. and Shevlin, M. (2001) *Applying Regression and Correlation: A Guide for Students and Researchers*, London: SAGE.

Roger Tarling's book is an ideal introduction to a range of common methods of statistical modelling, many of which are extensions of regression analysis. It covers 10 different types of modelling, as well as providing an introduction to more basic issues:

Tarling, R. (2009) *Statistical Modelling for Social Researchers: Principles and Practice*, Abingdon: Routledge.

Richard Berk has written a great deal about the possibilities and limitations of regression analysis. This book addresses some of the more controversial issues relating to what regression can and can't do, and what it should and shouldn't be used for. It's not a book for those new to statistical modelling, but is recommended reading if you pursue regression analysis further:

Berk, R.A. (2004) *Regression Analysis: A Constructive Critique*, Thousand Oaks, CA: SAGE.

Judea Pearl has pioneered a new approach to thinking about causality in statistical analysis. This is his most accessible work, although it's still quite technical in places. Judea Pearl and Dana Mackenzie discuss some of the issues I raised in this chapter about cause and effect in much greater detail:

Pearl, J. and Mackenzie, D. (2019) *The Book of Why? The New Science of Cause and Effect*, London: Penguin.

Answers to exercises

Exercise 8.0
a) Children's weight would have to be the dependent variable, and their height the independent variable, because your height can affect your weight, but your weight can't affect your height. As you get taller, your weight will tend to increase. However, putting on weight isn't usually responsible for making you taller.

b) There are many examples where the intercept can be useful information on its own. An example where a value of the independent variable being zero makes sense will produce an intercept that also makes sense. If we were interested in whether the amount of time people spent training influenced their finishing time in a marathon, for example, a zero value for the independent variable makes sense. It probably wouldn't be wise to try to run a marathon with zero hours training, but various celebrities have famously attempted this (although, at the time of writing, 2023, none have made it to the finishing line).

For any example where the independent variable equalling zero doesn't make sense, the intercept will only be useful if you want to use the regression line equation to make predictions. However, some examples are trickier than others. If age is our independent variable, you might think that the intercept would always make sense, as we are all age zero at our birth. This would certainly be the case if we were looking at the relationship between age and height or weight. But zero age makes less sense if we were looking at age and alcohol consumption because, although it technically makes sense to have an age of zero, in most countries it's illegal to give alcohol to young children (and certainly new-born babies!). We need to think through any specific example carefully before we can decide what role the intercept can play in our interpretation of the results.

9

A graph is like a joke: if you have to explain it, it isn't any good

WHAT IS THIS CHAPTER FOR?

The previous chapters in this book have all focused on analysing your data. In this chapter I introduce some principles for displaying numeric data in tables, charts and graphs that will help you present your data clearly and effectively.

Clear and effective data display is very important, but something that is often done badly. Displaying your data well can be quite straightforward if you follow a few guiding principles and, in general, simpler ways of displaying data are usually better. But some methods of data display are frequently misused, and others are rarely very useful.

WHAT DOES IT COVER?

In this chapter we'll see how you can use different methods of displaying your data to help you understand and analyse your data, and to present your findings to others. We'll look at the strengths and weaknesses of some of the most common ways that numeric data are displayed. I explain how to use different methods of data display appropriately and effectively, and help you to avoid common mistakes. I also provide some guidance on making decisions about when it's useful or necessary to display your data visually, and when using a table or incorporating numeric data into your text is a better option.

WHAT WILL YOU LEARN?

- How to make decisions about whether you need to display data graphically or in a table, or whether it can be incorporated into the text
- What types of data display and visual effects to avoid
- How to effectively create the following methods of data display:
  - Tables
  - Bar charts
  - Line graphs
  - Scatterplots

Why we use graphs and charts

You'll see numeric data displayed in tables, graphs and charts in all sorts of places: the news media, academic publications, on webpages and on social media. As

I discussed earlier in this book, journalists, politicians and researchers all like to use numbers to support their arguments, and this numeric data is often displayed visually. But while charts and graphs are used very frequently, they are not always used well. Sometimes the most effective method of displaying data hasn't been chosen, and at other times the type of chart or graph that is used isn't appropriate for the data. In this chapter we'll explore the different methods you can use to display your data, their advantages and disadvantages, and when they should and shouldn't be used. But before we look at specific methods for displaying numeric data, I want to help you decide when you need to display your data in a table, graph or chart, and when it's not necessary, or may even be counterproductive.

How do I know when I need a graph, chart or table?

One of the most frequent mistakes my students make when they're writing up a research report is to have too many tables, graphs and charts. Just as some of them believe that they need a particular number of sources in their bibliography, others think that there is a 'standard' number of tables and graphs that should be included in a report. As a result, they usually have far too many in their first drafts. If they ask me how many they should include, my answer is always the same: 'It depends'.

A good principle to follow with data display is to always start with the simplest options. The first option you should consider is to simply include the figures directly in the text. If you only have a few numbers, this might be your best option. There are several reasons for this.

The first reason relates to what is called your 'narrative', or the story that you're telling about your data. Whatever kind of research you're doing, when you write up your findings you are telling a story (hopefully one that's as close to the truth as possible). We look at this process in more detail in the next chapter, but for now it's enough to say that we want that story to flow smoothly, so that the reader can follow our argument easily and without unnecessary interruptions.

Every time you include a table, graph or chart in your report you break the flow of your narrative and interrupt the story you're telling. A reader will have to stop, examine the table, chart or graph, digest the contents, and then move on to the next paragraph. Ideally, you should keep these interruptions to a minimum, so any table, graph or chart that you include needs to compensate for the disruption by being a worthwhile or necessary interruption. You should only be using a table, graph or chart because you can't tell part of your story properly using only text and numbers, or because it allows you to tell that part of your story much more effectively. And you shouldn't include any table, graph or chart without first thinking about whether you really need one.

So how do you make this decision? I recommend a simple test: try to write up one of your results and include all the necessary numbers in the text. Then get someone else to read what you've written and ask them if they can follow both your argument and the figures you used to support it. If they can't do this

– because they can't hold all the numbers in their head – then you probably need to use some kind of table, graph or chart.

You might not always be able to use this test, as you won't always have someone around who's willing to read your work. The second-best thing is to read over your writing yourself, and try to put yourself in the shoes of someone who is reading it for the first time. This exercise is as much of a thought experiment as anything else – a way of you thinking about how many numbers you can incorporate in your text before it becomes too difficult to read. Sometimes it will be obvious that you need to display your data visually and at other times, when it's less clear, the guidance provided in the rest of this chapter will help you come to a decision about how best to present your data.

What should I include and what should I leave out?

Once you've decided that you need a table, graph or chart, your next decision is what you need to include in it. We'll look at specific examples later in this chapter, when we examine each of the commonly used types of data display, but there's a general principle of balance that it's important to follow. You should include all the data needed to support your argument and for your readers to assess any claims you are making, but no more data than is needed to do this.

We'll look in more detail about how to make this kind of judgement over the course of the rest of this chapter. The most important point to emphasise here is that tables, graphs and charts should be primarily used to help your narrative, rather than being for 'reference'. This doesn't mean that you need to discuss every number or **data point** you've included in a graph, as some of this information will be needed for context. But try to avoid showing more data than are needed when you display data visually. If you feel that you need to include some more detailed information about your dataset or findings – for reasons of transparency, for example, or to include things that wouldn't fit into the main report – consider putting them in an appendix at the end of your report rather than in the middle of a narrative describing your findings.

How do I make sure my table, graph or chart is as clear as possible?

Choosing the most appropriate method for displaying your data is one of the most important steps in making sure that you are telling your story as effectively as possible. However, once you've decided on a type of table, graph or chart, there are many more decisions you will have to make about exactly how it should be designed.

Modern software packages make it very easy to add textures, colours and other effects, but, as we'll see when looking at some examples later in this chapter, simpler is usually better when it comes to displaying data visually. Remember that the primary goal of displaying your data visually is *communication*, not *decoration*. It may be fun to create full-colour 3D graphs and charts with fancy backgrounds, but this won't necessarily help, and can often hinder, communicating your findings effectively.

Tufte's (2001, p 92) famous advice is to 'above all show the data'. He distinguishes between **data ink** and **non–data ink**, and recommends keeping non-data ink to a minimum. 'Data ink' is anything in your table, graph or chart that provides information about your data. This isn't restricted to the numbers in a table or the bars or lines on a chart or graph, but also things such as labels and titles. Non-data ink doesn't just include obviously decorative things like logos or background textures, but also everything else that doesn't contain a direct message about the data: things like grid lines in a table or reference lines on a graph. While it's fairly simple to get rid of the decorative non-data ink, it's much harder, for example, to decide on a suitable number (and thickness) of grid lines in a table. Few (2012) advises keeping only what is absolutely necessary to understand the data ink. There are no hard and fast rules for this, so you need to use your judgement: experiment with taking things out and adding them back in to help you decide what really *needs* to be included. It's much more important that you pay attention to this matter than it is that you get the 'right' answer (as there probably isn't one best way of doing this).

More difficult than minimising the amount of non-data ink is making sure there is no unnecessary data ink in your table or graph. Few (2012, p 143) warns that 'not all information is equally important', and recommends that you 'give your readers what they need, and all that they need, but nothing more'. This means being selective about what data you include without leaving out crucial information. In the next section we'll look at what to include and exclude from your tables and graphs in more detail, when we look at some of the most common ways of displaying data.

Some common ways of displaying data

Data display is a huge topic and there is only space to touch on the basics in this chapter. As usual, I've provided some recommendations for further reading at the end of the chapter. Here, I'm going to focus on the following commonly used methods of displaying numeric data:

- Tables
- Bar charts
- Pie charts
- Line graphs
- Scatterplots

There's a section on each of these methods later in the chapter. But before we look at each of these in more detail, we need to discuss one of the most important decisions that has to be made when displaying your data: table or graph?

Box 9.0: Graphs, charts and plots

So far in this chapter I've used the general terms 'graphs' and 'charts'. The terms 'graphs' and 'charts' both refer to ways of displaying data visually and, although there may technically be differences between them, I use them interchangeably as general terms throughout this chapter. They are used fairly loosely in the literature with, for example, some people using terms such as 'bar chart' and others calling the same thing a 'bar graph'. My view is that the important distinction is between displaying data visually and displaying it as numeric values in a table or in a text. The exact terms used to describe different methods of data display aren't nearly as important as using the techniques effectively.

Tables or graphs?

Once you've decided that simply incorporating your data directly into the text isn't the best way of presenting your story, you'll need to work out which method of displaying your data is the most appropriate. The first decision you'll have to make is whether to display your data visually, in a graph or chart, or numerically, in a table. Few (2012) provides some useful guidance on this, and suggests that a good starting point is to think about how the reader will use the information. I've adapted his discussion to create a series of questions that can help you make this decision. Answering these might not always give you a definitive answer about whether you should use a graph or a table, but it will help guide your thinking.

Does the reader need to look up precise values?

Tables are primarily made up of numeric values, and sometimes these numbers are very important to the story you're telling. Graphs and charts communicate visually, and while a limited number of individual values are often added to them, they are best used when the pattern or shape of a relationship is of more concern than the precise values that make it up. Numbers in a table can be as precise as is needed, and being able to see these values allows your reader to make comparisons and do further calculations. If particular, precise values in the data are the most important element in your story, this is one reason why a table might be more suitable than a graph or chart. If there are only small differences between groups, for example, but these differences are consequential, the precise values might be important information for your readers.

How complicated is the relationship I am trying to show?

While tables are fine for showing simple relationships, graphs are usually better when the relationship is complicated. As Few (2012, p 49) notes, graphs have a 'unique power to reveal patterns of various types, including changes, differences, similarities, and exceptions'. It's much easier to see a trend over time on a line graph, for example, that it is when looking at the figures in a table. And as we'll see later in this chapter, a bar chart can immediately convey differences between many different categories. If your story is primarily about a relationship you have discovered, or differences between a large number of groups, a graph or chart might show this relationship or these differences much more effectively than a table.

How many different units of measurement do I need to show?

Graphs generally work best with only one or two different measures and can become difficult to read with multiple measures. Tables, on the other hand, can include lots of different measures because, unlike graphs, they're not limited by having only two (or maybe three) axes. It's quite common, for example, for a reader to want to see exact frequencies and exact percentages, which can be easier to present clearly in a table. When the exact values of three or more different measures need to be shown, a table tends to be a better option.

How large is the dataset I am presenting?

While it's possible to show very large datasets in tables, when you have more than a relatively small number of data points to display, it will usually be easier to see patterns and relationships in the same data displayed as graph or chart. In general, large tables aren't an effective method of telling a story. If you have a dataset that covers a large number of years, for example, any changes over time will be much easier to follow on a line graph. Few (2012, p 48) notes that 'the patterns revealed by graphs enable readers to detect many points of interest in a single collection of information' in a way that would be very difficult in a table. He uses the example of a **scatterplot** (which we will discuss in detail later in this chapter) to show how patterns and relationships can be clearly shown, even when many hundreds – or even thousands – of data points are included in a graph. A table showing the same data would be much more difficult to interpret, and would take up a great deal of space.

Table 9.0 is a modified version of the one Few (2012) provides, and summarises the key considerations when deciding whether to use a table or a graph.

Table 9.0: Reasons for using tables and graphs

Use tables when ...	Use graphs when ...
• Individual values are important	• A complex relationship is being shown
• Comparing individual values is important	• Patterns and trends are being shown
• Precise values are needed	• A large number of values need to be shown
• There is more than one unit of measure (eg, individuals and households)	
• Both detail and summary are needed	

How to create a good table

As I wrote at the beginning of this chapter, modern software packages make it very easy to create graphs and charts with all sorts of colours, textures and effects. This can be a fun distraction from writing your report, but doesn't usually result in better data display. Unfortunately for those of you with artistic flair, simple displays are usually best.

I don't imagine that many people find creating tables to be fun. But while they're not particularly exciting in a visual sense, it's still important to pay attention to their design. Fortunately, there are probably fewer pitfalls in designing tables than there are with graphs and charts. There isn't the room in this book to look at table design in detail, but, if you're interested in pursuing this topic further, Few (2012) provides an extremely comprehensive discussion of all aspects of the process.

Here are a few ways that you can avoid common issues with table design:

- *Only include the figures needed for the narrative:* Tables should be essential for the narrative and shouldn't be included just for reference. This doesn't mean that you only include the numbers in a table that you refer to in your text – some numbers will be needed for context and comparison – but you shouldn't include information that doesn't relate to the point you're making in your discussion. This requires some judgement, but, as always, thinking carefully about this decision will usually result in a better table.
- *Be consistent with decimal places:* It's best to use the same number of decimal places for each measure in your table. You might use a different number of decimal places for different measures, but the important thing is that in any particular measure of variable, the same number of decimal places is used. This means that, if the numbers are also aligned properly, comparing the figures will be easier.
- *Align the text and numbers:* Numbers should usually be aligned ('justified') to the right side of each column. This means that they should all line up on the right, so that they can be easily compared. For this to be effective, you need to use the same number of decimal places for the figures in a particular column. Aligning the text is less crucial, but doing this in a thoughtful way makes a much neater looking table. Text is often aligned to the left in the first column of a table but can be centred in subsequent column headings.
- *Keep the design simple:* A general principle running through this chapter is that simplicity is usually better in data display. An important part of this is keeping non-data ink to a minimum. With tables this relates mostly to grid lines, so try to only include lines that are necessary, and don't make lines too thick or too heavy.

Now that we've covered the basics of creating a table, in the next section we look at some methods for displaying data visually. We start with one of the most common methods: pie charts.

Pies are for eating, not for displaying data

When asked to display some data showing the distribution of a categorical variable, many people's first instinct is to create a pie chart. Pie charts are very popular and are often people's 'go-to' preference for displaying this kind of data. It's easy to see why they're attractive, as they have an intuitive appeal: most people have cut up a pie, cake or pizza. Pie charts are often presented in colour and sometimes also with textures, and it's quite common to see three-dimensional (3D) versions. It's easy to create charts like this using software packages that are used in most offices or educational settings, such as Microsoft Excel or Google Sheets.

Given their popularity, you might be surprised to find out that I *never* recommend using a pie chart to my students or colleagues. This isn't because they don't work (no one would use them if they were completely ineffective), but because I have not yet encountered a situation where they are the best method of data display. Where they do 'work', they are either unnecessary or could be replaced by a more effective way of displaying the same data.

I could easily end this section of the chapter here, by telling you never to use pie charts. But given that pie charts are so popular, I don't want you just to take my word for it that pie charts aren't often very useful. I want to *show* you why they aren't. And if I haven't convinced you by the end of this chapter, feel free to use them whenever and however you want.

I'm going to use some example data to demonstrate the weaknesses of pie charts. Most of this will be from the National Survey of Sexual Attitudes and Lifestyles (Natsal) dataset that I've used in previous chapters. I occasionally use hypothetical data to make particular points, but I'll point out when this is the case. I realise that I'm spending quite a lot of time discussing a method of data display that I'm advising you not to use, but I think that it's justified given the popularity of pie charts and the number of problems with them. I hope you find my arguments convincing, and save the pies in your life for eating.

Problem one: there are no axes on a pie chart (and only figures if you add them)

One of the problems inherent to pie charts is that, in their pure form, they don't have any axes or contain any numbers. Axes are the lines on the edge of a graph that usually have labels and/or a scale. I discussed the **x-axis** and the **y-axis** in the last chapter (and will come back to these later). The axes are important on a line graph, bar chart or scatterplot because they help us estimate the values in that visual display. Because there are no axes on pie charts, this means that the numbers behind the visual display are either invisible to the reader or have to be added on as an 'extra'.

Figure 9.0 shows a very basic pie chart. It displays the answers from a question about alcohol consumption from the Natsal dataset. The four categories each represent a different range of alcohol consumption. As you can see, there are no axes and no numbers on the main part of the chart.

Figure 9.0: A basic pie chart

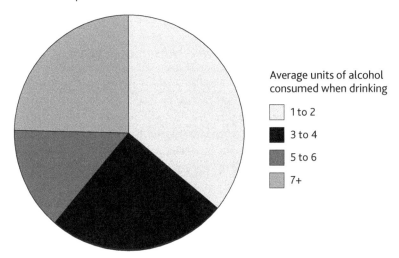

Average units of alcohol
consumed when drinking

- 1 to 2
- 3 to 4
- 5 to 6
- 7+

One problem with pie charts is that estimating accurate figures from the pie 'segments' isn't easy. We can get a rough sense of proportion in some cases, but this isn't always possible. You can probably guess that the section for '1 to 2 units' is about a third of the whole pie (it's actually 36%), for example. And the '7+' and '3 to 4' sections look like they each represent around a quarter of the whole pie, but it's much harder to come up with a percentage or fraction for the '5 to 6' segment (have a try). This is because we're generally not very good at estimating angles and turning these into proportions, at least not unless they are obvious and simple (a half, a quarter, one third, and so on).

Unlike tables and other kinds of graphs, there are no figures that are an inherent part of a bar chart that can help us with this task. Frequencies and percentages can be added, of course, but I'll discuss why this isn't an ideal solution later in this chapter.

Problem two: it can be difficult to compare the size of different segments

As discussed earlier, the main advantage of displaying data visually is that the story — what is going on in the data — can be perceived almost immediately because of our brain's ability to understand size, shape, order, and so on. A pie chart can give us a good idea of when the segments are *very* different from each other, as you can see in Figure 9.0 if you compare the segment representing '1 to 2' units of alcohol consumed with the segment showing '5 to 6' units of alcohol: the '1 to 2' segment is clearly much larger than the '5 to 6' segment.

However, comparing the '3 to 4' units of alcohol with the '7+' category is more difficult. We can see that they are quite similar, but which one is bigger? And how much bigger is the larger segment? It's quite hard to tell, and our interpretation can be affected by the colours or textures used in each segment. Judging proportions and comparing categories in pie charts can be quite hard, especially when segments are a similar size. But small differences can sometimes be very important in our research findings.

Problem three: pie charts don't work well with lots of categories

The problem of both working out an approximate proportion of a segment and comparing segments of different sizes tends to get worse as more categories are represented in your pie chart. Figure 9.1 shows Natsal data on preferred source of contraception. As before, some of the segments are quite similar in size and are hard to differentiate, but, in this case, the number and size of the segments make this problem worse. Judging the approximate proportion taken up by some of the larger segments is reasonably straightforward. If you look at the largest segment in Figure 9.1, you might guess that it's a bit larger than one-third of the whole 'pie' (it's actually 38%) – but what about some of the smaller sections? Can you easily work out what proportion they represent? It's quite hard to do. Interpreting graphs and charts should be easier than interpreting the figures in tables – the whole point is that they tell the story more immediately. If you have to struggle to work out proportions, differences or approximate figures from a graph or chart, it hasn't served its purpose very well.

Figure 9.1: A pie chart with lots of categories

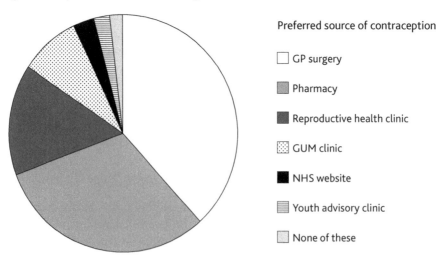

The more categories you have in a pie chart, the greater the chance that some segments will be small, hard to compare and difficult to interpret as proportions. As the number of segments increases, it also gets harder to create a pie chart without using colour – something that is less of an issue for bar charts, as we'll see. Although most things we now read are available electronically, some are not, and we can sometimes only use black, white and grey to draw graphs and charts. This makes pie charts a bit less flexible in terms of where they can be used.

Problem four: three dimensions makes things worse, not better

Modern software has made it easy for anyone to make graphs and charts, and to add colours, textures and effects. Creating three-dimensional (3D) graphs has become very popular, and it's common to see pie charts presented this way. As we shall see, however, 3D pie charts are even more difficult to interpret than conventional ones. This is because they distort the proportions that would be correctly shown in a two-dimensional (2D) graph, and make it almost impossible to judge the correct size of segments by eye.

Figure 9.2 shows the same data as we saw in Figure 9.0, but in a 3D rather than a 2D bar chart. In Figure 9.0, we saw that the segments for '3 to 4' and '7+' were very similar in size and difficult to tell apart. In the 3D bar chart, however, the same two segments look very different. The segment closest to us, representing '7+' units of alcohol, looks much bigger than the segment at the back right of the pie, which represents '3 to 4' units of alcohol. But these two segments each account for 25% of cases: they should appear to be exactly the same size (as they did in Figure 9.0).

Figure 9.2: A 3D pie chart

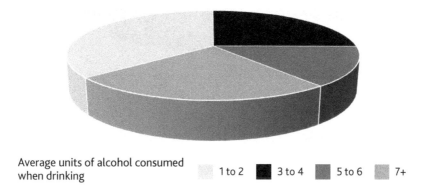

Average units of alcohol consumed when drinking   1 to 2   3 to 4   5 to 6   7+

Presenting the data in a 3D pie chart has distorted the true proportions of the segments. It has achieved the exact opposite of what a graph or chart is supposed to do: accurately tell the story of the data. This has happened because a false sense of 'perspective' has been added to the pie chart. You might remember from your art classes that things that are further away appear smaller than things that are close to us. So if we draw a field of cows, the ones in the distance would be drawn smaller than the ones nearby, even if they were actually the same size. This is good practice if you're painting a view of the countryside, but it doesn't work with graphs and charts because there is no 'close by' or 'far away'. Graphs and charts are an abstract representation of data rather than an attempt to capture what we see when looking at the material world.

Figure 9.3 shows the same data in a different 3D pie chart. The only difference is that the pie has been rotated, so the segments that were previously at the front are now at the back. As you can see, the '3 to 4' segment, which is now at the front, looks much larger than the '7+' segment, which is now at the back. Compared to Figure 9.2, it gives the opposite impression of the relative proportions of these two categories. The story told by the data has changed just because I have changed the order in which the categories are represented in the pie chart.

I hope that you can see how this could potentially mislead readers, and how 3D pie charts could be manipulated to misrepresent research findings. While I may be able to be convinced that there are occasions where pie charts could be useful, I don't think that this will ever be the case for 3D pie charts.

Figure 9.3: The same 3D pie chart from a different angle

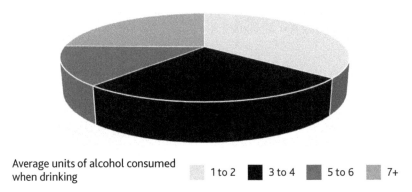

Average units of alcohol consumed when drinking 1 to 2   3 to 4   5 to 6   7+

Can we improve pie charts by adding numbers?

You might think that I've been a bit unfair to pie charts because, so far, the examples I have used haven't had any numbers attached to them. Most of the pie charts you see have numbers attached to them, to help readers see the exact values, either as frequencies or percentages (and sometimes both). This is particularly helpful when some of the segments are of similar sizes or are very small.

If you're going to add numbers to a pie chart, it makes most sense to add frequencies. The whole point of pie charts is to show proportions visually, so you should be able to see these by comparing relative size of the different segments. However, I'm going to argue that adding numbers to pie charts both reveals their inherent weaknesses and also detracts from much of their value as a visual display.

Let's look first at adding percentages to pie charts, which is a fairly common practice. Figure 9.4 shows the same data on preferred source of contraception as we saw in Figure 9.1. The difference here is that I've added percentages

Figure 9.4: A pie chart with percentage values added

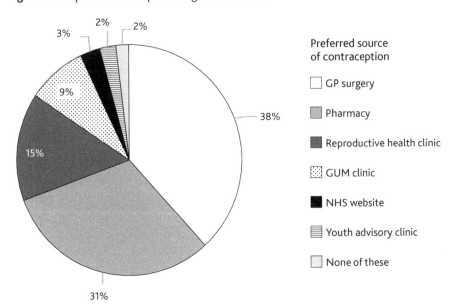

to each segment. This makes it easier for us to compare the sizes of the different segments and to judge the proportions represented by some of the smaller segments.

Has adding numbers solved some of the problems I raised earlier and transformed our pie chart into a useful way of presenting our data? Yes and no. It's true that you can now make comparisons more easily and have access to exact percentages – but notice where your eyes go when you first look at the pie chart. I bet that most of you are drawn straight to the percentage figures themselves, rather than the pie. This almost makes the graphical part redundant, as you could have just presented the percentages in a table. There doesn't seem to be much advantage to using a pie chart rather than a table in this case, and a table would have the advantage of presenting the percentages in a more orderly way.

Let's try adding frequencies instead. As the pie charts already show proportions, frequencies add some additional information, rather than just helping you interpret the proportions more accurately. But, as you can see in Figure 9.5, where I've added frequencies to the pie chart we've been looking at, the numbers have to be scattered across the chart, rather than being in neat and easy-to-read columns like they would be in a table. And it's still difficult to judge the proportions of the smaller segments.

A solution to this could be to add both frequencies and percentages. However, this makes your pie chart very cluttered. It would be much more effective simply to put the frequencies and percentages into a table, as it is these figures that you're paying most attention to. But tables aren't always the best way to display data, so what other options do we have?

Figure 9.5: A pie chart with frequencies added

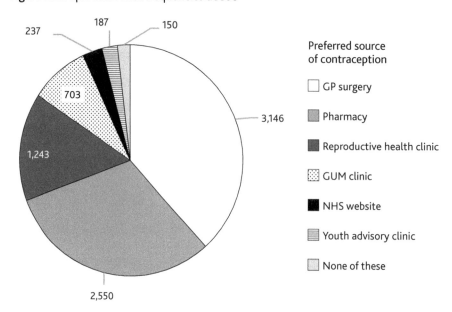

What are the alternatives to pie charts?

Although tables are good for presenting precise figures and multiple measures – such as frequencies and percentages – they do lack the immediacy of graphs and charts. They're not as good at telling the story of your data, and can be more of an interruption to your narrative if your readers have to spend time studying them. So what are the alternatives to pie charts for showing how many cases there are in different categories?

As I discussed earlier, if you only have a few figures, you may simply be able to incorporate them into your text. The data in Figure 9.0, which only relate to four different categories, could be incorporated into your text without providing too many numbers for the reader. There would be a maximum of four frequencies and four percentages, which you could present in pairs (for example, '25% of respondents [N = 2,656] consumed three to four units of alcohol when drinking'). But incorporating the data in Figures 9.4 and 9.5 into the text would probably result in a long list of numbers that would be hard for your readers to follow. There are seven different sources of contraception, which would result in up to 14 different frequencies and percentages to discuss. In this case a table or a graph would be a better option.

Figure 9.6 shows the same data as Figures 9.4 and 9.5 presented in a bar chart rather than a pie chart. This has several advantages. One important difference is that a bar chart has two axes: the one on the left with numbers (the y-axis) and the one on the bottom with the labels for each category (the x-axis). Both these axes help us interpret the data in the chart more easily.

Figure 9.6: A simple bar chart with frequencies

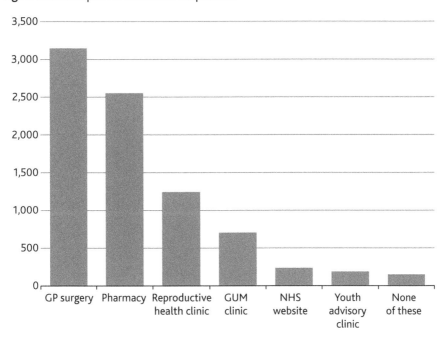

Preferred source of contraception

The y-axis, which on this chart shows frequencies, allows us to read off an approximate value from each bar. You can see, for example, that the number of people whose preferred source of contraception is a GP surgery is just over 3,100. It's easy to find the data for this category because the label, on the x-axis, is directly below the relevant bar.

These two features give bar charts several advantages over pie charts. First, you can read off the approximate value for any category without having to attach the appropriate figure to the bar (as you have to do for a pie chart segment). Second, you can immediately see which bar relates to which category, something that is much less immediate with pie charts, where you need to match the category label from a list (called a **legend**) to the appropriate segment. And last, because of the way bar charts are laid out, and unlike pie charts, you don't need to use different colours, shades or textures to differentiate between categories, which can get increasingly complicated the more categories you are trying to represent.

It's also the case that it's much easier to judge the relative size of the bars in a bar chart than with the segments in a pie chart. For example, without referring to the frequencies shown on the y-axis, we can easily see that the 'Pharmacy' bar is roughly twice the size of the 'Reproductive health clinic' bar. And even when the difference in the size of the categories is very small, you can easily see which ones are larger and smaller. The bar for the 'NHS website' category is only slightly larger than the one for the 'Youth advisory clinic' category, but it's immediately clear which one is bigger than the other. This is because bar charts work with our innate ability to recognise some kind of patterns or differences, and seeing how much a bar is 'sticking out' compared to another bar is something we can do well.

When you have more than a few categories, it's not straightforward to estimate the percentage that each bar represents, but if this is the most important information, the y-axis can be used to indicate percentages rather than frequencies, or if frequencies are also needed, a y-axis indicating percentages can be added to the right side of the chart.

Figure 9.7 demonstrates how much more effective bar charts are at showing the difference in size of each category compared to pie charts. It's difficult to distinguish the differences in sizes of the segments in each of the two pie charts. However, when looking at the bar charts, it's much easier to see the relative sizes of each of the different categories in each chart. We can also see any differences between the two charts in the sizes of the categories A to E and we have the added advantage of being able to read off frequencies from the y-axis.

Figure 9.7: Pie charts versus bar charts

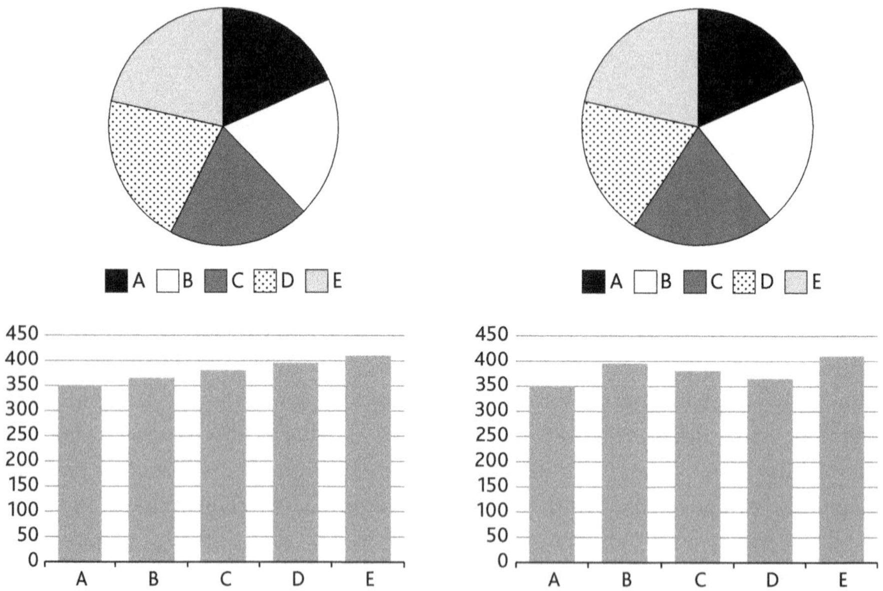

Source: Data invented by the author

The flexibility of bar charts in their different forms

As well as being better at showing us the difference between the frequencies and percentages associated with different categories in a variable, it's also the case that bar charts are much more flexible than pie charts, and can be used for a much wider range of purposes.

One of the most useful types of bar chart is the clustered bar chart. These charts allow you to look at the relationship between two variables, rather than only looking at one variable at a time. Figure 9.8 compares the contraception source preferences between male and female respondents. You can immediately see that there are substantial gender differences, with GP surgeries being the preference of more than half of the female respondents, but only just over one-fifth of the male respondents. In contrast, over 46% of men preferred to get their contraception from pharmacies, whereas only just over 20% of women indicated this preference.

Clustered bar charts have the same desirable properties as simple bar charts: the key advantage being that it's very easy to compare the relative size of the bars. They still work well with a large number of categories, and can be used with both frequencies and percentages.

Figure 9.8: A clustered bar chart

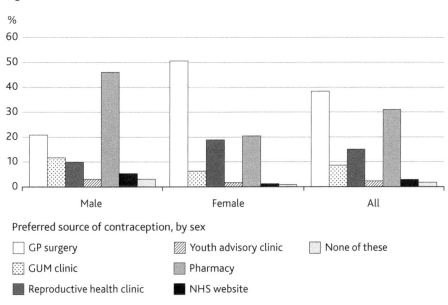

Preferred source of contraception, by sex

☐ GP surgery   ▨ Youth advisory clinic   ▨ None of these
▨ GUM clinic   ▨ Pharmacy
▨ Reproductive health clinic   ■ NHS website

A commonly used alternative to the clustered bar chart is the stacked bar chart. These can be used to show both percentages and frequencies but are most commonly used to compare proportional differences between groups.

Stacked bar charts work best when there are relatively few categories for each group. In Figure 9.9 we have three categories of smoking behaviour – 'Never smoked', 'Ex-smoker', 'Current smoker' – and have compared two groups, male and female respondents. A stacked bar chart allows us to easily see that there are only very small differences in smoking behaviour between the male and female respondents.

Figure 9.9: A stacked bar chart with three categories

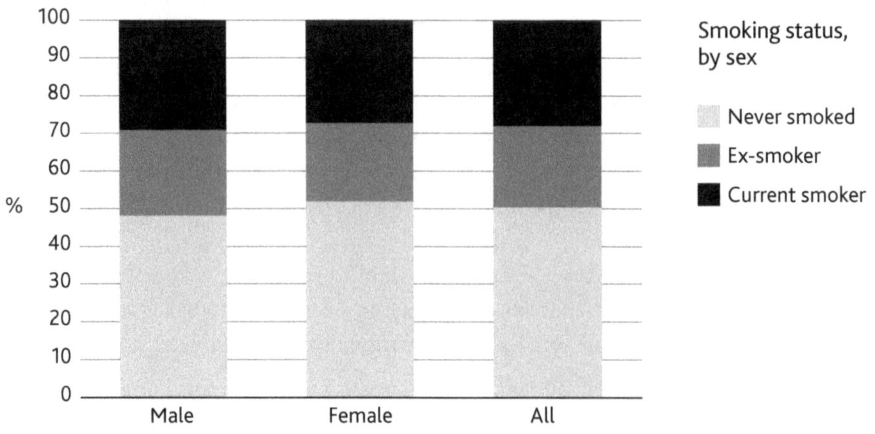

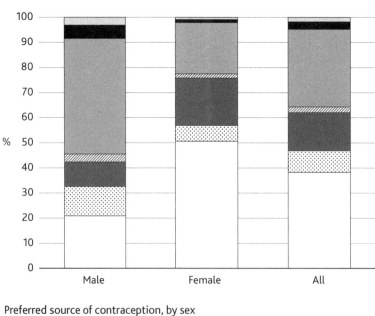

Figure 9.10 shows a stacked bar chart with seven categories. However, as you can see, when the number of categories increases, and when some of the bars are quite different in size, it becomes more difficult to compare the size of the segments between different bars.

Figure 9.10: A stacked bar chart with seven categories

Stacked bar charts vs clustered bar charts

The key advantage of clustered bar charts is the same as for simple bar charts: the bars all start from the same baseline. This means that they are easier to compare because it's clear which bars stick out further and how much further they stick out. We lose some of this advantage when we use stacked bar charts because this is only the case for the category at the bottom end of each bar. The sections that are stacked on top of the bottom one don't necessarily start at the same point, so aren't quite as easy to compare. Reading values from the y-axis to help work out the size of each category is also harder for these sections.

Stacked bar carts can have their place, however. When used with percentages, they are better for comparing proportions than pie charts, as the figures on the y-axis make it easier to judge the proportion of the categories. They can also be used effectively with frequencies, as an alternative to clustered bar charts, although, for the reasons I have already explained, I tend to prefer the latter.

As you may have gathered from what you've already read, I believe that bar charts are one of the most useful and versatile methods of displaying data visually. I only have the space to introduce them very briefly in this chapter but have included further reading at the end of the chapter for those of you who may want to read more about them.

In the next section we're going to look at another important method for data display: line graphs.

Line graphs

Line graphs can be a very useful method for displaying data. However, they have a very specific use, and are commonly misused. Figure 9.11 shows an example of the appropriate use of a line graph. The important feature of this graph is that is shows *change over time*. Line graphs are intended to show change over time and are very effective at doing this.

The simplest type of line graph has only one line, as is the case in Figure 9.11. This shows how one thing has changed, in this case, the number of COVID-19 vaccine doses given at different points in time over a two-year period. The line gives us the idea of the trend – when there have been the highest and lowest numbers of doses administered, and during which periods there has been the most change. Our eyes follow the line from left to right, following the 'story' as it unfolds over time.

We can see, for example, that there was a rapid rise in the administration of vaccines shortly after they were authorised for use, in early December 2020. This peaked in the summer of 2021 and again in December 2021, perhaps because people were getting additional doses.

Figure 9.11: A line graph with a single line

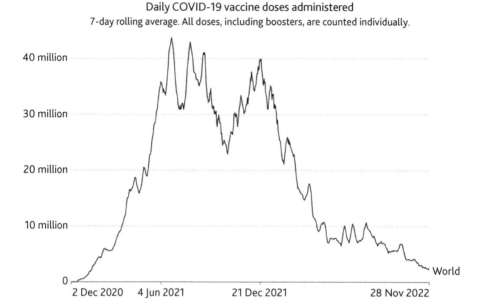

Source: Our World in Data

Line graphs can have more than one line, however, and this allows us to compare different groups over time. Figure 9.12 shows the number of people using different social media platforms. Each of the lines represents a different social media platform, and, as you can see, you can include several different groups in a single line graph without making it difficult to read.

We can see that there has been a general growth in the overall use of social media, but that some platforms have grown faster than others. Facebook was the most popular platform in 2018 and has been the largest platform since it overtook YouTube in 2010. However, the popularity of Twitter has stalled, and newer platforms such as WhatsApp and TikTok have grown very quickly.

Apart from the different number of lines, there are some other important differences between these two line graphs. You'll notice that there aren't data for the entire period for any of the platforms. For TikTok there are only data for two years. There are two reasons for the different amount of data available for each platform, one of which you might have already guessed.

The most obvious reason for the differences is that Facebook is the only platform that has existed for the whole time period. Other platforms, such as Reddit, have been around for almost as long, but those such as Pinterest or TikTok are much newer. As it's only possible to have users if a platform exists, this explains some of the data that are missing. Another reason why there is some **missing data** is because there wasn't up-to-date data for all platforms when this graph was produced – there's only data for 2019 for Facebook,

Figure 9.12: A line graph with multiple lines

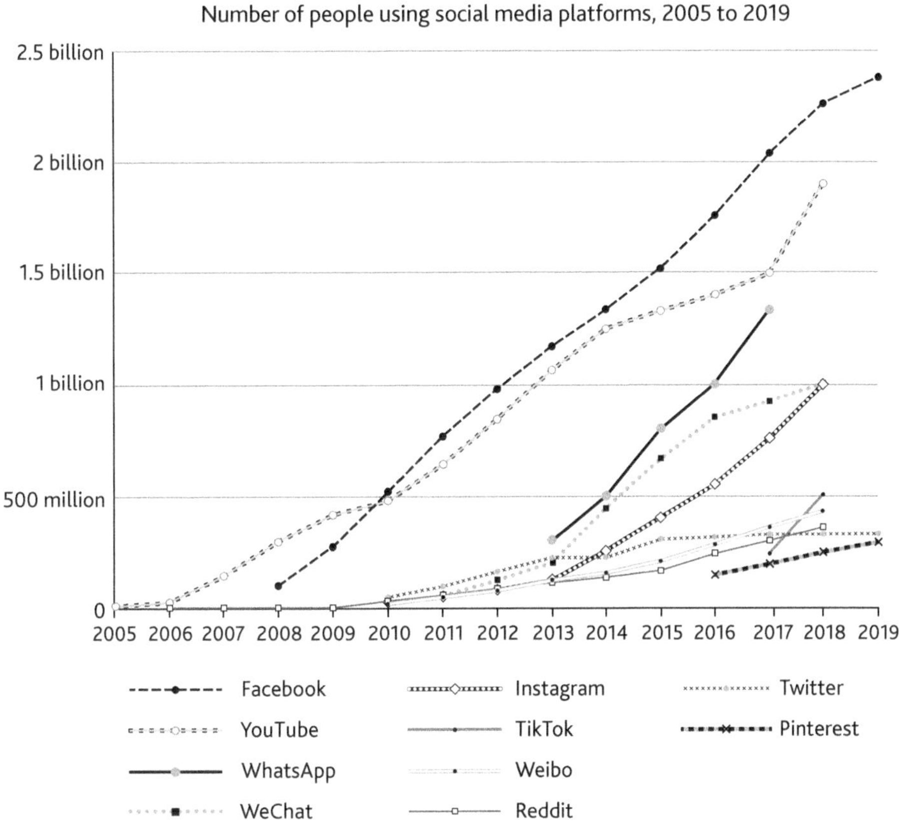

Number of people using social media platforms, 2005 to 2019

Source: Our World in Data

Twitter and Pinterest. Despite this, the graph gives us a very good overview of the popularity of different social media platforms and how this has changed over time.

An important difference between the line graph shown in Figure 9.11 and the one in Figure 9.12 is the number of data points making up each line. In Figure 9.11 there are data for each day of the year, meaning that the data points are so close together that you can't see any lines that join them. In contrast, there are only yearly data points in Figure 9.12, and it's easy to see the dots and the lines that join them. Strictly speaking, we have no data between each of the data points, so we don't really know what the trend was between them. However, we usually accept that the line is a simplification of what has happened between the data points, as we're more interested in the longer term trends.

Misuse of line graphs

The two examples we've looked at so far are both appropriate uses of line graphs. This is because they show change over time, and it makes sense to follow the progress of the line from the left to the right of the graph. But it's quite common to see line graphs misused, and sometimes it's tricky to work out whether a line graph is an appropriate way to display your own data.

Figure 9.13 shows the Natsal data on contraception sources that we've seen before. This time it's presented in a line graph. A line graph isn't appropriate here, because there is no 'progression' from left to right in relation to the categories. If we put the categories in a different order, the shape of the line would change even though we would be using the same data. Line graphs don't work as they're supposed to if the line doesn't show progress from one time period to the next. Also, each line in a line graph represents a single category, whereas the line in Figure 9.13 appears to link all the seven different categories of contraception source.

I hope that you can see that the data in Figure 9.13 are better suited to the bar chart we used earlier in this chapter. It would even be better to display them in a pie chart than in a line graph! The problem with the line graph is that it invites us to follow the line across the graph, and it suggests that there is some kind of change over time.

Figure 9.14 shows another line graph using Natsal data. This time it shows the number of participants who drank different amounts of alcohol. This example is a bit trickier because, unlike the data in Figure 9.13, there is an order in the categories of alcohol consumption (that is, it is an **ordinal** categorical variable). So it makes sense to have the categories in the order that you see in the graph.

Figure 9.13: An inappropriate line graph

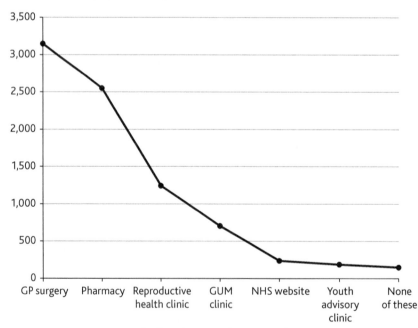

Figure 9.14: Another inappropriate line graph

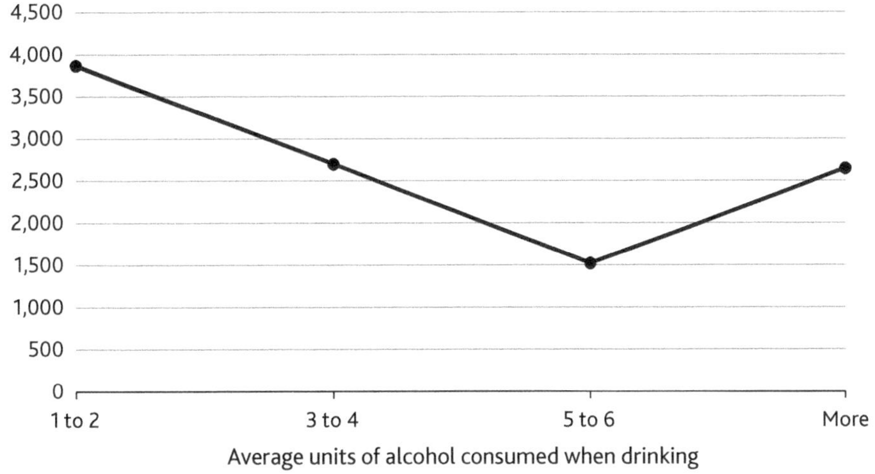

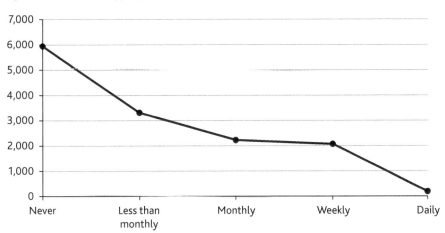

However, just because they are ordered doesn't mean that they should be joined with a line, as they are in Figure 9.14. Remember that in a line graph, the line represents how a single category has changed over time. But these data were all collected at one point in time, so there is no change over time to be shown in a graph. And each participant could only pick one category of alcohol consumption, so the line is joining up the responses of different participants even though there is no link between them.

Figure 9.15 shows results from another question in the Natsal study. Again, deciding whether a line graph is appropriate is not straightforward because

Figure 9.15: A final inappropriate line graph

there is an element of time in the data: how often people drank more than six units of alcohol. But, like the previous two examples, the data doesn't measure *change* over time, and there is no link between each of the categories that relate to time. The people in the 'Daily' category, for example, are not the same people who are in the 'Weekly' category, and so these two groups shouldn't be joined by a line.

Line graphs are a bit of a niche method of displaying data. They are very effective at displaying trends over time and can be used to compare change over time for many different groups in a single graph, and so it's very useful to be familiar with them. But they shouldn't be used in other circumstances.

Next we're going to look at a type of graph that you'll be familiar with if you've read the previous two chapters: scatterplots.

Scatterplots

In Chapters 7 and 8, where I covered **correlation** and regression analysis, I used scatterplots at various points to show the relationship between two continuous (or discrete) variables. I want to briefly revisit them here to discuss their uses, and also to highlight their limitations. There will be some overlap with what I covered in the previous chapters, so if you've read those you might want to skip over some of the content here, but I've tried to be reasonably comprehensive to make sure that this discussion works as a stand-alone section for anyone who hasn't read the rest of the book.

Figure 9.16 shows the relationship between two continuous variables: household income and expenditure. Each of the dots on the scatterplot represents a particular case, and in this example that means a household. For any one of

Figure 9.16: A scatterplot showing the relationship between two continuous variables

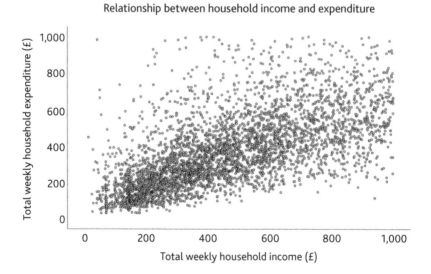

Relationship between household income and expenditure

these cases, you can estimate the approximate value for the household income and household expenditure by seeing where each dot sits in relation to the y-axis and x-axis.

Although you can see every case in your dataset on a scatterplot, we're not usually interested in looking at all of these cases individually. Scatterplots tend to be used to give an overview of the relationship between two variables. This allows you to check whether the relationship is linear which, as we saw in Chapters 7 and 8, is very important if you're going to go on to conduct any correlation or regression analysis. However, they can also be useful in identifying **outliers** – cases that are unusual (and that may even be errors).

Scatterplots can be very useful, but they work best in particular circumstances. They're ideally suited to showing strong relationships in relatively small datasets. When there are thousands of cases *and* the relationship being shown is weak, it becomes difficult to see patterns in a scatterplot.

Figure 9.17 shows a scatterplot with 8,297 cases. The correlation between the two variables is very weak ($r=0.09$), and the graph doesn't add much to our understanding. It's not possible to see whether the relationship is linear (this is difficult to ascertain when relationships are not reasonably strong), and there's so much overlap of the data points on the graph that we can't tell how many dots are sitting on top of each other. (There are technical workarounds to this issue but they don't always solve this problem and are beyond the scope of what is covered in this book.)

Figure 9.17: A scatterplot with thousands of cases and a weak relationship

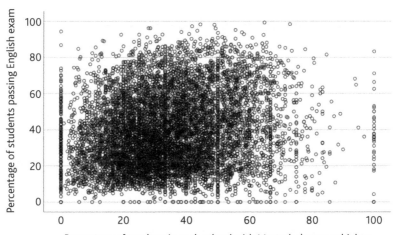

If you've read Chapters 7 and 8 you'll remember that although, strictly speaking, correlation and regression analysis require you to have continuous variables, it's usually fine to use these techniques when your data are discrete. This means that, while your data may be 'equal interval', in practice you only collect data that take certain values (it might be helpful to refer to Chapter 2 if these terms are unfamiliar to you). Data on the number of people in a household are discrete (you can't have half a person), and a variable such as 'years in full-time education' would also be discrete. Unfortunately, discrete variables don't always work as well in scatterplots as continuous variables.

Figure 9.18 shows an example of the relationship between one continuous variable (current salary) and one discrete variable (whole years of education completed). You can see that years of education is a discrete variable because the data points form lines running vertically on the scatterplot. These data are from the USA, and the lines correspond to the points at which people have left full-time education. There are some older people who left school after eight years of education, but most stayed for 12 years or longer since the law changed. You can see that quite a few data points fall at 15 years and 16 years of education, representing people who have graduated from three- or four-year degrees.

As you can see, the scatterplot works reasonably well, even though one of the variables is discrete (and is restricted to a small number of possible values). The spread of the data suggests that the relationship may not be linear, as it appears that salary increases disproportionately with each extra year of education. This is useful information, and in this case, the scatterplot has served the purpose well of allowing us to visually examine the relationship that we're interested in.

Figure 9.18: A scatterplot with one discrete and one continuous variable

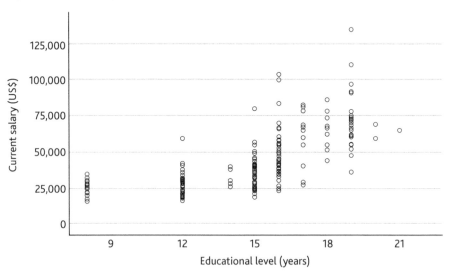

Source: SPSS® demonstration data

Figure 9.19 shows us a relationship between two discrete variables. The data I used to create this graph comes from the 2011 ONS Opinions and Lifestyle

Figure 9.19: A scatterplot with two discrete variables

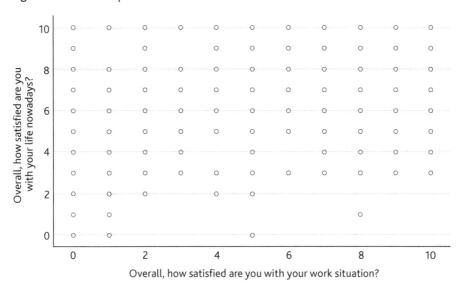

Survey. The questions ask respondents to rate their satisfaction with various aspects of their lives on a scale from 0 to 10. (I realise that, in Chapter 2, I warned about the issues with assuming that such data was 'equal interval', but we'll ignore that here, as we're only concerned with how discrete data are displayed on a scatterplot.)

The scatterplot shown in Figure 9.19 looks a bit odd, with the data points forming a grid pattern. It's important to point out that there are 1,124 cases in the Opinions and Lifestyle Survey, and they are all represented in this scatterplot. The problem is that many of these cases are sitting in exactly the same place on the scatterplot, and it's impossible to see how many are represented at each point on the grid.

There are techniques that you can use to solve this problem, one of which is **jittering** the data. This randomly moves the data points by a very small amount, so that they don't overlap in a perfect grid pattern. Figure 9.20 shows the same variables as Figure 9.19, but the data have been jittered. This is something that may be possible with the software you are using to analyse your data or create a graph, but isn't always an easily accessible option.

Scatterplots can be a very useful technique for data display. They are sometimes used when reporting findings, but are more commonly used in the exploratory stages of analysis to examine a relationship visually and check for things such as the linearity of the relationship or whether there are any outliers. They work best with continuous data but can be used when one of your variables is discrete. If both variables are discrete, however, they aren't useful unless you manipulate your data with techniques such as jittering.

Figure 9.20: A scatterplot with two discrete variables and jittered data

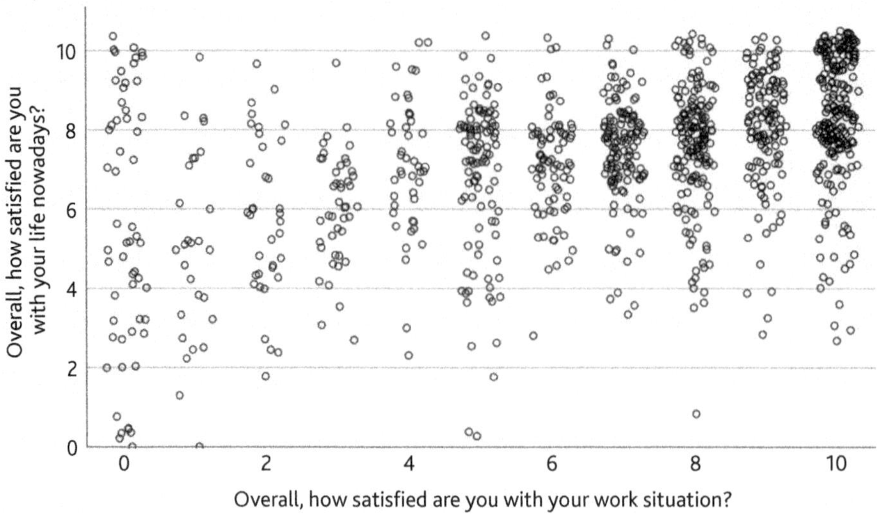

Summary

This chapter has provided an overview of the pros and cons of some of the most commonly used methods of displaying data. It has only scratched the surface of a vast topic, and I have provided some suggestions for further reading below.

The next, and last chapter continues this theme of presenting your results, and examines how best to write up the results of a statistical analysis.

References

Few, S. (2012) *Show Me the Numbers: Designing Tables and Graphs to Enlighten* (2nd edn), Burlingame, CA: Analytics Press.

Tufte, E. (2001) *The Visual Display of Quantitative Information* (2nd edn), Cheshire, CT: Graphics Press.

Sources

Figures 9.0 to 9.6, 9.8 to 9.10 and 9.13 to 9.15 were based on analysis of the British National Survey of Sexual Attitudes and Lifestyles, 2010–2012 Teaching dataset:

University of Manchester, CMIST (Cathie Marsh Institute for Social Research), UK Data Service (2021) *National Survey of Sexual Attitudes and Lifestyles, 2010–2012: Teaching dataset* [data collection], University College London, Centre for Sexual Health and HIV Research [original data producer(s)], SN: 8735, DOI: 10.5255/UKDA-SN-8735-1

Figures 9.11 and 9.12, sourced from Our World in Data, are available under the Creative Commons license, and can be found at:

https://ourworldindata.org/grapher/daily-covid-19-vaccination-doses?tab=chart&time=earliest..2022-11-28&country=~OWID_WRL, https://ourworldindata.org/grapher/users-by-social-media-platform

Figure 9.16 was based on analysis of the Living Costs and Food Survey, 2013: Unrestricted access teaching dataset:

ONS (Office for National Statistics), University of Manchester. CMIST (Cathie Marsh Institute for Social Research), UK Data Service (2016) *Living Costs and Food Survey, 2013: Unrestricted access teaching dataset* [data collection], 2nd release, UK Data Service, SN: 7932, DOI: 10.5255/UKDA-SN-7932-2. Contains public sector information licensed under the Open Government Licence v2.0.

Figure 9.17 was based on analysis of the California Department of Education 2006 Adequate Yearly Progress (AYP) data files, www.cde.ca.gov/re/pr/aypdatafiles.asp

Figures 9.19 and 9.20 were based on analysis of the ONS Opinions Survey, Well-Being Module, April 2011: Unrestricted access teaching dataset:

University of Manchester, Cathie Marsh Centre for Census and Survey Research, ESDS (Economic and Social Data Service) Government (2012) *ONS Opinions Survey, Well-Being Module, April 2011: Unrestricted access teaching dataset* [data collection], ONS, Social Survey Division [original data producer(s)], SN: 7146, DOI: 10.5255/UKDA-SN-7146-1. Contains public sector information licensed under the Open Government Licence v2.0.

Useful resources

The most immediately accessible text I know of on data display that covers a wide variety of issues and techniques is by Naomi Robbins:

Robbins, N. (2005) *Creating More Effective Graphs*, Hoboken, NJ: John Wiley & Sons.

Stephen Few's hefty text on display data is as comprehensive and detailed a guide to this topic as you could ever need:

Few, S. (2012) *Show Me The Numbers: Designing Tables and Graphs to Enlighten* (2nd edn), Burlingame, CA: Analytics Press.

W.E.B. Du Bois is often overlooked as an innovator in data display. Du Bois was working at the beginning of the 20th century, and developed and refined many different methods for displaying data, exposing the inequalities experienced by

Black Americans. Whitney Battle–Baptiste and Britt Rusert provide an important overview of Du Bois' work:

Battle-Baptiste, W. and Rusert, B. (eds) (2018) *W.E.B. Du Bois's Data Portraits: Visualizing Black America*, New York: Princeton Architectural Press.

Alberto Cairo provides an interesting critique of some of the most common misuses of graphs and charts:

Cairo, A. (2019) *How Charts Lie: Getting Smarter about Visual Information*, New York: Norton.

10

Telling statistical stories: how to present your findings and conclusions

> ### WHAT IS THIS CHAPTER FOR?
> Most of this book so far has been about how to conduct statistical analyses. In Chapter 9 we also looked at the use of tables, charts and graphs, and started thinking about how to present your results. In this chapter we take this one step further and look at how to write up your findings and conclusions as a coherent narrative that readers will find both accessible and appealing.
>
> ### WHAT DOES IT COVER?
> I provide some basic guidelines to help you present your statistical 'story', and point out some common mistakes made by those who are new to writing about statistics and presenting numeric data. I discuss what you must leave in and what you can leave out when writing up your findings and conclusions, and how to best structure your narrative.
>
> ### WHAT WILL YOU LEARN?
> • How to avoid a 'shopping list' approach to presenting statistical findings
> • What you should write most about and what you can write less about
> • The technical details that you need to include and those that you can leave out
> • How to make sure that your conclusions are justified by your findings

All statistics textbooks tell you how to analyse your data and show you what the results of these analyses look like. You'll see these results presented in their pages as lists of figures and as tables and graphs. Some, but not all, texts also cover the principles of good data display that we looked at in Chapter 9. But very few textbooks provide any guidance on how to turn all these figures, tables and graphs into a coherent and engaging narrative – the 'story' of your research findings. This is what we're going to focus on here.

Remember that you're telling a story

When you write up your results you're telling the 'story' of your research. This is the case regardless of what kind of data you've collected and what type of analyses you've conducted. When I use the term 'story' or 'narrative', I don't mean that you'll be making something up and creating a work of fiction. Most researchers try to report their findings as truthfully as possible (while realising that all research involves making judgements, and you can only ever give a partial account of what's in your data). By writing up your results you're telling the story of what you found out, and it's useful to think of your writing as a narrative because this will help you present your findings in a way that is engaging and appealing to readers.

Presenting the results of statistical analysis is different in some ways to presenting the results of other types of analysis, but there are also some similarities. Statistical results will contain more numerical data and probably more tables, graphs and charts, and so they'll look different to the results of, for example, the thematic analysis of interview data. But deciding how to present any research findings always involves making decisions about what you show the readers, in how much detail, and in what order. We'll look at these differences and similarities in more detail throughout this chapter.

Curating your findings

To present the results of your research in a way that creates the best possible narrative, you need to 'curate' your findings. A curator uses their expertise to select, organise and present a collection of things, and 'curate' is a term more often associated with the contents of a museum or art gallery than of a research report. A well-curated exhibition will tell a good story about a collection of things. When you carry out a piece of research, you become an expert on your data, analysis and results, and when you're writing up your findings, it's useful to think of yourself as curating them. Seeing your results as a collection of ideas that need to be selected, organised and presented will help you build a good research narrative.

Being selective

Being selective about what you present to your readers is probably the most important consideration when writing up your findings. There are practical reasons why you might need to be selective – such as meeting a word limit – but being selective is also essential to creating a good narrative.

Writing up any type of analysis requires you to be selective

Being selective about what to include when reporting your results isn't something that just applies to writing up statistical analyses. Regardless of the kind of data you have collected or the method you've used to analyse them, you'll have to make decisions about what data you present to your readers. All analysis involves processes of selecting and summarising data, and it isn't possible to show readers all the data *and* all the information on exactly how it was analysed. Before we look in detail at presenting numeric and statistical results, it's useful to think about how we might present the findings of research using other kinds of data.

If your research is based on analysing interview data, for example, you could find yourself with many thousands of words of interview transcripts. You're also likely to have other important information about how you coded and analysed the data. If you presented all of this to readers, you'd give them a complete picture of the data and the analytic process, but it's unlikely that it would be an engaging narrative. You'd end up with a very long document that probably wouldn't be very interesting to read.

When writing up their results, researchers who analyse interview data usually present extracts from interview transcripts alongside a discussion of the importance of these extracts, how they relate to each other and to broader themes in the data, and how they relate to their research questions. They won't usually have the space to include all the relevant extracts from the interview transcripts, and so they have to choose only the most important ones and will, by necessity, leave out some others. As with any analysis, readers only get to see some of the data, but researchers should try to make sure that what their readers see is a faithful representation of the most relevant information. Most of my students who analyse interview transcripts understand that they shouldn't try to include all their data and all the details of their analytic process when they write up their results. And they usually realise that they need to tell the reader the most important details.

However, when students first present me with a report of the results of research based on statistical analysis, they are often less sure about what they should include. This means that they sometimes present me with a discussion of the results of every single analysis they have conducted. I call this the 'shopping list' approach. Not only do they include all the information about every analysis they have conducted, they provide roughly the same amount of detail for each one, and usually present these in the order that they conducted them.

Why doesn't this approach work? Isn't it best to include as much information as possible about your analysis so that it's clear to your readers what you have – and haven't – done? Not really. The problem is that this kind of report tends to be very long, is usually quite dull to read, and often doesn't give a clear sense of the story they're trying to tell. While being transparent about your data and analysis is important, it's very hard to create a good narrative without being selective about what you include. In the following sections we'll look at the different types of analysis, what they tell you, and how you should write them up.

Exploratory analyses: what they are for and how to write them up

As I noted earlier, writing up a statistical analysis isn't completely different to writing up any other kind of analysis. Just as a researcher using interview data must decide which extracts to include or leave out in the write-up of their results, if you're writing up the results of a statistical analysis you need to make similar decisions. But rather than thinking about which bits of an interview you're going to put in your report, you need to make decisions about which results of statistical analyses your readers need to see, and in how much detail. Just like with interview data, there usually simply isn't the room to include everything (and tables and charts can take up a lot of space), but there are other reasons why you shouldn't include all your analyses in your report, even if you do have the space.

Regardless of the kind of data you have, or the type of analysis you're doing, you'll probably start with some **exploratory analysis**. It's important to start any analysis by 'getting to know' your data. With interview data this might involve reading through transcripts or listening to recordings and perhaps making some summary notes about each interview. With statistical analysis it usually involves conducting some univariate and bivariate analyses, and displaying your data using graphs and charts.

As we saw in Chapters 3 and 4, one reason we conduct exploratory statistical analysis is to work out whether there are any issues or problems with our data. It can be useful in flagging up any **missing data** or **implausible values**, for example. But you also want to know what our data look like in terms of the distributions of our variables and relationships between them. For example, you might want to look at the distribution of ages among your respondents to see how **representative** they are of your population. Or you may want to look at the relationship between two independent variables, to check whether they are both measuring something similar (for example, the number of years in education and the highest level of educational participation). The findings from your exploratory analyses can highlight any problems or issues with your data and put you in a better position to conduct further analyses in a thoughtful and considered way.

But many of these exploratory analyses will be 'for your eyes only'. They are often fairly routine and don't reveal anything unexpected or exciting. Because of this, your readers won't need to know about all of them in detail, and will mostly just need to be reassured that you did explore your data thoroughly at the beginning of your analysis. You do need to tell your readers if you find something that affects either the analyses that you can conduct or the conclusions that you can draw, however. If there's a large proportion of missing data for a variable, or if a variable is distributed in a way that you wouldn't have expected, these are things that you should discuss at some point. But you don't need to show the results of every single analysis that you've conducted. Writing up your exploratory analyses is definitely an area where you need to be selective, particularly in the amount of detail you go into.

Analyses that answer your research questions: why you still need to be selective

After you finish your exploratory analyses, you'll start to conduct those analyses that directly contribute to answering your research questions. The results of these analyses are central to your statistical 'story' and are something your readers will need to know about. However, this doesn't mean that you should report all of them in the same amount of detail. Being selective about how much you say about each of your findings is as important as being selective about which analyses you include in your report.

Working out which results to include and how much detail to devote to each finding can be quite tricky. I understand why students think they need to include all the information about everything they've done. After all, we spend a lot of time telling them to be thorough and transparent. But writing a good narrative requires you not just to be thorough and transparent; it also requires you to make judgements about where you need to be comprehensive and where your readers need less information.

Thinking about your story

One way we can learn about effective narratives is by looking at some examples of those we encounter in our everyday lives: novels and news coverage. If we think about how a novel is written, we can get a good idea of what a good story looks like.

In a novel you'll usually find lots of different characters, but the author doesn't spend the same amount of time discussing each one. There will be characters that are central to the story that the author will write lots about and that will feature very regularly in the plot. But there will also be minor characters that don't appear as frequently and aren't discussed in as much detail. It doesn't matter that we don't find out as much about these characters as we do about the main characters, as they're less important to the story. The same will be true for events that occur. Some events will be covered in great depth because they are very important to the plot, but lots of other things that happen are described in much less detail because they are more mundane but are necessary to make the plot make sense. And some things aren't mentioned at all: we don't need to know what every character had for breakfast each day!

In novels, not every event is presented in the order in which it occurred. You might get 'flashbacks' to events that happened in the past, for example. Or the focus might shift to a character or group that are doing something in one location, then back to some other characters that are somewhere else at a previous point in time, at the same time, or in the future. All these techniques are used to create a more interesting story.

If you look at news coverage, you'll find that information is presented in a similar way. Some news stories will have more time or space dedicated to them than others because they are considered to be more important. In broadcast news, the most important stories are also presented first, regardless of how recently the events they report occurred. In the print media or on news websites, the most important stories are at the top of the front page and are given the most space. Just like the plot in a novel, the presentation of news is organised in a way to highlight what the editors have decided is most important and what they want their readers or viewers to pay most attention to.

When writing up your research findings, it's useful to adopt the mindset of other kinds of story-writers, such as novelists and journalists. Presenting your findings is very different from generating them, and so you need to take a different approach when writing them up.

What to keep in, what to leave out, and what to spend most time on

Before you present the results of your analyses, it's worth trying to write down a short summary of the 'story' of your findings. What were your most important findings? Did you find what you had expected or were some of your results surprising? How do your results compare to those found by other researchers? The answers to these questions will help you decide what you keep in and leave out, and how much space you dedicate to discussing each of your findings.

You might find that what you thought were going to be the most important analyses turned out to be less exciting when you looked at the results. Some of your other analyses could have revealed unexpected findings and suddenly become the focus of your discussion. How you write up your results should, to some extent at least, be structured around what you have found out, and which of your findings are most important. What you judge to be the most important findings – for whatever reason – should be what you discuss in most detail. Other results can be reported in less detail, and you may even have some findings that aren't interesting enough to be worth reporting at all.

There's no magic formula for this. As is the case with using tables, graphs and charts (or not using them), the most important thing is to spend some time thinking about what are the most important parts of your findings, and to devote some time to planning how you structure your narrative.

Linking your results to the wider literature

Although you'll probably be most interested in the results of your analyses, it's important not to ignore how your findings relate to what is already known about the topic you're researching. How interesting or important your findings are will depend to some extent on how similar or different they are to those from previous research, so you need to discuss your results in the context of the wider literature in the area. It's usual to present your research findings after a review of the literature (and a discussion of your methods), so making links to what others have found out can help you place your own research findings in a broader context.

There are two common ways in which your research results can be linked to the wider literature. The simplest way is to present your results and then follow this with a separate discussion that compares them to existing research in the area. This is the approach that most of my undergraduate students take, and it's reasonably easy to plan and write. A more ambitious approach is to discuss how your research fits with the wider literature as you are presenting your results. This is more difficult but creates a more coherent narrative and is, arguably, a more sophisticated way of writing the story of your research.

Making judgements about your results

Engaging with the literature on the topic you're researching doesn't just allow you to link your results to previous findings. It also helps you make judgements about the implications of your own results. A common misconception among people who don't do statistical analysis is that it's the computer that does all the analysis. After all, as we have software to do all the hard work, when it comes to the maths, is there really much left for us to do in the way of thinking?

Computers can't 'think', and doing statistics isn't just a mechanical process

I hope that, if you've read any previous chapters of this book, you'll have seen that doing statistical analysis isn't just a 'mechanical' process, and that at every stage you need to make subjective judgements about things such as **levels of measurement** and how the data are distributed. These decisions are ones that aren't always straightforward, but they also help keep things interesting. And even when you've got the 'results' of your analysis – all the tables and statistics the software has generated – the process doesn't stop there. As I explain below, that's when the real work of analysis really starts!

Computers are really good at crunching numbers. They can do it much faster than us and they don't make mistakes. But, at this current point in time, computers aren't very good at thinking. (We're beginning to see more and more advances in artificial intelligence, but these haven't yet impacted how we interpret basic statistics.) Most importantly, they don't understand concepts, so they don't know what your variables *mean* in any real sense. The data that you enter into a spreadsheet are just numbers to a computer. You might label them as 'income' or 'occupation', but a computer has no understanding of what 'income' or 'occupation' are.

As well as not knowing what 'income' is, a computer also has no understanding of what a 'good' income might be, or even why we think that income is an important thing to study. So it can't interpret the numbers that it generates. That's our job as researchers.

How do we start to interpret the results that the software generates? And how do we know which of our findings are most important? Or whether any of them are important at all? This is where our understanding of the social world and the work of other researchers comes in.

Where our understandings come from and how they can help us interpret our results

When we begin researching a new topic, we sometimes start with only a 'common-sense' understanding of that area. For example, when I started studying education, my initial ideas for research were guided by my own experience of teaching and learning, and the experiences of students and teachers I'd spoken with. These led to me being curious about a number of questions, as well generating some hunches (or **hypotheses**) about what the answers might be.

But the social world isn't always easy to understand, and unfortunately, we can't just rely on our common sense to explain everything in it. Our experiences are always partial and some of the things that happen are counterintuitive, so we need to investigate the world in a systematic and transparent way. And we do that by conducting research.

As I noted in the last section, one of the first things we do when we start to study a new area is to read the literature on that topic. The 'literature' includes academic studies and writing, but also research conducted by other types of organisation, and also covers things like policy documents. Becoming familiar with this literature helps us to make sure that the research we're planning hasn't been done before, tells us what has already been found out, and helps us develop good research questions (see White, 2017). Most importantly for our current discussion, it can help us interpret the results of our statistical analysis in a more informed and considered way. In the next section we'll look at how expert knowledge can help us make sense of statistical outputs.

Why context is essential for making judgements and interpreting results

As I've noted in previous chapters, guidelines in statistics textbooks about what are 'large' or 'small' differences or 'weak' and 'strong' **associations** are always arbitrary. It's impossible to formulate general rules about what is a 'large' difference, or a 'strong' relationship, because this varies according to what is being researched and what we already know. We've already seen that computers can't help you with these decisions because they don't understand what you're researching. So how can we make them? The simple answer is that it's not always easy. This is another part of statistical analysis where you need to use your judgement.

The easiest way to demonstrate this is by using an example. Table 10.0 shows guidance from the Food Standards Agency (FSA) on different nutrients in food. The figures show how much or little of these nutrients a food product can contain before they consider it to be healthy or not.

This example demonstrates several important points. The first, and most obvious, is that particular quantities mean different things depending on the

Table 10.0: Food Standards Agency guidance on nutrients

Per 100g	'A lot'/'Too much'	'A little'/'Healthy'
Sugar	10.0g	2.0g
Fat	20.0g	3.0g
Saturates	5.0g	1.0g
Salt	1.3g	0.3g
Sodium	0.5g	0.1g

Source: *The Times* (2004, p 9)

quality they represent. A food can have 2.0g of sugar per 100g and still be considered healthy. But 2.0g of sodium per 100g would be considered way too much. However, 2.0g looks the same in the output of statistical analysis, regardless of what is being measured. It is up to you, as the analyst, to recognise that this number means different things depending on what it refers to (in this case, sugar or salt content).

The second point is that this table contains *specialist* knowledge. These aren't numbers that could be worked out with 'common sense' or ones that are widely known. It's the type of information that you find in the specialist literature (academic or otherwise) and without which you couldn't interpret your data properly. Having access to information like this is why you need to do a literature review before you collect and analyse your data.

The last point relates to the status of the information included in Table 10.0. You might have noticed that there's a relatively large gap between the nutrient content of 'Healthy' foods and those that have 'Too much' of a certain nutrient. As we've seen already, a 'Healthy' level of sugar is 2.0g or less per 100g. And 'Too much' is 10g or over per 100g. But what about foods that fall between 2.0g and 10.0g per 100g?

There are several things going on here. One is that there isn't a 'tipping point' where healthy foods suddenly become unhealthy. In terms of the content of different kinds of nutrients, foods will fall somewhere on a continuum, from healthy to less healthy, in terms of that particular nutrient. Researchers are sometimes asked to present their research findings in terms of 'limits' or 'thresholds', but most know that any such figures will be arbitrary to some degree. It's also the case that there are disagreements among researchers, particularly in some areas, and that it's sometimes difficult to find consensus on important issues. (There are several different competing measures of 'poverty', for example.) The figures in Table 10.0 aren't 'set in stone' and may be contested among experts or change over time as we learn more about nutrition.

Although I've used a reasonably simple example here, relating to food and nutrition, the same principles apply regardless of the topic you're researching. When you interpret the results of a statistical analysis, you need to bear all these things in mind. Each statistic will need to be interpreted in terms of what is being measured, counted or compared, and what this figure means in relation to what we already know in the field. You'll need to use your judgement for this, and you also need to be prepared for other people to have slightly (or even very) different interpretations of the same statistical results.

Other factors that might affect the interpretation of your results

There are other contextual factors than can also influence the interpretation of your findings. The size of a difference or strength of a relationship is important, but, as we saw in the previous example, this size or strength can only really be judged in relation to what we already know or expect. Researchers often get excited about larger differences and stronger relationships, but they aren't always more interesting than smaller or weaker ones. The direction of a relationship is important, too. A small difference or weak relationship that is in the opposite direction to all the previous evidence would be more interesting than a large difference or strong relationship that just confirms existing findings. For example, middle-class students have been considerably more likely to attend university than their peers from the working class for the entire history of higher education. If, next year, a researcher analysing the most recent data discovered that working-class students were now slightly more likely to attend higher education than middle-class students, this would be an extremely important finding, even though the difference was very small and the relationship between class background and higher education entry could now be described as a weak one. What we expect to find can be an important influence on how we interpret what we actually discover.

There is another side to this coin, however, and 'only' finding out what we expect can also be important. The more often we find the same kind of differences or relationships in different contexts, the more confident we can be about some of our more general understandings about the social world. Poverty, for example, has been found to be related to reduced life chances in lots of different areas, such as education and health outcomes and being a victim of crime. The more times we confirm this with repeated studies, and the more areas in which we have evidence of the adverse effects of poverty, the more we can be confident that it is an underlying cause of disadvantage in other areas. Persistence and consistency can be important in building our confidence in our research findings, even if our results aren't dramatic or surprising. But knowing what is considered as large or small and strong or weak, and knowing whether our research confirms what we already suspected, or whether our findings are dramatically new and different, all depends on being familiar with the work of other researchers. Only once you've put your results into the proper context can you move on to drawing conclusions about the implications of your research.

Discussing the limitations of your study and being modest about your claims

Constructing a convincing argument to support your conclusions is a process known as **warranting** your claims. It involves you acknowledging the weaknesses in the way your data has been collected and analysed, and requires you to consider alternative explanations for the results that you observed. You'll probably need to qualify some of the claims you make, being clear that they might only apply in certain circumstances or be subject to other types of uncertainty. It's important for all kinds of research, not just studies using statistical analysis, and isn't a topic that's often covered in research methods text. Although there isn't space to cover warranting in detail in this chapter, I've written in more detail about this topic (White, 2017), and Gorard (2013) also provides some useful guidance.

Summary

If you've got this far in this book, then you're probably ready to go and conduct some statistical analysis for yourself. You'll have learned some important statistical concepts and found out about the techniques you can use to analyse different types of data. You'll also have learned how to present your data visually and, having read this chapter, may have started to think about how you will tell the story of your results.

I hope I've delivered on my promise to make learning statistical analysis as straightforward as possible. While there are some very tricky issues to consider when doing any kind of research, I've tried to show that the conceptual side of doing statistics isn't as difficult as most people fear and that, with the help of computers to do the maths, most people can do useful statistical analyses themselves. Some of you might even have been surprised to find out that you enjoy doing statistics!

References

The Times (2004) 'Stores in pledge to cut salt', 26 February, www.thetimes. co.uk/article/stores-in-pledge-to-cut-salt-jpwwhhfwpwl

Useful resources

I write in more detail about how to answer your research questions here:

White, P. (2017) *Developing Research Questions* (2nd edn), London: Palgrave [Chapter 5: 'How Do I Answer My Research Question?'].

I also discuss hypotheses on pages 61 to 65 of the same book.

Stephen Gorard provides a useful discussion of warranting research claims:

Gorard, S. (2013) *Research Design: Creating Robust Approaches for the Social Sciences*, London: SAGE [Chapter 4: 'Warranting research claims'].

Glossary and index

This is a combination glossary and index. All the terms listed below are highlighted in bold in the main text, generally when they are first used in a chapter. Although most of these terms are explained in detail somewhere in the book, I have also provided a short definition of each term here that may be sufficient for readers who are not reading the book from start to finish, and only need a basic understanding of the term in order to progress with their learning.

Absolute deviation 66
This is the distance of a value from another value as an absolute number. The absolute deviation of 10 from 5 would be 5. The absolute deviation is used in the calculation of the mean deviation.

Absolute number 44, 66
An absolute number is one where the sign (negative or positive) is ignored. It is always treated as a positive number.

Aggregate data 43
Information about individual values that has already been summarised, for example, as frequencies and percentages. Aggregate data do not contain any information about individual cases in isolation.

Anchored response 35
Questionnaire questions often ask respondents to select an answer from a range of options arranged in a hierarchical order. Anchored response options have a label attached to them, whereas 'unanchored response' options require respondents to select a number or position on a scale. The following is an example of a set of five anchored options: 'Strongly agree'; 'Agree'; 'Neither agree nor disagree'; 'Disagree'; 'Strongly disagree'. This set of anchored response options is commonly used to collect data on respondents' levels of agreement to particular statements.

Association 12, 91, 192
This is another word for a relationship between two or more variables. It can be used to describe a correlation, but is also used to describe differences between groups. The term 'association' is sometimes used to show that there may be uncertainty over whether the relationship is a causal one.

Central tendency
50, 63, 99

A measure of central tendency is an average. The common measures of central tendency are the arithmetic mean, the median and the mode. The term 'central tendency' is sometimes preferred over 'average' because of the many different ways the word 'average' is used in everyday conversation, only some of which correspond with the way the term is used in statistics.

Coding
43

This is used to describe how data are organised and classified by researchers, either before or after they have been collected. It is used in all kinds of analyses with different types of data. Coding textual data involves sorting text into themes and categories. Numeric labels or values are often attached to different response options in questionnaire data as part of a process of coding that precedes statistical analysis.

Coefficient of determination
127

The technical name for the statistic more commonly known as r-squared. This is the proportion of variation in the dependent variable that is matched by variation in the independent variable(s) in a correlation or regression analysis. It can take a value between 0 and 1, with 0 corresponding to 0% and 1 corresponding to 100%.

Constant
11, 134, 147

The opposite of a variable: it is something that doesn't vary. Researchers are usually interested in variables, rather than constants, as things that stay the same aren't often as interesting as things that change or differ. A regression line equation will always contain a constant term. This is sometimes useful information in its own right, but is always needed if the results of a regression analysis are used to make predictions about values of the dependent variable.

Correlation
13, 136, 178

A correlation analysis is a statistical procedure for determining the predictability of a relationship between two variables. Correlations are most commonly calculated between continuous or discrete variables, but correlational techniques are also available to determine the relationships between ordinal variables and binary categorical variables.

Where the relationship between two (usually continuous or discrete) variables is not constant over the range of the values of those variables. An example might be the relationship between the number of hours students studied for an exam and the marks those students gained in that exam. The first hour of study is likely to be more valuable than the 100th hour of study, with extra hours of study having diminishing returns in terms of marks gained in the exam. As students can get no more than 100% in the exam, there is also a limit to the extent that students can gain marks with extra study.

A term used to describe the parts of a graph, chart or table that show information. This can include data points, bars, data lines, and so on, but also labels. This is contrasted with 'non-data ink', which refers to the features that do not directly provide information on the data itself.

Strictly speaking, a data point is one piece of information about the value of a variable for a single case. However, it is often used to refer to a point on a graph or a figure in a table, which may represent more than one piece of information (such as a point on a scatterplot that shows the values of two variables for a single case).

The background characteristics of the people who often make up the cases in a sample or population. Characteristics relating to age, occupational and social class, ethnicity, religion and place of residence are often related to other aspects of people's lives and life chances, and are commonly included in statistical analyses by social researchers.

Any measure that summarises the extent to which the dependent variable is affected, or changed, by the independent variable. Different types, or 'families', of effect sizes are used with different types of data. Standardised mean differences are used when comparing the distribution of a variable in two different groups, whereas coefficients are used in correlation and regression analysis. Odds and risk ratios can be used to judge the effect sizes in analyses using only categorical variables.

Expected counts
88

These are numbers that are sometimes included in a table showing the results of a cross-tabulation. Expected counts are usually shown alongside, and compared with, 'observed counts'. Observed counts show how many cases there are in a particular sub-group in the data you have analysed. Expected counts, in contrast, show you how many cases you would 'expect' to have in that sub-group, if there was no relationship between the two variables you are analysing. If the expected counts are different from the observed counts, this shows that there is some kind of relationship between the two variables.

Explanatory power
146

This refers to how well the results of a statistical analysis can predict values of the dependent variable. It is frequently used in relation to techniques for statistical modelling, such as regression analysis, where statistics such as r-squared are used to measure explanatory power.

Exploratory analysis
188

Any analysis that is not aimed at addressing your research questions directly, but is intended to identify any issues with the data, and to prepare the ground for analyses that address the research questions more directly.

Gaussian distribution
70

See 'normal distribution'.

Grouping variable
110

A different name for a categorical variable.

Histogram
54, 100

A type of graph that shows the distribution of a continuous variable as bars, in a similar way to how a bar chart shows the distribution of a categorical variable. The difference between a histogram and a bar chart is that bar charts are not always ordered and have discrete categories (so are used with categorical data). The bars in a histogram represent different 'ranges' of the values of a continuous variable, and the size of these bars (technically known as the 'bin size') can be changed as required, in order to best represent the distribution of the variable graphically. Histograms are often used to check whether a variable is normally distributed or has a 'skewed' (or other shaped) distribution.

Hypothesis
192

Simply a 'guess' or 'hunch' about an answer to a question. It's not necessary to have hypotheses for all research questions and research with hypotheses is not necessarily superior to research that starts with no hypotheses. I write more about hypotheses in my book about research questions, *Developing Reseach Questions*.

Implausible value
44, 188

A value of a variable that appears unlikely to be valid. An example, for the variable 'age', would be someone with an age of 141 years. As no human has so far been recorded as living that long, this value would be suspected of being the result of a typographical or transcription error, rather than representing the true age of one of the participants in a study. Univariate analysis can help identify potential implausible values, which should be checked and amended or removed if they cannot be verified.

Intercept
139

The point at which a line on a graph crosses one of the graph's axes. It is an important concept in ordinary least squares (OLS) regression analysis as the regression line equation includes the intercept of the line of best fit with the y-axis.

Jittering
181

This is a method of randomly changing the values of the data points on a scatterplot by a very small amount. This allows relationships to be seen between variables where the data can only take certain discrete values.

Legend
169

In a graph or chart, a legend is a label that provides information about one of the variables shown in that graph or chart. It could, for example, describe the categories shown in a pie chart and show which categories are represented by which colours or textures in the chart.

Level of measurement
25, 118, 191

A way of distinguishing between the different ways we use numbers with different types of data. The key distinction for most analyses is between data that are measured on a continuous scale and data that can only be assigned to categories. In 1946 Stanley Stevens proposed a typology with four different levels of measurement. This typology is widely used today, but is not without its critics.

Line of best fit
119, 137

A line that is drawn through the points on a scatterplot, showing the relationship between two variables in a way that minimises the distance from those points and the line itself. A line of best fit is usually calculated mathematically, and is also known as the regression line.

Mean deviation
65, 102

The mean absolute deviation, or mean deviation, is a measure of spread (dispersion). It is the mean of the absolute distance of all the data points from the arithmetic mean of that variable. As it has an intuitive interpretation as 'the average distance from the average', it is easier to understand than the standard deviation, which is a much more commonly used measure of dispersion.

Measures of spread
101

Measures of spread, sometimes called measures of 'dispersion', are statistics that show you how spread out the data for a variable are. Some of these are fairly simple, such as the minimum and maximum values, or the range – which is the distance between the minimum and maximum values. Measures such as the mean deviation and standard deviation are more complicated but give a better indication of how the data are spread out overall.

Missing data
44, 113, 174, 188

Data that are missing from a dataset at the case or variable level. Missing data can be caused by participants not completing all the items on a data collection instrument, such as a questionnaire or test, or by declining to participate in a study. Missing data can reduce the number of cases that can be included in an analysis. The effect is cumulative in multi-variable analysis, and can affect representativeness in sample-based studies.

Monotonic relationship
129

A relationship where a change in one variable tends to be accompanied by a change in another variable, either in a positive or negative direction, but this relationship is non-linear. Correlation coefficients such as Spearman's *rho* and Kendall's *tau* were developed for analysing these kinds of relationships.

Multi-variable analysis
12, 42, 131

Any analysis where there is a single dependent variable but more than one independent variable. It is often confused with multivariate analysis, where there is more than one dependent variable.

Negative relationship
122, 136

A relationship in which the values of one variable increase as the values of the other variable decrease (or vice versa).

Negative skew
76, 100

Data are negatively skewed when the majority of cases have relatively high values but there is also a 'tail' made up of a smaller number of cases with low values. It is also known as 'left skewed'.

Nominal data/ variable
28, 45, 94

Categorical data that do not have a hierarchical order. Religious affiliation is an example of nominal data because, although people may be affiliated with different religious groups, these groups are not seen as 'higher' or 'lower' than each other.

Non–data ink
158

Anything in a graph or chart that does not directly show information. This includes lines, grids and other features that do not represent data. Non–data ink should be kept to a minimum, both in terms of its amount and its visibility.

Normal distribution
55, 70, 89, 100

The normal distribution (also known as the Gaussian distribution, after Carl Friedrich Gauss) is the distribution of values of a continuous variable that take on a symmetrical bell shape when shown on a histogram. Many phenomena in nature – such as people's height – are approximately normally distributed. Some statistical procedures assume that a variable is normally distributed, and the normal distribution is used as a comparator in some types of diagnostics to check if the data meet certain assumptions.

Observed count
88

The number (or frequency) of cases in a particular group or sub-group. When cross-tabulating data, the observed count is sometimes compared to the expected count, which is the number of cases that would be expected in the group or sub-group if there was no relationship between the variables being analysed.

Observed values
150

These are the actual values for particular variables for each case. They are what are 'observed' in the data. In regression analysis, observed values for the dependent variable are contrasted with the values that would be predicted, or estimated, using the line of best fit.

**Ordinal data/
variable**
29, 45, 94, 128, 176

Categorical data that have a hierarchical order. The level of someone's education is an example of ordinal data in which subsequent levels of education are considered 'higher' than previous ones (for example, 'university degree' being higher than 'high school diploma').

**Ordinary least
squares (OLS)**
131, 136

This is a method for calculating the line of best fit in a linear regression model. It works by calculating a line of best fit that minimises the sum of the squares of the differences between that line and all the data points.

Outlier
49, 100, 130, 179

A value for a variable that is very different from the values for most of the cases. An example could be a student taking an undergraduate degree at university who is 82 years old. Most students would be much younger than this, with the majority being in their late teens or early twenties. Outliers need to be checked to make sure they are valid data, rather than being the result of a transcription error or typo. In small datasets outliers can influence the results of some analyses, so are sometimes removed from the dataset before these analyses are conducted.

Placebo
107

A placebo traditionally refers to a treatment that is designed to have no therapeutic or beneficial value, and is used to provide a valid comparison for the effect of a treatment. While this term originated in medical research, its use has expanded to include any studies with experimental designs.

**Positive
relationship**
15, 91, 120, 136

A positive relationship is an association between variables in which the values of one variable increase as the values of the other variable rise (and vice versa).

Positive skew
54, 75, 108

Data are positively skewed when the majority of the cases have relatively low values but there is also a 'tail' made up of a small number of cases with high values. This distribution is also known as 'right skewed'.

Predicted values
150

The values predicted by a statistical model. One common example would be the values on a line of best fit produced by a regression analysis. In this example, the values of a dependent (outcome) variable can be estimated, to varying degrees of accuracy, using the values of the independent variable or variables.

R-squared
127, 139

The r-squared, technically known as the 'coefficient of determination', is a measure of the predictability of a relationship. It is related to Pearson's *r* correlation coefficient and is simply this value multiplied by itself (squared). It is easier to interpret than Pearson's *r* as it has an intuitive real-world interpretation as the proportion of variation in one variable that is matched by variation in another variable or variables.

Representativeness
10, 43, 188

This is the extent to which data from a sample reflect the data in the population that the sample was selected from. Not all samples aim to be representative, but techniques such as random sampling are used to maximise representativeness when this is an important aim of a study.

Residual
140, 150

The difference (or distance) between the value observed for a case in a dataset and the value predicted for that case by a statistical model. This term is usually used in relation to techniques such as regression analysis, but can also be applied to the results of univariate analysis using 'models' such as the arithmetic mean.

Scatterplot
119, 136, 160

A graph showing the relationship between two continuous variables. It can provide an indication of the direction of a relationship (positive or negative), how predictable the relationship is (the correlation) and whether the relationship is linear or non-linear. Scatterplots are usually drawn in two dimensions and show the relationship between two variables. However, it is possible to draw them in three dimensions to show the relationship between one dependent variable and two independent variables. Scatterplots are not only used to determine the relationship between variables, but are also used for diagnostic purposes in multi-variable analyses.

Skew
54, 75, 99

This is a measure of how a variable is distributed. It is usually applied to continuous variables, but can also be used with discrete and ordinal data. The distribution of a variable is skewed if, rather than having a symmetrical or flat distribution, the values are concentrated in the upper or lower ends of the distribution. A distribution concentrated in the upper ends of the distribution is described as negatively skewed (or left skewed) and a distribution concentrated in the lower ends of the distribution is described as positively skewed (or right skewed).

Standardised mean difference
105

A measure of effect size that can be used when comparing the distribution of a variable between two groups. Cohen's *d* is an example of a standardised mean difference. To calculate Cohen's *d*, the difference between the arithmetic means of the two groups is divided by the standard deviation of the two groups combined to provide a standardised measure. Other measures of standardised mean difference, such as Glass's delta and Hedges' *g*, are variations on this type of effect size.

Sub-group
81

A group within a group. If a variable is categorical, cases will be allocated to different groups. For example, we might divide people up into groups according to their religious identification. We might be interested in the way that people from different social classes are distributed between different religions. We could conduct an analysis using cross-tabulation that would produce data showing this. Hinduism would be a religious group, but members of the working class who identify as Hindu would be a sub-group.

Unanchored response
35

An answer option for a questionnaire or test item where the respondent must select an answer that isn't labelled but falls on a scale of some kind. The respondent is often asked to select a number on a scale that attempts to measure, for example, agreement or disagreement. There are usually 'anchors' at each end of the scale ('Strongly agree' and 'Strongly disagree', for example), but the answer options between these extremes do not have descriptive labels. Unanchored responses are more common when scales have a greater number of possible answer options. For example, a question in the Office for National Statistics (ONS) Opinions and Lifestyles Survey asks, 'Overall, how satisfied are you with your life nowadays?' Respondents can pick an answer that is a whole number ranging from 0 to 10. At one end of the scale, 0 is 'anchored' with the label 'Not at all' and at the other end 10 is 'anchored' with the label 'Completely'. However, the numbers from 1 to 9 do not have labels attached to them and so are 'unanchored'.

This refers to the type of case you are researching. In social research it is common for individual people to be units of analysis, but families, groups, organisations, institutions and events can also be units of analysis. A researcher studying crime, for example, may be interested in the experiences of victims of crimes. They could treat individual victims as their unit of analysis, but a different approach would be treating each crime as the unit of analysis. The choice between the two would be dependent on their research questions and would affect how the data were analysed.

If something is volatile, it can change rapidly or unpredictably. In relation to statistical analysis, it is important to consider that small numbers are volatile. Analyses with small numbers of cases are considered volatile, as small changes or differences in absolute terms can be very large proportionally. For example, if a religious group is comprised of only the founding member in one year, but has five members the next year, the membership has increased by 400%.

The argument linking the results of your research to the conclusions that you draw from them. Some principles of warranting your conclusions are widely agreed, but others are more controversial. A good warrant will consider the design of a study, any weaknesses in both the data collection and analysis, the logic of the link between the findings and conclusions, and alternative explanations for those findings.

Sometimes called the 'horizontal axis', the x-axis runs from the left to the right of a chart or graph. It is usually placed at the bottom. Conventionally, it represents the values of independent variable (usually denoted by the letter 'x').

The y-axis is sometimes known as the 'vertical axis' of a graph or chart. It runs from the bottom to the top of a graph or chart, usually on the left side (and less often on the right). It is called the y-axis because it usually shows values for the y-variable, which, by convention is the dependent variable.